KILLED AT THE GAP

By

Donald Colson

A
DonMarLu
Book

7272 Lindale Drive , Sacramento, CA 95828
Phone: (916) 421-5063

Library of Congress Control Number: 2003091221

ISBN 0-9729784-0-2

PRINTING HISTORY

First Printing	March 2003
Second Printing	July 2003

Printed in the United States of America

To

Marilou

This book is dedicated to the memory of your Grandfather George and his brothers, Johnny and Willie.

"Nothing Without God"

This is the Scottish Motto for the name Litster

"Litster"

There are a few spelling variation of the Litster name.
In Latin documents the name was rendered Tinctor.
It has been spelled, Littester and Lyttister.
Litster is the older spelling of the surname Lister

Acknowledgments

I want to thank Lander County Clerk and staff for the help they provided as well as the staff at the Nevada State Library in Carson City. Without this help the old case records would not have been found. This was especially true for the trial transcripts. Fortunately, these were recovered from the top of an old book case in the Archives Building. These transcripts had not been microfilmed. The old dusty binders containing the trial transcripts provided the needed insight necessary to tell this story.

The following individuals have taken time to help me with this effort by assisting with the field work and or by reading and commenting on parts of the text:

Marilou Colson, the great granddaughter of the Boone Canyon Litster family.

Phillip Colson, Airline Pilot, Flight Simulator Instructor and Genealogist.

Dieter Dahmen, Civil Engineer and Public Speaker for: "Sovereign Citizens of America"; and "Anatomy of Freedom".

Marie Jeanne Ansolabehere, Rancher and Owner of the Boone Creek Ranch

Angie Elquist, Lander County Archives

Author

While researching my wife's family history a sad story was found about two brothers. They were killed on their father's ranch. My wife's great grandparents were early settlers to the Nevada frontier. They came to Lander County in 1874. This book has been compiled from the historical records of the homicide that occurred in 1893.

Donald Colson
Retired Civil Engineer

Foreword

by
Marilou Colson

Why did my husband write this book? I asked him to see if he could find the details about the killing of my great grandfather's two sons. I was told a young man from a neighboring ranch shot them. My adopted father was also my grandfather and he told me that his brothers Johnny and Willie were killed. Therefore the book is the result of compiling information about the murder. My husband's motivation really came from an old article in Austin's newspaper, the Reese River Reveille. He discovered this murder was at one time Lander County's most famous crime story. The old newspaper that began publishing on May 16, 1863 and continued till 1993, had several articles about Alfred Vaughan's three trials. Alfred was tried for killing Willie Litster.

Memories have faded; only a few people now can say they have heard about a Litster boy being shot. In addition to the Austin and Reno newspaper articles; field trips to the old ranch site; the original transcripts found for the first and second trials as well as the appeals to the Nevada State Supreme Court formed the basis of the story. The book is more than just a murder story. It is about a feud that reached the boiling point and about Nevada's early criminal justice system. It is a tragic and heart breaking story. Therefore the objective of my husband's book has been to preserve this history.

A reconstructed timeline for day of the killing, December 28, 1893, was used to study the crime. You can read about the events from the perspective of those that testified at the trials. The State's Supreme Court overturned the verdicts of the first and second trials. The third trial was moved from Austin to Reno where Alfred Vaughan was again found guilty.

There are many myths from Nevada's frontier days in the 1800s. The historic background of the book covers part of Lander County's early history. The book should clarify some of the County's history.

KILLED AT THE GAP

CONTENTS

Introduction

This story is about justice and how it was administered nearly a century ago for Lander County's famous double murder. Alfred Vaughan shot and killed two brothers, Johnny and Willie Litster. This happened on their father's ranch in Boone Canyon. The shooting occurred shortly after Vaughan's big lumber wagon stopped in front of a fence gate on a cold winter morning. Alfred was traveling with his brother, Charlie, and a hired man named Nick Rast. They were going to a mining claim located in the Water Canyon. This canyon branches from Boone Canyon at the upper end of the Litster Ranch. Here they found Johnny and Willie standing with their arms crossed in front of the gate commonly known as "The Gap".

Headlines from the Reese River Reveille on Saturday, December 30, 1893: *"A HORRIBLE TRAGEDY - John and Willie Litster shot and killed by Alpha Vaughan. The slayer surrenders to the Sheriff and is in jail. Nick Rast and Charlie Vaughan arrested as accessories."* Why did Alfred shoot them?

Alfred admits to the shooting but he claims it was in self-defense. Alfred stood trial not once but three times for the Grand Jury's Indictment for killing Willie Litster. The trials were spaced about a year apart. The question before each jury was whether these brothers were shot down in cold blood or did Alfred act as he continued to claim self-defense?

The story begins by providing a few of the details for the historic setting and the immigration of the Litster family to Nevada from their native Scotland in 1874. Most of the immigrants that came in the 1800s were from Europe. Gold and silver caused many to seek a fortune in the west. Others like the Litster's were just seeking a new life on the frontier. Transcontinental rail service began in 1869 and the Litster family used the portion from Oakland to Battle Mountain where they were met by relatives, George and Isabella Watt. They would complete their long journey traveling south by wagon towards Austin, Nevada.

The first chapter provides background information and a summary of Lander County's early history. The second and third chapters cover a chronologically reconstructed scenario of the day of the killing, December 28, 1893 and conclude with the arrest of the three men from the Vaughan Ranch. The fourth chapter commences with the Coroner gathering evidence, the funeral and the burial of Johnny and Willie. Next the men from the Vaughan Ranch appeared at the Preliminary Examination. Following this hearing the Grand Jury issued indictments and the subsequent chapters cover the trials and appeals.

Conflicting statements and testimony about what actually happened or might have taken place should be expected. The first trial is covered in the fifth chapter. In the sixth chapter you will find why the State Supreme Court ruled for new trial. You can read the actual opinions written by the Justices.

The opportunity to use two old trial transcripts from the 19th century seemed to be an obligation to preserve this small history from Nevada. Memories have grown cold, but still a few in the County will say they have heard about the shooting of a Litster boy, yet none were aware of the grim and sad details.

You might agree with the Supreme Courts rulings regarding Judge Fitzgerald's instructions to the jury as well as their decision to overturn Judge Mack's ruling to restart the second trial with the original eleven jurors by adding a new twelfth juror. Was justice served following the jury's verdict at the third trial in Reno? Did Alfred really cheat the gallows?

The sequence and time of events that took place on the day of the shooting was reconstructed from newspaper accounts by the Reese River Reveille, Reno Gazette-Journal and the Trial Transcripts. The research includes the written opinions by the Supreme Court Justices, as well as the information from a great-granddaughter of the Boone Canyon Litster's. The rulings by the Justices regarding Alfred's appeal from verdicts rendered after the first two trials are important and the written opinions provide objectivity to the presentation of the story.

Chapter 14 is titled, "Closure". Here is a brief summary of

the impact of the tragic shooting. Is there such thing, as "Closure" when life is taken from a loved one?

Chapter 15 is the author's "Epilogue". Our criminal justice system has evolved. However, United States Constitution still remains the powerful connection to our nation's true heritage.

The Appendix was added to compliment the story. It includes: a Bibliography; three Biographies of prominent men from Lander County; a few old photos including the Litster family and relatives can be seen along with a copy of Johnny's letter written two days before his death. Many of the characters in this story can be found listed in the census for: 1870, 1880, 1900, and 1910 in Lander County. A summary of the 1894 Lander County election results indicates other characters could easily have filled the elected positions. There is a short history of the Nevada Central Railroad. Also, two maps are included, one showing the boundary of the Old Litster Ranch and the other, a Vicinity Map to aid readers not familiar with Lander County.

The casts of historical characters were just ordinary citizens. Their story was not news outside of the County; until the third trial, which took place in Reno. A change of venue was necessary. Even by today's standards, this case would be more than just another murder. You can compare this case to the current criminal justice system, but this book is not intended to be a legal treatise in anyway, just an historical account of hatred coupled with an unbridle rage and a sprinkling of comments from the author.

It was interesting to follow W. D. Jones, Lander County's able District Attorney prosecuting this case for the State as well as James F. Dennis; the aggressive lead Defense Attorney. I will point out it wasn't to many years before that perhaps the law of the old west would have had Judge Lynch presiding. Such a case did occur in 1881, where a. lynching took place on the front steps of the Austin Courthouse late one night. It came close to that here, but this time the taxpayer would not be spared the cost of these trials.

The little Litster boy that rode for help that cold December morning was just eight years old. He had a vivid memory of that day for his entire lifetime. The impact of his big brother's being murdered produced suffering that can only be fully understood by others that have had to bear up when love ones are murdered. And when a loved one commits such an act of murder, how too does his family suffer?

While the story can be nothing more than a lesser part of the State's great history, it is an interesting story. Many historical characters did participate. A few of the notable names are: Judge L. A. Fitzgerald; Judge C. E. Mack; Judge A. E. Cheney; District Attorney, W. D. Jones; Sheriff, William Easton; Ranchers: George Watt, Thomas Dunsdon and the widow Mrs. Alexander Eason. I must add to this list the German immigrant, Nick Rast, without his guilty conscience, Willie Litster's deathbed declaration may not have been enough to bring guilty verdicts at each trial.

By writing this story, I learned a great deal about a family living on a remote ranch in Nevada. It is hard to imagine their life style as compared to current living conditions.

As you consider the historic setting you should think about the fact that in this same century Jedediah Smith, the famous American explorer first passed through Nevada in 1827. John C. Fremont explored this vast area that would become the State of Nevada in 1843-46. The territory now encompassing Nevada was ceded by Mexico to the United States in 1846 following our war with that country. In 1858, the Mormons were first to establish a permanent settlement in Nevada. In this same year silver was discovered at a place that would become Virginia City. The rush produced a population boom. Four years later there was another rush to Austin. The population of Nevada during the two Silver Rush's, one 1858 and the other in 1862-63, is unknown. However, at the turn of the century in 1900, the State's population was said to have dropped to approximately 42,000. Nevada became the 36th State in 1864.

Many of those rushed from one discovery and then to another seeking a fortune that few ever found. Some of these treasure seekers gave up and sought work building the transcontinental railroad while others returned east to volunteer as soldiers for the Union or the Confederacy. Railroad construction began in 1863 by laying track eastward from Sacramento. The tracks being laid passed Battle Mountain in 1868. The connection with the railroad tracks being placed in a westerly direction from Omaha, Nebraska was made on May 10, 1869, at Promontory, Utah.

In 1874, William Litster with his family came to Lander County following the persuasion of his sister Isabella She was George Watt's wife. The Watt's are listed on the 1870 Census. George Watt was one of the first Scotsman immigrating to Lander County. He came to California in the 1850s and later to Austin in 1863. He acquired his ranch at Silver Creek in 1866.

In 1881, William Litster purchased his ranch in Boone Canyon. Today the Litster Ranch is known as the Boone Creek Ranch. You can still drive to the ranch house via the dirt road bypassing the Silver Creek Ranch, formerly the Watt Ranch. Boone Canyon is approximately 25 miles from the junction US Highway 50 and State Route 305. Here a road sign reads: "Boone Canyon, Vaughan Ranch". The site of the Litster's ranch house is four miles east of the highway.

William and his wife Elizabeth were 29 and 28 years old respectively when they made the journey from Scotland. They heard about the beautiful mountains, green meadows and the creeks with trout as well as the wild horses to numerous to count and the vast open range land for cattle and sheep. Here the Litster's hoped to find a better life and yes freedom from that English cast system with all its nobility.

Characters

The following persons are introduced as the prominent characters of this story. These characters are listed in alphabetical order and where ages are shown it is for the year 1894.

William W. Christian: William was 32 years old. He ran a store at Cortez and in Austin before becoming the Clerk of Lander County in 1895. His wife Mary was the older sister of the two Litster brothers that were killed. I have his hand written notes that he made during the second and third trials. He assisted the County Commissioners with the jury pool selection. The Defense felt that he influenced the jury selection process.

James F. Dennis, Esq.: He was the defense attorney for Alfred Vaughan. Most of his clients lived in the Austin area even through his residence was at Battle Mountain. He spent many hours at clients expense riding or should I say commuting on the narrow gauge Nevada Central Railroad. The train departing Battle Mountain at 7:30 a.m. would travel the 93 miles before arriving at the Clifton Station just below Austin at 1:10 p.m. Was he considered a skillfully attorney by winning two appeals before the State's Supreme Court? Perhaps he could have gotten a lesser sentence for Alfred Vaughan if he had been able to talk to him and his brother before they concocted two different stories about a gunfight?

Thomas Dunsdon: Tom was 52 years old. Tom was the best friend and neighbor of William Litster. On the day of the shooting, Tom sent his two sons for the doctor in Austin. His boys made the sixteen-mile ride to town in about ninety minutes. Tom and his wife, Emily spent the night at the Litster ranch consoling Elizabeth and the children. They also helped the Litster's take the bodies of the brothers into Austin for the funeral and burial.

William Easton: William was 40 years old. He was the Sheriff and Assessor of Lander Country. His salary was $104 per month. He arrested the Vaughan brothers and Nick Rast on the day of the shooting with the help of George Watt, Jr. His testimony seemed show that there may have been some conflict between himself and the District Attorney. Perhaps this was just a little professional jealousy. He later served two terms in the Nevada State Senate as a Republican. He married Lucy Stow from a wealthy San Francisco family. He would live his final days in that big city but he requested his burial be at the only town he loved, Austin. (See Appendix for Biographical Summary)

Mrs. Alex Eason: Mary was 48 years old. William Litster called her Mollie. She was Alexander Eason's wife. He had died leaving her as widow in 1891. Her husband was the nephew of Christina (Eason) Litster who was the Grandmother of Johnny and Willie. Her home was about a mile and a half from the Litster's. Her son, Joe Eason, was visiting with James Litster when the Vaughan wagon came back down the road after the shooting.

W. D. Jones: William Dudley Jones was 43 years old. He was Lander County's District Attorney. He was very definitely the outstanding citizen of Austin and leading character of this story. He was a self-made lawyer. He came to Austin 1868 at the age of eighteen. Here he studied law books and became a member of the Nevada State Bar. He was the prosecuting attorney in all three trials, State of Nevada vs. Alfred Vaughan. His monthly salary was $150 in 1895. He was very active in the community as well as being a sportsman. His fishing trips would take him to Big Creek and Birch Creek. He liked hunting above Kingston along the Toiyabe Crest. He attended all the social activities in Austin, such as the stage plays, the annual

Costume Ball and the annual Burlesque Show. The later was a fundraiser and it was a respectable show in those days. Was he responsible for the loosing the two appeals to the Supreme Court? (See Appendix for a his Biographical Summary)

Elizabeth Litster: Elizabeth was 48 years old. She was mother of seven children. Johnny and Willie were her two oldest boys. She helped her husband and Jimmy carry Willie back to the house while he was in great pain. She saw the Vaughan wagon drive by on that tragic day and she was concerned enough to insist that her husband go and check on her boys. Why did she wait until her husband came back to the house? She could have gone to him thirty minutes earlier. She would live on the ranch with her youngest son Louis until her death in 1926. She also witnessed the death of her 19-year-old beautiful daughter. Lizzie's death was two years before the death of her husband's in 1903. How did she bare the pain of watching life slipped from Willie, as her first-born son was lying dead in the next room?

James Litster: He was a few months shy of his 14th birthday when his big brothers were killed. He probably would have been shot too except for that fact that his mother sent him for the mail that morning. On his return he had stopped to visit his friend Joe Eason. Nick Rast jumped off the Vaughan wagon and told Jimmy and the widow Mrs. Alexander Eason that there had been trouble at the Litster Ranch. Jimmy returned home to helped his Papa carry his brother's back to the ranch house.

Johnny Litster: He was the eldest of William and Elizabeth's sons. He was nineteen when he was shot. He was just reaching manhood. He was a tall lad at six-feet one-inch. He had the classic high Litster forehead. He and his bother Willie were very close. His father depended a great deal on him to for a lot of the work at the ranch. The local young girls from neighboring ranches as well as Austin were attracted to him and they all like to dance with him. Johnny liked to write and receive letters. (See Appendix for Letter dated December 26, 1893)

Willie Litster: He could always been found with his older brother. He was sixteen when he was shot. Willie too was also tall for his age, just an inch shorter at six-feet than Johnny. Willie was an outstanding horseman and perhaps the best buckaroo in the County. He found it challenging to break mustangs into good saddle horses. He loved the opportunity to lasso these mustangs and bring them to the ranch. Willie resented the men from the Vaughan Ranch passing through his family's ranch.

William Litster: He was 49 years old. His family moved to their new beautiful Boone Canyon ranch in 1881. His two eldest sons were doing a lot of the work at the ranch. His family was happy to be living near their relatives; Watt's and Eason's; and his best friend Tom Dunsdon as well as the Steiner's, and Duffy's. William found both of his sons lying on the snow, one dead and the other near death. Did a day ever pass without him wondering why he let his boys ride off that morning when he saw the Vaughan wagon coming?

Charles E. Mack: Judge Mack presided over the second trial. He seemed to be a very competent judge. His salary was $333.34 per month. By comparison, the State Governor's salary was $416.67 per month. The highest paid State Official was the Chief Justice at $550.00 per month. The Judge lived in one of Austin's best homes. He seemed frustrated by Mr. Dennis's continuing objections and exceptions; yet he praised his work for trying to save Alfred.

Nick Rast: Nick was 43 years old and he spoke with a heavy German accent. The Vaughan's hired him the day before the shooting to work at their mining claim. Nick had worked most of his life as a miner. He was living with his brother's family near Silver Creek. He casually knew both the Litster and Vaughan boys. He found himself in a situation that caused him to be charged with murder. He said he could not live with the lie that he first told about the shooting. When he changed his story during the first trial he became the State's star witness.

Charlie Vaughan: He was 24 years old. Charlie's best friend was his little brother and he must have loved him dearly. He always let Alfred be the boss. He liked to pack his bulldog six-shooter. He too was charged with murder. Did he know that Alfred was going to shooting the two brothers that morning? Why was his story about the shooting different from his brother's? He was very lucky; the Sheriff didn't arrest him for the attempted jailbreak. Was he just following his brother's request on the last day of the trial in Reno?

Alfred Vaughan: He was 21 years old. Alfred's nickname was Alfe, Alfa or is it Alphe? As a cowboy he was just beginning the prime of life. At one time he was a good friend with the two Litster brothers. This was prior to the feud that resulted when he pulled his pistol and pointed it at Mr. H. S. Starratt. Perhaps, Alfred was he just being foolish or stupid. He was eighteen at the time. Mr. Litster admonished him and told him to leave and never come back carrying a pistol. This embarrassed Alfred and his resentment soon became hatred. He deliberately left gates open at the Litster Ranch. The Litster's had a strong suspicion that he was stealing stock as well as the one who had poisoned their dog. Was he acting alone when he shot the brothers?

George Watt, Sr.: George was 62 years old. He was the patriarch of the Watt, Litster, Eason and Dunsdon immigrants to Lander County. He was 32 years old when he first came to Austin in 1863 with a herd of cattle from Yolo County, California. George purchased his first ranch at Silver Creek in 1866. He went back to Scotland 1869 where he married Isabella, the sister of William Litster. She was 17 years younger than her husband. George a successful rancher and he owned several ranches throughout Lander County. Through his financial help: the Litster, Eason and Dunsdon families were also able to purchase ranches. (See Appendix for Biographical Summary)

The following list shows these and other characters:

LITSTER FAMILY

William Litster, 49 yrs, Father
Elizabeth Litster, 48 yrs, Mother
John "Johnny" Litster, 19 yrs, Son
William "Willie" Litster, Jr. 16 yrs, Son
James "Jimmy" Litster, 13 yrs, Son
Elizabeth "Lizzie" Litster, 11 yrs, Daughter
George Watt Litster, 8 yrs, Son
Louis Litster, 5 yrs, Son

VAUGHAN FAMILY

Lee Vaughan, 70 yrs, Father
Mrs. Isabella Vaughan, 60 yrs, Mother
Frank Vaughan, 28 yrs, Son
Charlie Vaughan, 24 yrs, Son
Alfred Vaughan, 21 yrs, Son
Harry Vaughan, 19 yrs Son

LEGAL CHARACTERS

W. D. Jones, District Attorney
D. S. Truman, Assistant D.A.
James Dennis, Defense Attorney
J. H. MacMillian, Assistant Defense Attorney
William Easton, Sheriff
W. H. Bray, Coroner
Justice of the Peace, L. A. Weller, Preliminary Examination
Judge A. L. Fitzgerald, First Trial – Austin 1894
Judge C. E. Mack, Second Trial – Austin 1895
Judge A. E. Cheney, Third Trial – Reno 1896
Justice C. J. Bigelow, Opinion First Trial
Justice J. Belknap, Opinion Second Trial
Justice C. J. Bigelow, Concurring; Second Trial
Justice J. Bonnifield, Concurring; First and Second Trial

OTHER CHARACTERS

Samuel Crescenzo; International Hotel Owner
William W. Christian, County Clerk
Mary (Litster) Christian, Wife
Phillip Duffy; Rancher
Thomas Dunsdon, Rancher
Emily Dunsdon, Wife
Nathaniel Dunsdon, Son
John Dunsdon, Son
Mrs. Alex Eason, Widow
Joe Eason, Son
A. A. Flint; Perjured Juror, Second Trial
Dr. A. J. Huntsman; Doctor
James Kessell; Miner
Joe Moss; Public Administrator
H. S. Starratt; Regent University of Nevada
Nick Rast; Miner
Fred Steiner; Rancher
Miss Stina Wagner; , Silver Creek Schoolteacher
George Watt; Rancher
Isabella (Litster) Watt, Wife
George Watt, Jr; Son

14 Killed At The Gap

1

LANDER COUNTY

Is That Place In Nevada?

The journey from Scotland to Nevada in 1874 was long and tedious. Elizabeth was pregnant with her second child. Her little boy would soon be born on a far away ranch in Lander County, Nevada. She was twenty-eight years old and just about two years younger than her husband. William married Elizabeth six years ago. Their first child, Mary was now four years old. They would have five more children added to their family during the years following the move to Nevada.

Emigrating from one country to another was a major event and the Litster's were saying goodbye to their native homeland. They knew this was the last time they most likely would ever see those left behind. This was very sad and especially for William's parents, James and Christina as they kissed their two daughters Agnes, Helen and their grandchildren goodbye. They too were traveling with their son's family to Nevada. This type of farewell was common for those coming to America before the 1900s. Now day's people can easily take an airline flight and return to visit their homeland. William, Elizabeth and those traveling with them would soon learn Nevada is not at all like Scotland's wet, fogging and green landscape. The Eason and Dunsdon families were very close friends of the Litster's and they too were making the voyage to start a new life in America.

Why were the Litster's and their friends coming to Nevada? This was a mystery when the research started for this story. It soon became clear these families had been convinced by George Watt's wife to come to the place called Lander County, Nevada.

She was William's younger sister. Isabella Litster had married George Watt in 1869 when he returned to visit his family in Scotland.

No the Litster's and their friends were not part of the Silver Rush to Austin. They were not miners or prospectors either. They were just farmers or should I say ranchers? Marilou (Litster) Colson, a great granddaughter of William and Elizabeth Litster, said her grandfather, George Watt Litster, always made a point by saying his mother and father came by ship to San Francisco.

These immigrants were leaving the city of Dunfermline. The city's name means "fort on the wending stream", and it is the ancient capital of Scotland and burial place of Robert the Bruce. Now those names would become a distant memory.

Ships traveling to America from England with immigrant passengers could disembark at New York. This would be their port of entry to the United States. After the papers were processed they again could board another ship bound for Panama. Ships sailing from the East Coast generally made a few stops as they traveled south and into the Gulf of Mexico. Most of these ships would take on supplies at New Orleans before continuing the voyage to Panama. William had worked as a ships blacksmith as a young man so he knew what it was like by going to sea, but this was a new experience for the others. Nothing was ever said, but I'm sure Elizabeth with child was very glad to get back on solid ground.

The prospectors during the California Gold Rush had three basic routes to travel. The all season Panama route was the safest way to travel. Another route the rushers used was to cross the continent on land with one of the many wagon trains. These wagon trains traveled during the spring to fall season. A third route was very long and uncomfortable. This was the dangerous voyage around South America's Cape Horn. The Panama route was the way most people traveled to California during the Gold Rush following the discovery at Coloma in 1848.

A railroad was finally constructed across the Isthmus of Panama to handle the numerous travelers. It was completed in 1854. The train ride was far better than the fifty-mile trek walking through the jungle. It has been estimated that between 1848 and 1869, about 375,000 persons crossed this isthmus from the Atlantic to the Pacific and during the same period about 225,000 of these travelers returned to the east by using this route. Eventually the Panama route gave way to the transcontinental railroad that was completed in 1869. However, the Litster's and their fellow Scottish travelers in 1874 were told by George Watt to use the Panama route.

The book, "Letters from the Nevada Frontier", edited by William A. Douglas and Robert A. Nylen contains letters Tasker L. Oddie wrote to his mother during 1898 – 1902. Mr. Oddie became a prominent citizen in Nevada. This founder of Tonopah and later Governor of the State wrote about George Watt coming to California in the 1850s. George's name is listed in the California 1860 Census as a stockbroker in Yolo County. You might assume George came to sell beef to those rushing to the California gold fields. Mr. Oddie said, *"Mr. Watt drove a herd of cattle to central Nevada in 1863."* This is easy to understand; here again he could sell beef to the miners rushing from Virginia City to Austin. George was a wealth businessman. I wish I could tell you about how he took the cattle over the Sierra's.

George Watt was thirty-two years old in 1863 and he acquired his ranch along Silver Creek some sixteen mile north of Austin in 1866-67. The 1870 census shows that he had married Isabella, a woman from Scotland. This most likely happened during 1868-69 when he traveled to his homeland. George testified during the first trial of Alfred Vaughan that he came in 1866. The question in 1894 was about how long he has lived at Silver Creek and he answered 28 years. We learned from Oddie's letter that he was in Central Nevada in 1863. The 1870 Census lists George's age at 38 and his wife's age at 21. Isabella was born August 8, 1848. George's birthday is January 12, 1831, according to his gravestone at Austin. Their first child George Jr. was born in 1871.

Tasker Oddie said it was due to the efforts of George Watt that the Litster's came in 1874. I think it would be more correct to say it was Isabella's persuasion. Let us just give George credit for recommending the travel route.

Yes George Watt was a wealthy man. He owned the following ranches and other properties in Nevada: The 1500 acre Watt Ranch. This was his family's residence along Silver Creek. The 600 acre Fish Creek Ranch about 50 mile north of Austin; 150 acre North Fork property to the north of Silver Creek. The 100 acre China Ranch about two mile north of Silver Creek. The 100 acre Davey Creek property. The 100 acre Cottonwood Canyon property. The 160 acre Alex Eason Ranch in Boone Canyon. The 400 acre property three miles north of Silver Creek. The 150 acre Antelope Valley Ranch. And the 600 acre Hall Creek Ranch. He also owned a house in Austin. This is a very impressive property list.

The Litster and the Watt families had a very close relationship. George Watt Litster told his granddaughter, Marilou Colson that his Uncle George was a sheep man. George Watt owned 4000 sheep according to the 1893 tax recorders. No doubt the real number of sheep was much higher. George Watt has a remarkable gravestone at the Austin cemetery. It is in the shape of a tree trunk with all of the branches cut off. It has a Masonic emblem and a ships anchor with a rope carved at the base of the trunk. Is this not a strange sight for the middle of Nevada?

Those that journeyed across the isthmus to the Pacific Ocean re-boarded waiting ships for the voyage up the West Coast to San Francisco. Here they would ferry across the bay and board the eastbound train in Oakland. The Litster's would travel via Stockton, Sacramento, over the Sierra Nevada Mountains to Reno and continuing on to Battle Mountain. They would have had to wire a message ahead to George Watt about their arrival date at Battle Mountain. The Nevada Central Railroad's line between Battle Mountain and Austin had not yet been constructed. Therefore to complete the journey our travelers would now ride on a wagon.

George made arrangements to have several wagons there to carry all these immigrants back to his ranch at Silver Creek. It was a two or perhaps three day journey to Silver Creek. It is about 70 miles south of Battle Mountain..

A few years later the Nevada Central Railroad did become a

welcome addition in Lander County. It certainly made travel easier than the wagon ride. The 93-mile rail service between the two towns existed from 1880 to 1938. A terminal station was located at the base of Pony Canyon in the small settlement below Austin known as Clifton. There were several sidings along the way to load and off load passengers and freight. A brief summary of the railroad has been placed in the Appendix.

It might helpful to understand the setting better in Lander County by noting just a little more history. I'll keep the history brief. I think the background information will help you to understand the story's setting and the period of Nevada's history.

Austin, like several Nevada towns came into being following a silver discovery. The miners that founded this town built cabins as close as possible to the mining claims they were working. People walked to work, they didn't have cars to commute many miles. The Silver Rush to Austin started in the summer of 1862. By 1874, Austin's population had dropped from the peak years during the Civil War. Austin may have been good place to be during that war, especially for those that didn't find walking shoulder-to-shoulder across some soon to be named battlefield and perhaps being slaughtered acceptable. The west was a good place where many deserters also sought refuge. It was certainly a place to stay for those that didn't see the glory in fighting for either side.

I've often wondered how Austin was named. Finally, I found a good reference, "Nevada Place Names" by Helen S. Carlson, at the Nevada Historical Society's book store on the campus of the University of Nevada, Reno. Here, it is said that David Buel was in charge of surveying the town site. Now you citizens of Austin, you know the name of the man responsible for plotting the map that shows the lots for the property you probably don't entirely live upon. Sorry, I won't say anymore about his map. According to this reference, Mr. Buel might have named the town after his partner Alvah Austin. Also reference is given to another sources that claim's the name was given to honor the pioneer John Austin. The name is also said to commemorate Leander Kelse Austin, a mining developer and uncle of George

Austin. Another version has Mr. Buel naming the town after his native Austin, Texas. Take your pick.

The site of the town was first known as "Pony". I was told by Mrs. Joy Brandt, from the Lander County Commissioner's Office that it is a mistake to assume Pony Canyon was named after the Pony Express. She said it is her understanding the canyon was named for a lost and found pony. Was this pony owned by the Pony Express? Anyhow, the Pony Express riders used a trail a couple of miles north of Austin at Emigrant Pass. My professional engineering experience leads me to believe this would have been better route then the present U.S. Highway 50 alignment crossing the Toiyabe Range. You can find a sign showing the location of the Pony Express Trail 1.6 miles north on SR305 from the junction with US50. These riders changed horses a few miles to the west at the Jacob Station, later named Jacobsville located on the east side of the Reese River, about six miles west of Austin..

Lander County's name also came with the Silver Rush in 1862. According to "Nevada Place Names" the name honors Frederick W. Lander, Chief Engineer for developing a Federal wagon route known as the Central Overland Route from Fort Kearny to Honey Lake. Colonel Lander was also a Special Indian Agent and for this service the County was named in his honor. He was one of those that did return to the east during the Civil War. He was soon promoted to Brigadier General. and shortly he died from wounds received in the battle at Paw Paw, Virginia, on March 2, 1862. He was forty years old.

Austin and the area below the town in the Reese River Valley had a much larger population in the 1800s. The present day census for Lander County is less than 6000 people. An examination of the 1880 and the 1900 census confirms Austin was considerably larger at that time. It was surprising to see in 1880, the Chinese population in Austin was more than 350 people and the Indian population in Reese River Valley was even larger.

During the days of the Nevada Central Railroad, firewood was hauled to Austin from the Truckee area of California. This continued well into the early part of the 20th century.

Traveling in this part of the Nevada, you'll find US Highway 50 passing through Austin is locally called the "Loneliest Road in America". Today, Austin is a very small community. People living here will tell you they like it small. I'm told Austin would have joined the other ghost towns of Nevada. except for US Highway 50. Austin probably has less than 300 residents in 2002. Some say the dogs and horse out number the people.

The official version of the town's founding is somewhat different than a Pony Express rider's horse kicking a piece of quartz rock containing gold and silver. William M. Talcott, was an employee of the Overland Mail and Stage Company at Jacobsville. He is suppose to have went looking for a lost horse up Pony Canyon and accidentally found a ledge of silver ore.

As Jim Andersen states in his paper, "Lost in Austin", *"More than likely Talcott found the ore because he was prospecting and came up with the stray horse excuse to explain to his boss why he wasn't minding the Pony Express Station."*

The discovery on May 2, 1862, brought a Silver Rush that surged in 1863. I still like the story about Talcott's horse kicking the rock. I must admit that would be unlikely for a rider carrying mail to make such a discovery and besides the Pony Express ceased operation six months earlier and those riders did not travel in this canyon.

There is a better vision recorded about William M. Talcott's silver discovery by Thompson and West. They have a chapter for the history of Lander County in their 1881 book. It is said that Talcott was a former pony express rider before this mode of mail delivery gave way to the telegraph and the Overland Mail and Stage Company. He continued to work for the company at the Jacobs Station. On May 2, 1862, he was sent to gather and haul wood needed for station and while doing so he discovered a vein of ore bearing quartz. The ore was sent by stage to Virginia City for assay and the report for the sample was rich in silver. News of the discovery generated the excitement that led to Austin's Silver Rush.

Similarly, a book by Sam P. Davis, (1913?): "The History of Nevada", at the State Library in Carson City records:

"Early in the month of May, 1862, William M. Talcott an

> *attaché of the stage station at Jacob's Springs, while hauling wood from the hillside, now within the limits of the city of Austin, discovered a vein of metal-bearing quartz, and carried a small quantity with him to the station."*

Talcott named his first mining claim "Pony". No doubt to commemorate his days as a Pony Express rider and this is probably the true reason for the canyon's name. The Reese River mining District was organized on May 10, 1862.

Jim Andersen's speculation about Talcott doing a little prospecting seem to apply, but he may have accidentally noticed the quartz rock while cutting firewood for the station. Anyhow, I think history is better served by knowing that Talcott was collecting firewood rather than skipping work to go prospecting.

Just for the sake of western history the Pony Express used 183 riders. They were paid $25 per week, big money in those days. Pony Express operated from April 3, 1860 to October 24, 1861. The riders traveled 75 to 100 miles per day and changed horses every 10 to 15 miles. The fastest delivery time from St. Joseph, Missouri to Sacramento was 7 days and 17 hours, while the average time was 10 day in the summer and 12 to 16 days in the winter. For more information about these brave young Pony Express riders check out the following web site:
www.americanwest.com/trails/pages/ponyexp1.htm

It is estimated more than 10,000 people made the trek to Austin and by late summer in 1863, and some 400 buildings had been erected before winter set in over the Toiyabe Range. Other estimates have put the peak population of Austin much higher than the above figure for 1863. Comparing those days to the present day Austin's population makes the town very small in comparison. The 2000 Census figures lists Lander County's population at 5,794. Battle Mountain's population was 2,871 and it was the only listed town in the census for the County. Also, I've noted the County's population had dropped from the 1999 estimated figure of 6709. There is a web site that provides some pictures of Austin:
www.ghosttowns.com/states/nv/austin.html

Those miners that rushed to Austin in 1863 did not have a

railroad. That service came later. It was possible to ride a train from Reno to Battle Mountain by mid 1869. but the narrow gauge tracks south from Battle Mountain via the Nevada Central Railroad were not in place until the spring of 1880. Therefore these prospectors traveled 170 mile from Virginia City by following the old Pony Express Trail along the general direction of U.S. Highway 50 to Austin. If you have driven this highway, then you can imagine what that trip would have been like and then you would still be wrong. It was worse.

Let me add just a little more of the County's history. The seat of County government was first at Austin, but in modern times Battle Mountain became the larger town. The County Seat was moved in 1979.

Perhaps you haven't heard there was no battle here in the flatlands about ten miles east of the North Peak of the Battle Mountain. There is a story from a prospector by the name of Tannenhill. He was spinning a tale to the editor of the Reese River Reveille. while he recording a mining claim in Austin as he was showing off his rich copper ore specimen. He said he wanted to honor the 23 emigrants led by Captain Pierson in 1857 because they had to fight off an Indian attack. He suggested Battle Mountain for the name of a new mining district. No evidence has ever been found for this battle.

The only recorded battle happened when John Kirk's survey party had a fight that lasted about two hours with some 60 Indians at a place called Battle Creek. I assume this creek is near the mountain's where Tannenhill may have had his claim.

The Reese River flows in a northerly direction and like most of the larger valleys in Nevada they too are aligned in a north south direction. The Indian's had a good name for this river. They called it "Fish Creek". Perhaps that name should have continued with the creek identification. For those that haven't heard the story, well some eastern conmen were selling stock to finance barge shipments for ore on the river from Austin to Battle Mountain in the 1860s. They certainly would not have made any sales with a river named Fish Creek.

According to the reference "Nevada Place Names", Captain Simpson named the river after his troop's guide, John Reese in

1859. Personally, I like the name Fish Creek. This drainage channel flows to the Humboldt River at Battle Mountain. I hope the above history might generate some local interest but let's return to the story of the Scottish travelers.

Recall, it was my conclusion that Isabella Watt had written many letters to her parent about the new beautiful mountain country. Now at Battle Mountain, she again would see her parents and her brother's family. You can imagine the joy of the reunion they had at Battle Mountain. It must have lasted throughout the night. The next day they could visit and rest before traveling south to Silver Creek. The Watt's introduced these immigrates to the Nevada landscape. What a vast difference Nevada must have appeared in comparison to Scotland. Here there is no daily rain and fog to keep the vegetation green, except in mountain meadows that are fed by flowing springs.

George planned to travel to his northern Fish Creek Ranch for an over night stop. This ranch is about 35 miles south of Battle Mountain. George wanted to show William this ranch. He told William that this was the ranch he hoped to have him work until a better place could be found closer to Austin. They may have had to stop 19 miles south at the Bailey Ranch. Thirty Five mile is a little far for one days journey. Ranch's in those days were always a place where travelers could spend the night.

After stopping at the Fish Creek Ranch they proceeded south along the Reese River to the Watt Ranch at Silver Creek. Here Isabella had another end of journey and welcoming party planned for these immigrates. George already had collected all the items the Litster's would need before returning to the Fish Creek Ranch. But for now, he just wanted William to stay at Silver Creek until he could properly introduce him and the others to ranch life here in Lander County. Isabella was not about to allow her parents, James and Christina to leave the ranch at Silver Creek. They would stay on at the Watt Ranch for the rest of their lives.

William, Elizabeth and daughter, Mary did return to manage the Fish Creek Ranch. The Litster's remained at this ranch for the next six and a half years until George Watt was able the swing a deal for them to purchase the Hamilton Ranch in Boone Canyon in 1881. The ranch in Boone Canyon was composed of five 160-acre homesteads granted to the Hamilton's. The ranch boundaries for the 800-acre ranch follows Boone Creek for approximately three and a half miles.

The move to Boone Canyon surely was a happy move for Elizabeth. Now she would be closer to friends and relatives. Her only neighbor at the Fish Creek Ranch was the Steiner family. They lived on a ranch just a few miles south. Mary and Johnny could now go to the Silver Creek School with their cousins from the Watt Ranch. Willie was three years old when they made this move. A third son named James was born a few months before the move. William and Elizabeth's now had three sons: Johnny, age 8 year; Willie age 5 years; and James age 6 months. Their daughter Mary was now 11 years old.

The Litster's rebuilt the ranch house in Boone Canyon to fit the expanding family. A second daughter, Elizabeth, named after her mother was born August 1883. She would be nicknamed Lizzie. Two more sons would follow. George was born July 1885. He was named after his Uncle. Louis was born May 1888. These later three children were born in the ranch house at Boone Canyon.

It is hard to form a mental picture of Boone Canyon because it is not like the sagebrush flats that cover so much of Nevada. Their new home in Boone Canyon is one of the prettiest ranch sites that you can imagine. There is no shortage of water here or any need to pump water because of the gravity supply from mountain springs and especially the spring from the Water Canyon. The ranch currently is known as the Boone Creek Ranch. The above-mentioned reference for "Names and Places" is not accurate with regards to the old Litster Ranch, it was not known as the Boons (sic) in the early 1880s, perhaps before, but not when the Litster's had this ranch.

You can only speculate about daily life of the Litster's and the others living on ranches during the late 1800s. Story's have been passed down though families about those times can never give us the true picture of the conditions they faced daily. The

Litster Ranch was a place for cattle and horse breeding.

The winter of 1888-89 was severe and it changed a lot of the ways things would be done on ranches in the future. William reduced his cattle herd. Tasker L. Oddie wrote a letter on February 7, 1899, to his mother in New Jersey. He relates the story told to him about that hard winter. He said that George Watt lost $160,000 in cattle and sheep that winter. He told his mother that he went on the Litster Ranch before riding back to Austin where the thermometer was reading minus fifteen

During the 1888-89 winter the weather was cold and the snow didn't let up. This winter was following a dry summer. He said Mr. Litster showed him a pile of bones still there after ten years from the 4500 head of cattle he lost. I found a notice in the local paper where William sold some cattle at $33 a head. Therefore, the loss experienced by William was nearly the same a Watt's loss. The practice had been to let the cattle go all year grazing in the mountains. This winter there was no food and they just about all starved to death. In those days a salary of $100 per month was good wages.

I question the loss of 4500 head of cattle. The personal property tax records from that time do not support this figure for the Litster Ranch. However, it must be admitted, the tax recorders are not very accurate either. Perhaps 450 head were lost and that number would seem more reasonable. The tax records list 125 stock cattle in 1889 and 30 stock cattle in 1890 for the Litster Ranch.

Mr. Oddie said in his letter, William's two sons; Jimmy and George caught two large wildcats and two coyotes in their traps the day he was at their ranch. The bounty was $1 a head for the bobcats and 50 cents a head for the coyotes. In 1893, William owned 9 working horses; 40 stock horses, 7 milking cows, 30 stock cattle; one breeding stallion; and he did a little farming. The main crops were alfalfa and hay. While chickens were not mentioned we knew they had to have eggs. The people living on these ranches did provide much of their own food supplies. Still they needed flower, coffee, sugar, beans and other common items that we take for granted. Obtaining supplies for the stock and any building materials for these remote ranches must have been difficult. The winter of 1888-89 did reduce the stock at the Litster Ranch. He would no longer rely on cattle for his main source of income. According to family stories the Litster's focused on horse breeding; breaking wild horses; alfalfa; hay and firewood.

Just imagine raising a family with the following conditions: They had no refrigeration; no electricity; no telephones; no super markets; no TV; no Wal-Mart's; no hot showers every morning and let's not forget, no cell phone, and no cars. And what kind of education did the children receive? What about medical care? Yes, it is possible to raise children without videos. Marilou's grandfather, George went to the 5th grade. George had to leave school because his two older brothers were no longer there to work with his father. Recreation did play a part in their life, but there were no sporting events or movies. The fun times were social functions such as dances, stage plays and church.

The Litster's and six of their children were living at the ranch in 1893, the year the brothers were shot. Mary (Litster) Christian was now 23 years old. She had married and was living with her husband at Cortez in 1893. The ages of the children living at home were: John, age 19; William, age 16; James, age 13; Lizzie age 10; George Watt Litster, age 8; and Louis, age 5. The parents ages were 48 and 47 respectively at this fateful year, 1893.

The following is a transcribed letter written by Johnny Litster to his sister, Mary and her husband, William Christian. The letter was written two days before Johnny and Willie were killed. His letter provides a historic link to the families social life. I was thrilled when my wife accidentally found the old letter her Aunt Maine (Mary) had saved from her brother. It is not the type of letter that you would expect to survive all these 109 years. A copy of the original letter has been included in the Appendix.

Boon (sic) Creek, December 26, 1893

Dear Brother and Sister:

I thought I would write you a few lines tonight as I have plenty of time. We had a fine time last Friday night the entertainment was fine. Miss Wagner shok (sic) two peaces her self they was fine the school house looked fine she had the blackboards all full of drawings we started to dance about seven o'clock and danced till about four in the morning they wasn't any one from town it was a stormy day or they would have been a good many come out. Sam Cresenzo said he was going to bring out a buss(sic) load. We plained (sic) the floor and cut six wax candles on it, I tell you it was fine, wish you only were here. Miss Wagner's sister and husband and his brother and cousin were there we would send you a program when we get an envelope all the neighbors was there but Aunt Isa. Uncle George went home with the girls after the entertainment was over.

We received your letter Friday but you forgot to put in the samples of Will's shirt it must be pretty good cloth for 10 cents a yard. Mama says she hopes you will have a good luck with them. The steers are doing fine they are fat as hogs now the stock cattle are looking fine too, we feed them one lode (sic) a day that is when it is storming when it is good weather we don't feed them. Willie has got two colts up breaking. They are daisies to buck. They are pretty gentle now.

Is Will Shultes back to Cortez yet he said he was going to try to be back for Xmas? Lizzie is writing to Reto tonight and sending her a New Years card. Jane Eason got home yesterday she is going to stay till the fifteenth. Mama got the cover for your bowl when she was in town from the Daltons. I guess I will close, as I haven't any more news wishing you both a Happy New Year and many of them.

Your Loving Brother;
John G. Litster

The letter was post marked, Battle Mountain, Dec. 26, 1893. The envelope has a two-cent stamp. Johnny mentions a social function last Friday, December 22, 1893. Miss Wagner was the teacher at Silver Creek and she had an entertainment program that was followed by dancing. I don't think many people today know how people socialized before movies, sporting events, radio and television. They didn't sit around doing nothing. I can recall from my own youth, yes that was before TV, going to potluck dances with a girl friend that was a member of the 4H at a local Grange Hall.

The Christmas program had been planned for weeks and a little snow wasn't going to keep these people in the Silver Creek area home. We learned from Johnny's letter that it stormed on Friday and the people from Austin didn't make the 16-mile wagon trek to Silver Creek. What did Johnny mean when he said? "Sam Cresenzo said he was going to bring out a buss (sic) load." To bad the people from Austin could not make it to the dance. What is a "buss load?" Perhaps it was a wagon rigged with benches to carry several people. Surely, the evening's affair started with a potluck dinner. The schoolteacher, Miss Wagner had the kids put on a short program before the dancing started.

The music would have been live. Perhaps a guitar or two, a piano and a bass fiddle may have been used. People who played these instruments loved the opportunity and they would play as long as the people would dance. The dancing that evening lasted till 4 a.m. Tasker Oddie relates in a couple of his letters about dancing till 5 a.m. In the 1950s we danced until 2 a.m. Now days young people will dance only to about midnight. There was something special about dancing in those days. The girls love it and so did the older boys once they realize how nice it is to hold hands with a girl and may be these boys did steal a kiss before the evening was over.

I can only guess what Johnny means when he says: "We plained (sic) the floor and cut six wax candles on it". We use to make our dance floor slick with cornstarch. A slick floor is more fun for dancing. I wonder, do you think they did the Chicken Dance, Mexican Hat Dance or maybe the Hokey-Pokey?

Johnny told his sister and brother in-law that Willie has the two colts nearly broken to ride. This letter also confirms that Mamma and Papa Litster did not go to Cortez for Christmas. Sending and receiving mail was a very important part of family life. As Johnny closed his letter he never knew it but his sister would have seventy more New Years Eves to celebrate and that he had his last a year ago, in two days both Willie and he would be dead because Alfred Vaughan could not control his hatred or was it self-defense?

Marilou's grandfather said, everyone that knew his mother,

except for the kids called Elizabeth, "Mother". The kids called her "Mamma". She liked to read aloud the Bible after the family dinner to everyone. She also helped by letting the kids read aloud. Many kids learned to read and write this way.

There is no doubt in my mind that it was early to bed and the get up call came very early too. The brothers loved horses and it was a big challenge for the older boys to break-in a good saddle horse. Many of the their horses came from wild mustangs. The better horses were bred with their big stallion. Marilou said her grandfather always had a way with horses and could ride very well even into his sixties and he always preferred a frisky horse.

George Litster was eight years old in 1893 and he still remembered the events of that December 28th when his two big brothers were killed. George didn't talk much about the details of that day to his granddaughter, but he did tell her several times that his brothers, Johnny and Willie were shot and killed by Alfred Vaughan. This is an event that any eight year old would remember the rest of his or her life because of the impact on their family's life. There are many lessons in a tragic story such as this one.

The murder of loved ones can deeply impact a family and while emotions run high, people often fall for a liberal lie: "you don't need guns for self defense". That is another subject; please excuse the digression. Still we must sympathize with people dealing with such a loss from the criminal act of murder. The hurt is no less today than that hurt experienced in 1893 by the Litster family.

My wife and I made a trip to the Boone Canyon near the site of the old Litster Ranch in the September 1996. There we found a beautiful narrow valley along Boone Creek with green grass and the creek was still flowing. This property is currently part of the Boone Creek Ranch. We could drive no further than the site of the old house at the Eason Ranch. This was the dry time of the year and we were surprised with what we saw. Also, this answered my questions about why the Litster's had a ranch here. Deer were in the valley and they didn't seem to mind our presence. I wonder what hunting was like in those days a century ago? Probably not as good as today considering the fact they had no hunting regulations and at that time there were more people living in the area.

A second trip was made to the Boone Canyon Ranch in May 2001. This time we found the owner, Marie Jeanne Ansolabehere, a very nice French Basque lady. Her name is pronounced "An-so-la-bear" for us English language users. She came to the ranch from France at the age of nineteen in 1959. She has been the owner of this ranch for most of the intervening years. She knew my wife's adopted mother Ida "Pat" (Miles) Litster, who was a long time resident in Austin. Pat passed away in 1986 at the age of 86 after living here for 30 years .

Quite by chance as some would say we found Marie Jeanne driving her big tractor towards her ranch, which was six miles or more away on a dirt road near the Silver Creek Ranch. This time we were able to see the ranch in its entirety and take pictures. I was very impressed with the ranch and especially the water supply at the upper end of the ranch. The Water Canyon offers a natural gravity water supply for all downstream uses. Again, I don't know if I have ever seen a prettier little ranch. That is if you consider 960 acres little. She owns both the old Litster and Eason ranches.

We drove up the old wagon road that the Vaughan's travel on the fateful day in 1893. We found a gate crossing the main road about a mile above the ranch house. I thought this was the location where the shooting occurred. I later learned this was not the case. We needed to find a side road from the main road into the Water Canyon. I hoped to find the fence with a gate that would have been known as "The Gap" to match the trial testimony. I believe we must have been very near to the location, perhaps within a 100 yards of the actual site, however I was not sure.

This trip certainly helped me to imagined the conditions on the day of the shooting in 1893. It seems surprising that Litster's did not hear the two shots fired that morning. We left the ranch by driving down Boone Canyon on the old main road towards Highway 305 and through the old Eason Ranch. We stopped at the mouth of the canyon in the Reese River Valley to take pictures of the old Vaughan Ranch.

Still I wanted very much to find location of the gate called "The Gap". After studying the trial testimony. I was sure I understood the whereabouts of the location. This did require another trip to the ranch in Boone Canyon. We arranged to meet Marie Jeannie at 9 a.m. on October 11, 2002. She invited us to have bread pudding and coffee that morning. Marie Jeanne told us before we began our search that the sound of a gunshot does not travel far within the canyon. Perhaps this explains why no one heard those two shoots. She also said one morning last winter the temperature dropped to minus seventeen degree. That is cold!

We drove to the mouth of the Water Canyon and passed through the gate at the upper end of the pasture. We found a site of an old abandoned and destroyed wood bridge over Boone Creek. I'm sure the materials were from the original wood bridge. It was obvious the bridge had been moved upstream. This collapsed bridge has been replaced with a culvert just to the upstream. My engineering experience leads me to conclude the bridge was moved upstream for a stable road needed for motor vehicles. The original location of the wood bridge would have been about 100 yards downstream to correspond to the trial testimony. This is the site where I think the bridge was located 109 years ago.

The fence across the mouth of the Water Canyon does not exist and I could not find anything remaining from an old fence line. Still, I am confident I know the approximate location of the old connecting road to the Water Canyon and where the former fence would have crossed the road going up the Water Canyon with the opening that they called "The Gap". Also, I believe after reading the trial transcripts, William Litster removed the portion of fence crossing the mouth of the Water Canyon. He placed a new fence about 30 yard west of the old side road to the Water Canyon. This fence is the interior boundary of the upper pasture and runs in a northerly direction across the main road in Boone Canyon. It has the typical ranch gate with wire loops to hold the gate in place. You could asked why did he do this? I think the answer is simple. The memory of what happened here was something William Litster wanted to erase and he tried this by removing the fence with "The Gap". This probably did not help him. He was never the same after the murder of his two eldest sons.

Ranching in this part of Nevada has a longer history than Lander County. Most city people cannot accept or understand the lonely lifestyle of these ranchers out in the middle of Nevada. In a very limited sense, the Pony Express; the Silver Rush to Austin; the Overland Stage; and the Nevada Central Railroad helped to bring the outside world to this part of Nevada. The railroad was especially welcomed by the Litster's. Now mail could be delivered to the Vaughan Station, five miles from their ranch house. The Litster Ranch in Boone Canyon was approximately 22 miles north of Austin by way of the old wagon road along the foothills of the mountain range to the east. Yes, the Litster's were hearty souls. And this still applies today for those ranchers out in Nevada's big wide open country. Yes, these ranchers love Nevada and the freedom they once had to use the public lands without all the governmental regulations.

2

BOONE CANYON

Is there a Public Road?

An unpleasant situation occurred at the Litster home. Guests were visiting Mary Litster this evening. She was single and now nineteen years old. She had attracted the attention of the young bachelors in this part of the County. This was the time in her life when these young single men were finding excuses to visit the Litster Ranch. About a year later in 1891 she would become Mrs. William Christian. But what took place this evening was shocking and the details of story were about to be told during the second trial for Alfred Vaughan.

The District Attorney had called Mary to the stand as a rebuttal witness. The first question Jones asked:

"Mrs. Christian, I will ask you if at any time you witnessed Alfred Vaughan draw a pistol on a person?"

Dennis, Alfred's Defense Attorney quickly responded: "Your Honor please, I object to that on the grounds that it will be a collateral matter, one brought out on cross examination."

Judge Mack asked Jones to state his position.

"We offer it for the purpose of impeaching Alfred Vaughan."

"He said on examination the other day that he had never drawn a pistol on anyone in the Litster house."

Dennis argues: "You fixed the time indefinitely."

Jones replies: "I don't know the time myself, I asked him if he did at any time and he said he did not."

"I asked him if he didn't draw a pistol on Mr. Starratt when they were preparing a meal and when Mrs. Christian and the children were at the table, and he said no."

Judge Mack then said: "Objection sustained."

Mary was immediately excused and no more information was said about this occurrence. I am not an attorney and I must say that I don't understand the Judge's ruling. It was common knowledge at Silver Creek and Austin that a feud was raging between the Litster and Vaughan boys. Therefore, it seems logical that this was the occurrence where it all started in 1890. What actually transpired is subject to speculation. You can assume that there must have been an argument. Something was said that caused Alfred to draw and point his pistol at another man. The other quest was Mr. Starratt. The point you should remember is that Alfred was also a guest and he too had been invited to the evening meal. He was on good terms with the Litster family prior to this evening.

I have assumed Mr. Litster must have been standing, perhaps in another room away from these young people. He was still aware of what was happening in the kitchen dining room area of the house. Perhaps, he came from behind Alfred and stripped the gun from his hand. He could have thrown him out of the house. William would have unloaded the pistol and tossed the it to the ground. He might have told Alfred: "I don't want to ever see you here again with that six-shooter."

Alfred felt humiliated as he mounted his horse to make the four-mile ride down Boone Canyon to his home. Records from the trial indicate that William had complained many times since that evening about the Vaughan's deliberately leaving fence gates open as they passed through the ranch. Basically, it was only Alfred who was doing this. On more than one occasion cattle got out and at times the cattle went into William's garden, or in the hay field and sometimes a missing cow was never to be seen again. There is no doubt that this event started the feud. This feud would ultimately result in Alfred committing murder or was it as he claimed, self-defense.

This chapter and the next will describe my understanding of the events that occurred on December 28, 1893, the day Johnny and Willie were killed.

There was another event that took place about a week before this day and it demonstrates the fact that there was a feud. Had matters gotten worse? The answer is yes. The week before Christmas, a Litster calf came up missing as a result of gate being left open. The cows that had gotten out were all rounded up, except for one missing calf. Willie and Jimmy went in search of the missing calf. As they were going down the canyon, they passed the Eason's house. Here they saw Joe Eason. He was about the same age as his best friend Jimmy Litster, the 13 years old brother of Johnny and Willie. Willie was three years older than these two boys. Willie had his 16th birthday last August.

Joe said: "Ya, I saw your heifer heading down the road last night." "I was going to tell you about it later this morning."

The brothers proceeded down to the Reese River Valley below the mouth of Boone Canyon and while they were at the Nevada Central Railroad's siding or as they called it "the switch", they saw Mr. Fred Steiner. He said:

"Willie, I saw a heifer down the tracks standing in a pool of water."

The Steiner Ranch was about 35 miles north of Austin in the Reese River Valley and upstream from Mr. Watt's Fish Creek Ranch. Nothing was said about Mr. Steiner being here; most likely he was riding the morning train from Austin. He was a good friend of Litster's. They used to be neighbors.

Willie and Jimmy then rode down the Reese River as it borders the Vaughan Ranch. Here they found the calf wading in one of little pools where the ice was broken. They proceeded to head the calf back toward the Switch and then to the road to Boone Canyon. As they are going up the road the heifer jumped through a fence into the field with the Vaughan's cattle. Willie and Jimmy opened a nearby gate. Willie rode into the field to get the calf as Jimmy remained at the gate. Almost immediately, Alfred and Harry Vaughan saw Willie riding in their pasture. They both mount horses and rode out to confront Willie about being in their pasture.

Alfred demanded: "What in the hell are you doing here?"

"I am just getting our heifer out of your field."

Alfred replied: "Why didn't you sons of bitches ask before going in the pasture?"

Willie said: "I didn't think anyone was home."

Of course, he knew better but he had to say something as Alfred's horse came along to the side of Willie's horse. Alfred proceeded to belt Willie a couple of hard swats with his "quirt". If you are a non-horse person, a quirt is short whip used to get a horse's attention and they will sting if you are hit. Alfred was a strong young man, six-foot tall; 170 pounds and he had just whipped a boy five years younger than himself. Willie would not forget being hit by Alfred.

Alfred then decided to have some more fun at Willie's expense as he attempts to lasso Willie. As he chases after Willie's horse, he yelled:

"You son of a bitch I'm going to give you the fastest ride you'll ever have."

Fortunately for Willie, Harry Vaughan didn't close the gate and Willie escaped back to the road with Jimmy. Alfred was upset that his brother had spoiled his fun by not closing the gate.

At this point, Alfred yells at Willie: "Hey come on back here." "We'll get your cow out of the pasture."

The calf by now had mixed with the other cattle and shortly; Alfred and Harry came back to the gate and said:

"We don't see your damn cow so you guys can come in and find it for yourselves." "I never want to see you bastards back here unless I say it's okay."

Willie should have known better than to go into the field because of the existing hard feelings. This story gives credence to the feud and to say that these boys just didn't like each other would be a gross understatement.

The main road running up the canyon passes through the Litster Ranch. This Boone Canyon Road had been there long before the Litster's moved to the ranch in 1881. The Litster's had acquired the ranch from Jesse Hamilton. The Vaughan's have lived at their ranch near the mouth of the canyon since 1867 and to them the road up the canyon was a public road. Nevertheless, when traveling on ranch roads, the rule has always been that you leave gates the way you found them. A second rule is that you should get permission before entering or passing through another person's property, unless it is a public road. The second rule is violated more than the first. The Vaughan's never felt a need for any permission whenever they passed through any part of the Litster Ranch whether it was on the road or not.

William Litster was frustrated by Alfred Vaughan's rude attitude ever since the pistol incident with Mr. Starratt. Only, if he could have resolved the problem and they could again be friends. Alfred definitely lacked respect for his elders and his father's neighbor.

Johnny and Willie's parents had planned to travel the Cortez (pronounced Cor'-tus by Nevada people back then). They had hoped to visit with their eldest daughter and her husband, William Christian. They wanted to spend Christmas with them, but last Friday's storm canceled the planned trip. William Christian was managing the store at Cortez and it was not possible for Mary and him to come to the ranch this year for Christmas. Traveling at this time of year would have been difficult, especially for a two-day wagon journey over a mountain pass by way of the Hall Creek Ranch. The Litster's made this trip last August and at that time they stayed overnight at Mr. Watt's Hall Creek Ranch.

On a trip in October 2002 my wife and I drove from Battle Mountain to Cortez and then south on SR306 to Austin. Cortez is now one of Nevada's ghost towns. A lot of mining has been done in this area, especially a few mile to the north at Gold Acres. The road south from Gold Acres is unpaved. Cortez is within a mountain range and you really can feel the absence of humanity here. Later we were asked about the sharp rocks at Cortez that have caused many flat tires. Fortunately, we did not experience this problem. As we drove south it was amazing to me as I thought about a winter wagon trip in this country just to visit.

Friday's bad weather made the decision easy for William, now they will stay and he would help the boys milk the cows and care for the other animals. By staying they would be able to attend the potluck dinner dance at the Silver Creek School on Friday, December 22nd.

Johnny, Willie and Jimmy were old enough to tend the ranch had their parents traveled to Cortez. You cannot leave a ranch unattended when animals require daily care. Johnny was a young man. He was taller than his father and like all Litster's he had a high forehead. He was destined to have very little hair by the age of thirty. He was a handsome nineteen year old young man at about 165 pounds. Willie, at sixteen was nearly as tall as his six feet one inch brother and he too had the classic Litster high forehead. He was very much a teenage boy and he weighed about 145 pounds. Willie was extremely fit and could ride horses that other buckaroos would pass on. As for Jimmy, his fourteenth birthday a couple of months away and he looked like he was going to be taller than both Johnny and Willie in a couple years. People were already confusing Jimmy with Willie.

Thursday, December 28th was just three days before the New Years Eve Party at the Silver Creek School. A party that both Johnny and Willie were very much looking forward to attending, but it would be a party that no one would attend because of the tragedy occurring on this day. The following details are heart wrenching and extremely sad. It is a day that will change two family's lives forever. After studying the day the brothers were killed, I concluded that the best way to tell the story would be to reconstruct the daily events from a timeline. That timeline has been placed at the end of Chapter 3. You may refer to it as you follow the sequence of the events.

It was a brisk and cold Nevada morning. There was about two to three inches of snow covering the flats. When you think about the time of the year and that Nevada is high plateau country you can feel the chill in the air as our scene opens.

Even during the winter months, the typical Litster day started early. Elizabeth was the first one out of bed at 5 a.m. She started the fire in the wood stove and put the coffee pot on the stove. Her six children would be rousted out of bed shortly. These youngsters shared bedrooms. Let's assume Johnny, 19, Willie, 16, and Jimmy, 13 had one of the bedrooms. You know these older boys did not want to be sleeping in the same room with the two younger brothers, George, 8 and Louis, 5. As for Lizzie, she was now 11 and being the only little sister at the ranch, I think it safe to say that her Mamma had partitioned off an area for her to have as her separate bedroom.

The younger children were allowed to sleep in till seven o'clock. Elizabeth would see that the older boys and their father were called at 5:30 a.m. There was work to be done before breakfast. She needed more firewood, milk had to be brought from the milk house, and eggs had to be gathered. Breakfast came later. Johnny, Willie and Jimmy shared these daily morning chores. Afterwards, they would have breakfast with their mother and father. They would resume the daily chores after breakfast before starting any work assignment for the day.

At breakfast, William told the boys to hitch the two big draft horses to the utility sled. William told the boys to load it with eight hay bales and bring the sled to the house. The barn was where they kept the thoroughbred breeding stallion and other riding horses, as well as the big workhorses. The barn animals were in and out of the weather. They had it good compared to the cattle down in the upper corral below the house.

The little boys with their sister had breakfast at 7:30 a.m. Papa told his two youngest sons, George and Louis, they could go with him to feed the cattle and they could ride on one of the big horses. The horse drawn sled worked great while there was snow covering the frozen ground.

William gave Johnny and Willie their work assignment for the day at breakfast.

"I want the fence line checked around the upper pasture." "And I want the Gap closed at the Water Canyon" "Make all the repairs along the fence line so the cattle cannot get out."

He told them that he was going to let the cattle into the upper pasture to do a little foraging for food since the weather had improved. They have been couped up in the upper corral for more than a week. This day was not going to be a fun day for the boys like yesterday when Johnny, Willie and Jimmy rode over to Iowa Canyon, about six miles to the north of the ranch in search of wild horses. The cattle would surely find any opening in the upper pasture and William didn't want his boys wasting time searching like they did for the calf that got into the Vaughan pasture last week. The area of the upper pasture runs about a mile above the ranch house and this pasture has interior perimeter fence. There was an outer fence, but it wasn't very secure. The boys went to the barn about 7:15 a.m. to finish feeding the barn animals.

Jimmy was told that he had the morning off and all he had to do was to the ride down to the Vaughan Station and get the mail. Jimmy called this place "the Switch", as mentioned above, this was where the Nevada Central Railroad had a siding and it was the place where passengers could board and where freight could be loaded or unload as well as delivering and receive mail. It was a little after eight o'clock when Jimmy mounted his horse and started down the road. Elizabeth had told Jimmy he could stop and visit with Joe Eason on his return ride. Elizabeth knew it would be all right with his mother, Mary (the widow, Mrs. Alexander Eason). To friends, Mary was called Mollie.

After Johnny and Willie finished feeding the barn animals they hitched the two big horses to the sled and then drove it to the lower corral and loaded it with hay before going back to the house as their father had said. The hay was being stored under cover in the lower corral for these winter conditions. The brothers then gathered the tools for the fence work before saddling their favorite riding horses. Both boys were excellent horsemen. Willie loved to show off that he could ride better than Johnny and his cousins over at the Watt Ranch. Willie was very good at breaking wild mustangs into good saddle horses.

The two brothers mounted their horses and rode to the upper corral. William and the little boys were now feeding the stock cattle and the milk cows. Johnny wanted to tell his father they discovered two of the fence posts at the corral had been broken. They noticed this earlier while loading hay on the sled. William said he would take care of the fence posts.

It was now a little after nine o'clock and William tells his two older sons:

"Start your work at the Gap and work your way back towards the house."

"You should be able to hear your mother's dinner bell at noon."

She always rang the bell at noontime and again for the

evening meal, but never in the morning because the little one were still sleeping. It was the boy's responsibility to make all the meals or go without. Of course, the boys knew Mamma would always let them snack on some grub if they were late.

It was 9:20 a.m. when Johnny and Willie again mounted the horses after talking with their father. They rode past the ranch house to the main road on the north side and headed up Boone Canyon. This was about the same time that Mr. Litster saw the Vaughan wagon coming up the road. The wagon was about one half to three quarters of a mile down the valley. He saw them where the road turns toward the house and at this distance it is impossible to identify those riding on the wagon. Still, William immediately knew it was the Vaughan's.

On Jimmy's way to get the mail, just above the Vaughan Ranch near the mouth of the canyon he passed the big four-horse wagon driven by Alfred. It was about 8:45 a.m. Charlie was sitting on the bench beside his brother and Nick Rast was bundled up with a blanket setting on the wood stove they were hauling to their mine. That must have been a very cold place to sit and perhaps explains why Nick would soon get off and walk behind the wagon. Jimmy greeted them by saying "Good Morning". Nick responded by saying the same to Jimmy, but Nick didn't recognize him and probably mistook him for Joe Eason. The Vaughan brothers totally ignored Jimmy as if they never had seen him and that was not easy on this narrow road, just rude. They had left their ranch at 8:30 a.m. to go to their mining claim in the Water Canyon.

Jimmy was looking forward to talking to his cousin Joe about the dance last Friday at the Silver Creek Schoolhouse. Jimmy and Joe could talk about watching the girls. They even got enough nerve to try dancing with each other's sisters that night. They both thought it was real funny as they watched their older brothers dancing with all the girls. Elizabeth wanted Jimmy to have some time with his friend before school started next week. The Eason's house was about a mile and a half down the canyon towards the Vaughan Ranch. George Watt owned the 160-acre that the Eason's were using as their ranch and the Eason ranch house was actually on the Litster Ranch property.

Morning at Levi and Elizabeth Vaughan's also started very early. It was not a similar morning start here because the Vaughan's sons were all young men. The oldest was a half brother Frank 28; he worked most of the time with his father. The Vaughan's younger sons were Charlie 24, Alfred 21 and Harry 19. Harry also spent most of his time working with Frank and his father. Will Jackson was a half brother and he had went to Reno on horseback. He was only mentioned one time during the trials and he apparently never returned to the ranch. Albert Tipsword lived at the ranch. He was an old white bearded man and had worked several years for the Vaughan's. He and Charlie bunked together in the cabin beside the main house. They were both outstanding with their snoring and no one could sleep in the same house with these two.

Other than sleeping, Alfred and Charlie were inseparable and Alfred always played the roll of being Charlie's boss. You would not guess Alfred was Charlie's younger brother. Alfred liked to boss Charlie and whatever Alfred said Charlie did it. On this day Alfred was planning to work the mining claim above Boone Canyon. After breakfast Mr. Vaughan, Frank and Harry hitched the four horse team to the wagon while Charlie, Alfred and Nick loaded the wagon.

During the second trial, Alfred mentioned that they were in the process of building a cabin at their Blue Ledge Mine in the Water Canyon above the Litster Ranch. They were using a big Studebaker wagon to haul equipment and materials to the mine claim. This type of wagon was also called a lumber wagon and it was made for hauling heavy loads. And if you're a car buff, you know that Studebaker also made automobiles from 1902 to 1963. They were taking a cooking stove; lumber; bellows; an anvil; some other blacksmith tools and they had some grub to eat.

Shortly after leaving the ranch they pass a lone rider. Nick Rast responded when Jimmy said "Good Morning". Nick had been hired the just day before and he had spent the night snoring in the cabin with Charlie and Mr. Tipsword. You might assume this was going to be a bad first day on the job for Nick. Nick had no idea about the animosity that existed between the Vaughan and Litster youngsters.

Traveling to the mining claim would take them up Boone Creek about five miles to place where they would turn off the main road on the Litster Ranch and go about another mile up a canyon known as the Water Canyon. They would first pass through the Eason Ranch and then the Litster Ranch. Alexander Eason had died a couple of years ago in 1891 and Mary; his widow was living there with her children. Her husband was the nephew of James and Christina Litster.

The wagon road leading up Boone Creek Canyon was made during Austin's Silver Rush in the 1860s. It is noted that these ranches were on land that had been homesteaded. Was there such a thing as road easements in those days or was it just understood that they were public roads? Did the Vaughan's really have the right to use the road just because they used it before the Litster's moved to the ranch property? You can make the case for public use on main road because many others were also using the road. But the side road to the Water Canyon could never have been called a public road.

Charlie asked Alfred before they left the ranch:

"Alfe, should I bring the shotgun?"

"No, just the Winchester."

This was Alfred's 44-caliber lever action rifle and the magazine held sixteen rounds. When you go into the back country it is a good idea to have some means self-protection. Many of the cowboys carried a sidearm and that was the way Charlie and Alfred generally traveled. Actually, it is probably more dangerous today than in 1893. May be you haven't heard, but mountain lions no longer have any fear of man, as they did a century ago. I'm from California so please forgive me. I'm just disappointed that city people don't understand that people and lions don't mix. The problem in California will only get worse. This State outlawed lion hunting about twenty years ago and these modern lions have never been hunted. They are doing good job of eliminating California's the deer herd. I think it would have been unusual for the Vaughan's not to have at least a one firearm with them. Charlie liked to carry his pistol everywhere he went, so he didn't mention he had it in a holster under his coat. Alfred also liked to carry his bulldog pistol.

Workdays at this time of year are short and it would be dark when they returned home at five o'clock. Nevada's clear dry morning air can be very cold; but it is not a damp cold, like the kind that can go right through you even with a much warmer temperature. Nevertheless, this morning was cold enough to make them feel good about wearing long johns. These cowboys were use to the cold and to them it was not all that cold, it was just a little below freezing.

Alfred was not worried about getting the wagon stuck as the ground was frozen and besides he had four big horses pulling the wagon. They passed a lone rider coming down the road when they were about three quarters of a mile up the road. The boy they ignored had said, "Good Morning", was Jimmy. The Vaughan wagon continued up the road towards the Eason Ranch. Here Charlie saw a cottontail rabbit and he asked Alfred to stop so he could get a shot. Charlie jumped off the wagon and moved away so he would not frighten the horses. He fired off three rounds, which missed, as Alfred laughed:

"You didn't even come close."

Recall, Johnny and Willie went to tell their father about the broken corral fence posts before riding up the canyon about the time when the Vaughan wagon came around the bend in the road. A question could be asked: Who saw whom first? Did the Litster boys see the Vaughan wagon moving up the road towards their ranch before they rode off? I think they did. The wagon was about a half to three quarter's mile down the road when the Vaughan's also notice two riders leave the lower corral and from that distance they could not recognize anyone. The Vaughan's had entered through the lower gate and Nick Rast had opened and closed the gate. Johnny and Willie were the riders they saw mounting their horses at the corral and gallop towards the house and then up the main road.

I am sure Johnny and Willie saw the Vaughan wagon while they were at the corral before they rode off. If they didn't see the wagon here, for sure they would see it later as it traversed the road through the upper pasture.

Willie could have said:

"Look whose coming Jack, it's the Vaughan's."

"Ya and you know where they are going."

Their father didn't hear what the boys were saying just before they rode off and momentarily he too would see the Vaughan wagon coming, but not until the boys had left. The Litster's and the Vaughan's had been neighbors for nearly thirteen years and for about ten of those years they were on good terms.

As Vaughan's approached the Litster's house, Charlie called Alfred's attention that he just saw two riders leaving the corral area. They were about 500 to 600 yards above the lower pasture's fence gate. This is where the road makes a sweeping turn and from here they had a view of the house and the corral area below the barn. The corral was about 300 yards from the house and below the barn on the south side of the canyon opposite from the main road on the north side of the canyon.

Alfred said: "Nick didn't you say that the Litster's went to Cortez for Christmas?"

"Those riders could be some the Watt boys."

This seems strange because they had already passed James Litster on the road; perhaps they too were confused and thought the boy they had ignored was Joe Eason.

As they moved closer they could see William Litster with the two little boys. Alfred told Charlie:

"Just keep moving, he is on the other side of the canyon and we don't want to talk to him".

The canyon bottom is about 300 yards wide at this location. Charlie said: "Those riders must have been Johnny and Willie."

There would have been a gate separating the upper pasture from the lower pasture, however no mention was made about opening this gate as the wagon rolled by the house at 9:30 a.m. They could see the fresh horse tracks heading up the road.

Surely, William had time to confront the Vaughan's as they went passed the ranch house. This would have been a logical time to air any complaint about leaving any gate open. He could have told them the Gap was closed and if they wanted to go through they must close the gate at the Gap. But here is the impact of a feud; William didn't want to talk to the Vaughan's anymore than Alfred wanted to talk to him. Actually, I believe

William was intimidated by the Vaughan's.

A few minutes after the Vaughan's went by, about 9:35 a.m. William placed the two little boys on the back of one of the big draft horses and he mounted the other horse. The horses then pulled the sled to the barn where William unhitched the horses and put them back in their stalls before going to the house. It was about ten o'clock when Elizabeth asks:

"Did you see the Vaughan's?"

Of course she knew William had seen them. She was concerned for her sons and she knew they were closing the gate at the Gap. Elizabeth could have walked to the barn when William and the little boys first returned to the barn, but she waited for William to come into the house. She also knew the Vaughan's were going to use the road that went up into the Water Canyon.

"William you must go and see where the boys are working."

"There could be trouble with the Vaughan's if Johnny and Willie are at the Gap when their wagon gets there."

"You know this is where the Vaughan's will be going."

William reluctantly agrees to go. Instead of riding a horse or walking up the main road, he walks up the wood road that has a southern exposure on the north side of the canyon to get a view of the upper pasture.

In the mean time Alfred pulled the wagon to a halt. It was about 9:40 a.m. when he said his hands were cold.

"Charlie you can drive now."

"Holding these reins has made my hands cold."

"I am going to walk with Nick."

"You should have worn them gloves that were in the barn, Alfe."

Evidently, Nick had not got back in the wagon after closing the lower gate to the upper pasture.

"Walking will warm me up."

Charlie handed Alfred the rifle as he took the reins. Alfred and Nick continued to walk behind wagon for about twenty minutes. Alfred and Nick walked the remaining distance before they were stopped at the Gap. Nick testified that he was on the upper left side of the road and Alfred was on the lower right side when they came to the closed gate at the Gap. The Gap was only a short distance, about seventy feet going south on a side road from the main road leading into the Water Canyon.

While Alfred and Nick were walking they could easily see the fresh tracks made by the Johnny and Willie's horses. The brothers had obviously rode straight to the Gap to wrap the wires. These wires for the gate were laying loose under the snow. There is little doubt in my mind about whether they saw the Vaughan's coming.

William should have been aware of the problem that would occur when the Vaughan's found the Gap closed. Did William think the boys would let them pass through the Gap and then close it behind them? William knew about the calf situation from the week before. Willie and Jimmy surely told their father about Willie retrieving the calf from the Vaughan pasture and Alfred had hit Willie with a quirt.

William left the house to walk up the wood road to the ridge on the north side of the canyon. His decision to walk will forever remain a mystery, even more than not confronting the Vaughan's as the wagon passes the house and more than Elizabeth waiting for him to come to the house before demanding that he go and check on the boys. I can only assume he thought he could see where Johnny and Willie were working from the view up on the ridge. It was about ten minutes past ten o'clock when he left the house. It will take William about twenty minutes to get to the point where he could see the area of the Gap at the mouth of the Water Canyon. I'll never understand why William decided to walk when he could have saddled a horse and ridden to the Gap in less time. Why? On our October 2002 trip, I walked up on this ridge. It proved to be a poor place to view the Gap at the mouth of the Water Canyon.

A better description of the gate at the Gap might be helpful. This is a place along the fence line where the wires could easily be disconnected for passage between two fence posts. When the wires were reconnected you would not know it was a gate except for the wagon tracks that could be seen on both side of the fence.

Johnny and Willie saw the wagon coming up the road while they were at the corral and they knew exactly where it was headed. Did they really think they could stop the Vaughan's from using this side road to the Water Canyon? Did William tell his boys not to let the Vaughan's go though the Gap that morning? I don't think so. In the past, William had given Mr. Vaughan permission to use the road through the Gap whenever he asked with one exception. Mr. Vaughan wanted to use the road to haul firewood and William said no, he would not allow that use. However, Alfred and Charlie never asked at anytime when they wanted use the road through the Gap..

Now two young men or should I say boys, one 19 and the other 16 were about to stop the wagon. Charlie, age 24 was driving the wagon, while Alfred, age 21 and Nick, age 43, were both walking behind it. The time was now about ten o'clock and the sun was shining on the snow covered ground. It was considerably warmer now than when wagon pulled out of the corral at the Vaughan Ranch under the shadows cast by the mountains to the east of Boone Canyon. This situation had all the ingredients for trouble. Remember, this was Nick's first day on the job. Could anyone guessed the results would produce a double murder at the gate know as the Gap?

3

The Gap

Is There a Gate?

It was about twenty minutes after nine o'clock when Johnny and Willie galloped away from corral. They both had seen the Vaughan wagon slowly coming up the road just before they mounted their horses that had been hitched at the upper corral railing. The Vaughan wagon was nearly half mile down the canyon on the main road that traverses the north side along the lower pasture.

"Jack come on, get that horse of yours moving." "We got to get to the Gap and get it closed before they get here."

The crisp cold morning air blew in their face as they galloped along the road. They made the sharp turn to the side road leading to the Water Canyon. Here they tied the their horses to a fencepost, ten minutes had lapsed, and the time was now 9:30 a.m. They knew the Vaughan wagon would be there in about one half hour.

"What are you doing Willie?"

"I'm cutting a willow switch just in case Alfe tries hitting me with his quirt again."

"What are you going to do if he does?"

"You'll see, if he hits me, he's gonna get hit back."

"Alright, I get one too."

The brothers both cut the willow switches before they began to tie the wires to closing the Gap.

"Hey we got to put new staples in the posts to hold these wires."

"One staple is missing and the others are very loose."

"Willie, the bottom wire is a little short, give me a piece of the splicing wire."

"Hurry up Jack!"

After the brothers had the Gap closed they waited for the Vaughan's.

"I see them coming?"

"Yah, they are sure going slow."

"That's because two of them are walking behind the wagon."

"There's three of them, Alfe, Charlie and I can't recognize the other guy." "It doesn't look like Frank or Harry."

"Willie, you let me do all the talking."

"I'll tell them they can't use this Gap anymore, Okay!"

"Jack, what do you think they'll say?"

"They are going to be mad as hell and that is for sure."

Yes, William told them that he wanted the Gap closed, because he was going to let the cattle back into the upper pasture. Here the boys are bent on showing Vaughan's they resented their trespassing. Johnny and Willie's frustration had seized this opportunity to harass the Vaughan's. The scene is now set for the confrontation. It would prove fatal and neither of these brothers would have ever guessed that Alfred might shoot them. They carried only the small tools needed for the fence work. This included two hammers; a bag of staples, some wire for any needed fence splicing and they each had a pocketknife.

Boone Creek Canyon is a pretty place even at this time of year as it was then blanketed with snow. William didn't acknowledge the wagon as it passed the corral and the woodpile road. William acted about the same way as the Vaughan's did when Jimmy rode by their wagon about thirty minutes ago. There was no cordial wave. People often acknowledge others by waiving even to those they don't particularly like. This was not the case here. Did William ever think about how he could he change the situation from this feud back to friendship? He could have thought as long as they are traveling through ranch and there is no major damage, well he could live with that. Yet, he knew Willie was very upset, especially after the calf recovery situation last week when Alfred hit him. He didn't know it but the bad feelings would shortly cost the lives of his two eldest sons.

These boys had all went to the Silver Creek School together. The school was about three miles from the Litster Ranch going towards Austin. There was a fork from the main road below the Litster's house that was used for those traveling to Silver Creek or Austin. This is road the Litster's used when they traveled to the Watt or Dunsdon ranches as well as going to Austin.

Let me repeat the scene. Johnny and Willie galloped their horses along the canyon road and the Vaughan's could easily see the fresh tracks in the snow. It was about a mile from Litster's ranch house and the condition of the road made the traveling very slow for the big wagon. The gate at the Gap was not like most fence gates that you see on ranches today. Again, from a distance you might think that it was a continuation of the fence when it was closed, except for the rutted wagon tracks on both sides of the fence. It was really a place where barbwire between two posts could be spliced or should I say where the wires are warped together in the middle between these posts to close the opening. To open the gate at the Gap you just untied the wires and tossed each of them to the opposite side. This is the way the Vaughan's left this gate always open. Johnny and Willie often had to ride up and close the gate behind them whenever cattle were in the upper pasture.

Johnny and Willie knew about their so-called mine. They had ridden up the Water Canyon last month and all they saw was the Vaughan's sign posting the unpatented "Blue Ledge" mining claim. There was a hole in the ground that exposed a quartz ledge that might be silver bearing rock. The hole was about ten feet long and about five feet deep. The area had been cleared and it looked like the Vaughan's were planning to build a cabin. Did Litster's think the Vaughan's were going to squat on the land after building this cabin? If they did, perhaps they would have guessed correctly.

As the brothers watched the approaching wagon from behind the willows that concealed the area around the Gap, Willie said:

"Now Jack, the bastards can turn around and go back home."

"This is not their road."

Willie's statement was very true and this road was certainly not a public road. The Litster's maintained the lower part of the road on their ranch property. They used the road to haul firewood and to clean the spring from any from animal pollution. T. J. Perkins lived about four miles above the Litster in Boone Canyon, as well as Nels Haydon who also had a place near Perkins. These men were woodcutters. Whenever they used the Water Canyon road they asked William for his permission.

You can make a good case for public use of the main road. That road has always been used by those passing through the ranch as well as for the road that forked below the ranch house going towards Silver Creek. Why did William let the Vaughan's get away with using this side road through the Gap to the Water Canyon? I believe William had become afraid of these young gun packing Vaughan cowboys. He should have had the Sheriff put a stop to the Vaughan's traveling this way to the Water Canyon.

The ground at the Gap was frozen and covered with a few inches of snow. The exchange of words at the gate by these individuals will become the basis of the testimony by Alfred, Charlie and Nick Rast. Charlie turned the team pulling the wagon from the main road onto the side road and then across a small wood bridge over Boone Creek. It was about 10 o'clock when the big wagon came to a stop. It has been about a week since the Vaughan's were last here. Charlie stopped the big horses about six to eight feet from the closed Gap. The sun was shining and only a few shady spots remained. They didn't expect to find the Gap closed, but they were expecting to see the two Litster brothers because they had been following their fresh horse tracks. Still they were surprised to see them both standing with their arms crossed in front of the now wired shut Gap.

The Litster boys had been working for about a half hour and Willie had even taken his winter coat off. It was in his way, so he hung it over the fencepost. Willie was standing on the right downhill side of the road toward the ranch house. Johnny was standing on the uphill eastside of the road.

Johnny breaks the momentary silence:

"You guys need to find some other way to travel to wherever

you are going." "We are going to keep this fence closed."

Both boys were both holding the freshly cut willow sticks. Before the Vaughan's could answer Johnny, Willie yelled out to the men on the wagon:

"This ain't your road." "You can turn the damn wagon around and go back." "We are going to keep this gap closed and you can't go up here anymore."

So much for letting Johnny do all the talking.

Charlie now tells the brothers:

"Sorry boys, but we have to go through the Gap."

Again Johnny said: "You'll have to find some other way to travel to your mine."

The following situation gave way to an argument full of swearing.

Willie told Alfred: "You don't have a mine and if our Papa was here you won't even try to go through this fence."

Alfred responds: "I don't care who is here, we are going through you Litster sons of bitches."

Johnny and Willie recognized the third person in the wagon was Nick Rast and they were good friends of Nick's nephew Herbert. Nick had only known these youngsters casually during the last ten years and it seems Nick had no idea the feud was this bad. He couldn't believe what he was now hearing. He was probably thinking how did I ever get into this situation as these young hot heads continued to swear at each other.

Nick had walked up to Johnny on the left side of the wagon. Alfred had run up on the right side of the wagon and he was in Willie's face. Alfred and Willie continued swearing at each other as they were nose to nose. Nick was trying to be reasonable as he conversed with Johnny. And for a moment it looked like things were going to be okay. Johnny even asked Nick if his brother's son, Herbert, was going back to school next week. Nick could see new staples had been placed in the fence posts. But it seemed that Alfred and Willie were going to come to blows. Willie wasn't backing down to this older and larger young man. so Nick grabbed an axe handle from the wagon. He stepped between them. He was thinking that he might have to breakup a fight. Nick tried to cool the situation by stepping between

Willie and Alfred a second time as the swearing continued. Willie and Alfred finally stopped yelling and now they were just staring or should I say glaring at each other.

Nick resumed his conversation with Johnny. Remember the rifle, Alfred was still carrying that Winchester. Charlie was holding the reins and he was content to let Nick and Alfred do all the talking. Alfred took the Winchester when he got off the wagon. The rifle was loaded and ready to fire. Perhaps, if Alfred had just left the rifle in the wagon with Charlie their world would have been different.

Stories told later by Alfred and Charlie, as well as Nick, were certainly an attempt to justify a situation that had now gone bad. What Johnny and Willie had done was going to cause Alfred to loose control of the hatred he felt for the Litster's. While, Nick was still talking to Johnny, he took out his smoking pipe and lights it.

Johnny now relents and gives his consent to Nick to open the Gap:

"We will let you go through, but this will be the last time you can use this road."

Nick starts to get an axe to pull the staples at the left side fencepost. Johnny tells Nick that is not necessary.

"Nick just untie the wires at the center, you don't need to pull the staples."

Nick tosses his axe to the back left side of the wagon. This is an important point to remember, because Nick will testify to this fact. Johnny proceeds to help Nick with the wires as Alfred and Willie continued their cold stare at each other as they are facing off on the right side of the wagon near the lead horses.

Alfred was obviously thinking about what Johnny had just said about not being able to use this road anymore. Also, what did Willie say about them not having a "mine"? He knew how true those words were, if they could not use this access road they would have to travel much further to access the mine. Alfred was close to the edge and in a few seconds he would go over the edge as his hatred spilled out.

Nick and Johnny were in the process of undoing the second splice in the wires. **BANG**! The silence was broken, as the ear splitting ring came from Alfred's Winchester. And in a second the silence returned. Then panic, Nick starts to runs up the road looking for cover. As he glances back and he sees Charlie pulling hard on the reins to control the four horses. Alfred had now walked in front of lead horses to the left uphill side of the road.

Alfred fired the first shot at this point blank range from the hip at Willie who was now on his knees after falling and rolling over near the right gatepost. Charlie was doing his best to continue to steady the horses. Johnny was now backing away down the road to the rear of the wagon on the left side. Alfred has the rifle to his shoulder and he was pointing the gun at Johnny.

Johnny was waiving his hands and pleading:

"Don't shoot, Alfe don't shoot."

Charlie was also yelling at Alfred:

"Don't shoot him Alfe."

Nick starts to run back to stop Alfred. Johnny turns and starts to run just as Alfred fires the second shot. As Johnny falls down, he rolls over and was lying face up.

Nick was about six feet from Alfred when the second shot reported. Nick now goes to Willie and he asks:

"Are you bad hurt?"

Willie was gut shot and the pain was unbearable as he screamed for help:

"Get my father; Get my father."

Nick then ran around the wagon to Johnny. Johnny made one last groan as the air left his lungs. He was dead from the shot that passed through his lung and heart. Nick returned to Willie, who was up on his hands and knees vomiting a blood mixed with his early morning breakfast.

Nick walked to Alfred and with his heavy German ascent he says:

"For Christ's sakes why you shoot these boys?" "We have to get help."

Nick goes back again to Willie who is still crying for someone to go and get his father. Nick said:

"I will go."

Alfred interrupts: "I want you to get that last damn wire opened so we can turn the wagon around." Alfred had just previously grabbed Johnny by the boots and pulled his body back from the roadway. They would have to turn the wagon around on the other side of the fence because the bodies of the two boys were in the way.

"I'm going to Austin and turn myself in."

He was pointing the hot barrel of the Winchester at Nick when he told him to finish opening the Gap. No one feels comfortable with a gun pointed at them and Nick proceeded to remove the third wire to open the gap. Charlie whips the horses as they pull through the space between the fence posts. Charlie stepped on the left side wagon brake as the horses turned the wagon. He made two full circles before Alfred untangled one of the horses that got caught in the harness stretcher. Charlie was having trouble getting the horses back through the Gap. Alfred told Nick to climb on the wagon while he continued to point the rifle. Nick will testify that he was very much afraid of Alfred.

Charlie continued to have his hands full by keeping these horses from bolting. Charlie asks Alfred as he climbed on the wagon:

"Why did you shoot them?"

"I have to go to Austin to tell the Sheriff what happened here."

"I should have done this a long time ago."

Yes, Alfred meant to kill Johnny and Willie. Why didn't Alfred just put the rifle back on the wagon when it stopped? Why did he think shooting these two boys would make things better? The facts show that he acted alone in this situation. There was no threat to him that would have caused him to defend himself with deadly force, except for his claim you will hear shortly. He and his brother would claim self-defense with Nick's initial support. Can anyone guess what caused him to commit these acts of murder?

Yes, he just told us why he did it. Remember, Willie said:

"You don't have a mine."

Did he really think it would be better by shooting the Litster brothers? Perhaps, he did.

Generally, by the time a boy, now a young man twenty-one years old, well usually they have gained some common sense along with a little self-control. We've all heard about bar room brawls where the good guys and the bad guys had fights. Sometimes with guns or knifes. Liquor often was the cause for these young men to act with less than better judgment. Yes, we all know about feuds that have extended over many years. Some of these feuds eventually reach a boiling point. There can be no doubt that this is what happened at the Gap. Alfred lost control to his hatred for these two brothers and willfully with malice shot them. Is this Nevada's version of the Hatfield and McCoy's?

As the wagon came about Alfred and Nick climbed on board and Alfred tells Charlie:

"Get these horses moving fast."

The time was about 10:20 a.m. when Nick tells Alfred:

"We must stop at the Litster house?"

"No!" "Shut up, Nick, or do you want to be in a dead man's coffin too?"

Nick responded: "Mr. Litster might have heard them shots."

Why was Nick concerned about someone hearing the two shots? Was he thinking that Alfred would shoot and kill more people just to get off the ranch?

Nick asks: "Alfe do you have plenty of bullets?

"Plenty, didn't I say shut up?"

Remember, William started to walk along the north ridge fence line that goes up above the upper pasture. By examining the Quad Map it appears that he would have had to climb the hillside for about two hundred vertical feet and then walk about a half-mile before he would be able to see the area near the mouth of the Water Canyon. Again, I'll never understand why this was William's choice for the way to check on his sons. Assuming that he left the house about ten minutes after ten o'clock and considering the conditions with snow on the ground it would not have been an easy walk. The ridge has a southern exposure so there would have been less snow here and walking may have been somewhat easier. Still it probably would take him at least fifteen minutes to get to the point on the ridge to view the area of the Gap.

William was sure that his sons started the fence work at the Gap as he had told them. Did he think they might possibly have been working back along the north ridge fence line? He wasn't following any tracks as he made his way up to the ridge. Here William will see the Vaughan wagon coming back down the road from the ridge as it passes about 100 yards below where he was standing behind some small pine trees. The time was about 10:30 a.m. The horses were loping in a fast gallop and the riders in the wagon were being bounced around. Normally, you never drive a big wagon fast on a road like this.

What must have been going through William's mind? Why were they going fast and why were they returning? Remember, he didn't hear the two shots that were fired about fifteen minutes earlier. I can only assume he was huffing and puffing going up the ridge and with the snow crust breaking under his feet those shots did not register with his hearing or that he was still in the house where the shots were not audible. Also, Marie Jeanne states that sound is muffled within the canyon. We know Nick was very concerned about William hearing those two shots.

Personally, I just keep thinking about why didn't William ride a horse to check on his boys? Hearing the shots was never questioned during the trials. I have thought about the situation and I have concluded William too could have been shot had he arrived at the wrong time at the Gap or if he tried to stop the wagon come back down the road. Still he might have gotten to the Gap while the arguing was raging and he could have calmed the situation. It took William about another fifteen to twenty minutes to walk off the ridge and the remaining half mile to the Gap.

As he approached the Gap he could see both Johnny and Willie' horses tied to fence posts. Then terror set in as he saw the bodies of his two sons lying in the snow, one on each side of the road. Can anyone add words to what William was now thinking as he runs to Johnny's motionless body lying there in the blood stained snow?

Willie was aware that his father had come as he continued

moaning with great pain. You would think Willie would have passed out from shock.

"Papa, I thought you would never come."

"Who shot you?"

"Alfred Vaughan shot me." "He shot us both."

"You must lay here and stay quiet." "I have to go back for a wagon to carry you."

He covered Willie with the heavy winter coat that had been hanging over the fencepost and then he mounted Willie horse raced down the road. It is mile back to the house. William sees Jimmy riding towards him and he yells at Jimmy to return to the house with him.

William tells Jimmy: "When we get to the house I want you to get the spring wagon out of the barn". He knew what he had to tell his wife was going hurt. Elizabeth was standing in the door way and she knew by the look on William's face something terrible had happened. "The boys have been shot." Could she believe what he just said?

"We have to hitch the wagon and bring them to the house."

"Willie is alive."

"What about Johnny?"

William can only answer what his wife had sensed he was about to say: "Johnny is dead!"

The two little boys, George and Louis, seemed bewildered as their sister; Lizzie begins a screaming cry, as does her mother. Elizabeth held Lizzie as she collapsed in her mother's arms.

Elizabeth knew something bad had happened because Jimmy came home from the Eason's. He told his mother that Nick Rast said there was trouble up here and that Nick told him to go home which he did and she then told him to ride to the Gap. That was how he met his father galloping down the road. Jimmy's fourteenth birthday was just a couple months away. He was a big boy for his age. He would soon be William's oldest living son.

William told his wife:

"We have to hurry for Willie sake." "Send Lizzie and Louis to get Mollie."

This is the widow, Mrs. Alex Eason.

"I'm sending George to Tom's." "He can ride Willie's horse." "George you have to tell Tom that Johnny and Willie have been shot and we need him to get the doctor for Willie."

It was about a four-mile ride and little George should make it there in less than a half hour. George was eight years old and he was already a good rider. William helped George mount Willie's horse after adjusting the stirrups and then he tells George to go but don't work the horse to hard. The newspaper account said the little boy found Thomas Dunsdon, and that he and two other Dunsdon men, John and Nathan that made the ride to Austin for the doctor. Actually, it was just two riders, Nate and John Dunsdon. They are Tom's two sons.

William now runs to the barn to help Jimmy. As they start from the barn Elizabeth tells William she was going with them. William, Elizabeth and Jimmy proceed up the road to the Gap. William whipped the big horse as they went up the frozen bumpy ruddy road. That mile ride must have taken forever for Willie's, Mamma. Elizabeth and William must have been in a time warp as everything seemed to be in slow motion and she begged William to go faster. It was going to be very difficult for her and as she sees Johnny, she jumped off the wagon before it came to a stop and fell in the snow. Then she ran to Johnny. William stopped wagon and ran after her as she again fell on her knees beside her son. William lifts her from the snow:

"Mother, Mother look at me, we have to help Willie." "Johnny is gone."

"Jimmy and I will make a another trip for Johnny's body while you are caring for Willie."

Surprisingly, Willie was still conscious and seemed to be in less pain. That is until they moved him to the wagon. The three of them carefully lifted Willie and place him in a sitting position on the back of the wagon. The movement brought a great deal of pain to Willie. He did not want to lie down so his Mamma and Jimmy sat on each side of him with their feet hanging down at the back of the wagon. They covered him with a blanket, but the support they provided didn't help very much.

Elizabeth screamed: "William, you have to drive slower." "The bumps are hurting Willie."

Willie continued to cry out in great pain, as the wagon jarred him. He was still bleeding. He had lost a lot of blood and there was blood dripping from the wagon down onto the white snow covering the road.

When they arrive back at the house they saw Mollie's wagon. She had the kids and her son Joe was with her. I wonder if this is the Joe Eason that the mountain was named after. It is the big mountain a couple of miles north east of the ranch. Mollie told William the Vaughan wagon stopped at her place about an hour ago and Nick Rast jumped off and told her that they had some bad trouble. Jimmy was talking to Joe and he told Jimmy he'd better go home. She said, Alfred told Nick to get back on the wagon and he made Charlie drive off before she could ask any questions.

She was then told Johnny had been killed and Willie was shot too. He needs to be put in bed. Mollie helped them carry Willie to the bedroom. They tried to make Willie comfortable by removing is boots and they told Willie the doctor was on his way.

Willie said, "No use, he can't help me."

Willie's mother was again about to collapse with tears flowing. Later she tried to get Willie to take some medicine, but he said:

"It won't help, it is just a waste, I'm not going to make it."

"I'll be with Jack."

Willie liked to call his big brother by that nickname.

William again asks Willie: "Why did Alfred shoot you?"

"No reason, he just did." "All we did was to tell them that they can't use the Gap anymore."

"Jack said they could go through this last time." "Then he shot me; and then he shot Jack" "I knew he killed Jack, he never once moved."

Later Mrs. Eason will testify that she heard this declaration and she would say Willie did not have any firearms when he was brought to the house.

In the meantime little George arrived at the Dunsdon's. Here Tom's wife, Emily tells him that Thomas is rounding up some horses. Fortunately, Tom saw the boy racing his horse to their house and he thought he better check it out and see if there was a problem. George was sobbing as he told Tom and Emily: "My brothers...Johnny and Willie shot...Papa said...we need the doctor."

Tom's two sons were with him and they heard what George said. Tom told his boys to get fresh horses and ride hard to Austin and to get Doc Huntsman to come to the Litster's fast as he can. Then he told George to wait and to ride back with him and his wife.

"We're not going fast George and you need to be easy with that horse or he ain't gonna make it." "You can help me hitch the wagon George."

George began to cry. Emily tells Tom she is going to hold little George. She gave him a big hung and held him while Tom hitched the wagon.

Emily said: "George will you please ride in the wagon with me?"

Back at the Litster Ranch, William was now worrying about George. Did he find the Dunsdon's? William decides to send Jimmy to see if anyone did go for the doctor. William also tells Jimmy to go to the Watt's and tell them what happened. The time is about 1:35 p.m. when Jimmy rode out. He was about half way to the Dunsdon Ranch when he met the Dunsdon wagon with George riding on the bench between Tom and Emily. Willie's horses hitched to the back of the wagon.

"Yes, Nate and John went for the doctor."

"Papa wants me to tell Mr. Watt."

Jimmy proceeded to the Watt Ranch, it was a little before two o'clock when he arrived. George Watt couldn't believe what Jimmy was telling him, yet he knew the boy was telling the truth. Mr. Watt told Jimmy to go with his son, George Watt, Jr. to Austin and tell the Sheriff what had happened. George Watt, Jr. was a young man in his early twenties and he was very close to his cousins, Willie and Johnny. They left for Austin shortly after two o'clock.

Sheriff Easton had already received the news about the shooting when the Dunsdon brothers rode into town. Sheriff Easton told this deputy that he was leaving immediately for the Litster Ranch. As he was riding toward Silver Creek and he met

Jimmy and George Jr. galloping in his direction. It was about three o'clock when they greeted the Sheriff. All the Sheriff knew was that there had been a shooting at the Litster Ranch and that the Dunsdon's had been in town to get the doctor. After Jimmy explained to the Sheriff that Willie and Johnny were both shot and Johnny was dead. Alfred Vaughan had shot them. Sheriff Easton now understands this was a possible murder. That being the case he decided to send Jimmy back home to the ranch while he and George Jr. would go back to Austin. The Sheriff wanted to tell the District Attorney, W. D. Jones, they had a murder on their hands.

In the meantime George Watt, Sr. and his wife Isabella were traveling to the Litster Ranch. They arrived there a little after three o'clock.

An hour earlier at two o'clock William did greet the Dunsdon's as they came to the house. William told Tom that he had both boys here now. Tom said:

"What happened Billy?"

"The boys were shot this morning by Alfred Vaughan."

"Who?" "Johnny and Willie"

Tom knew, but it was a rhetorical comment as he too was still in a state of disbelief.

"Tom did anyone go for the doctor?"

"I sent Nate and John for the doctor." "They had fresh horses and they should be in Austin by now."

By way of comparison the Pony Express riders in 1861 rode 75 to 100 miles a day. They changed horses every 10 to 15 miles and their average speed was approximately 10 miles per hour. Tom's boys were faster. It was 18 miles to town and they made the ride in less than two hours. They would ride back to the Litster Ranch, 22 miles, in less than three hours including the stop to change horses at their ranch before continuing on to let the Litster's know the doctor was on his way.

William took Tom to see Willie. Here William said:

"Tom this is rough."

"It is pretty rough, Billy."

"Tell Tom who shot you Willie."

"Alfred did and he shot Jack too."

"Why did he shoot you?"

"We told him not to go through the Gap anymore."

"Did you do anything to him?"

"Did you hit him?"

"Did you have a gun?" "Did you threaten him?"

"No Papa! No Papa!"

Tom said: "Willie, the doctor will be here soon."

"No use, he can't help me." "I'm going with Jack."

Everyone hearing Willie's response to Tom could not hold back his or her tears. There would be more crying on this sad day.

Both Tom and Billy knew Willie was dying. It was getting harder for Willie to talk and he was still vomiting, though only a smaller amount of blood now. His voice was become more faint as another hour slipped away. The people at the house were talking less. They were just sitting and waiting and waiting. It was after four o'clock now. Willie's breathing grew so faint and then it stopped. His Mamma closed Willie's eyes as everyone wept openly. Mollie tried to comfort her dear friend, but she too was not handling the situation very well either. Tom took Billy's arm and led him out of the house and they just stood and starred down the long canyon for several minutes.

Finally, Emily came out and said:

"Billy, I'll fix the kids some food, they got to eat."

William thanked her.

It was dark when Doctor Huntsman's wagon came at about 5:30 p.m. Joe Moss was with the doctor, He worked for the Lander County's Commissioner's Office and was a member of the Coroner's Juror. Billy and Tom greeted him and proceeded to inform him that both boys were dead. The doctor offered his condolence. He then told William it would be necessary for him to examine the gunshot wounds to both boys' bodies. George Watt helped the Doctor and Joe Moss remove the boy's clothing for the examination. One of the items was Willie's vest. George Watt said:

"We need to store this vest." "It clearly shows the blood stain and the bullet hole for evidence."

Joe Moss assisted the Doctor as clothing was cut from the

boy's bodies.

There were a lot of people in the house that night, but there would be very little sleep. Most were content to sit and talk about what had to be done. The Doctor asked if he could spend the night and said all he needed was just a chair. George Watt told Doc Huntsman he should go with him back to the Watt Ranch, which he agreed to do. Joe said he would just sleep here because other members of the Coroner's Jury would be there tomorrow morning.

About three hours had passed before Jones arrived at the ranch. The hour was about 9:30 p.m. The sky was clear and there was a nearly full moon. Those wagons didn't have headlights and driving at night was not that easy, so the moonlight was a big help. Jones told William he had sent Sheriff Easton to arrest Alfred Vaughan. He told William he was going to need a statement about the shooting. He said, he had made arrangements for the Coroner's Inquest. Mr. Bray would be here in the morning to investigate the scene of the shooting. He said he would be leaving for Austin at first light and asked William if it was all right to sleep in one of those stairs not being used.

The people in town were shocked by the news. The Litster family had many friends in Austin. When the Sheriff first learned about the shooting, he only knew that there was a shooting and at least one of the Litster boys had been shot. The Sheriff headed towards Litster's after the Dunsdon brothers rode back towards Silver Creek. The Sheriff learned that Johnny was dead and Willie too was shot. It is late that afternoon when the Sheriff and George Jr. met with Jones and explained what they knew about the shootings. Jones told the Sheriff that he must go to the Vaughan Ranch and arrest Alfred and anyone that was with him when the shooting occurred. George Jr. said he would go with the Sheriff. This had the makings of a very long cold and dangerous night for the Sheriff and George Jr.

The sun was already beginning to set. They figured they could make the Vaughan Ranch in about four hours. No one really wants to be out on a freezing winter night with the temperature dropping into the teens or lower. They packed several extra blankets. They didn't have nice car with a heater to be adjusted for comfort. The Sheriff had no idea about what to expect or how he was going to approach the Vaughan family.

Fortunately, when they were about five miles out of town near the Nevada Central Railroad tracks in the Reese River Valley they saw two riders approaching in the opposite direction. As the riders came closer, the Sheriff recognized the two Vaughan brothers as Alfred and Charlie. They pulled up their horses up next to the buggy that the Sheriff and George Jr. were using. Alfred said:

"Sheriff Easton we are coming to town to see you." "I had a shootout with the Litster boys and we need to tell our story to you."

The Sheriff asked: "Are you boys carrying any guns beside that rifle in your scabbard?"

Alfred said it was the only gun he had. It was the 44-caliber Winchester. Charlie tells the Sheriff he has his bulldog pistol.

"I have to place you and Charlie under arrest." "You can give me your statement when we get back to Austin."

"Sheriff, I had to defend myself."

"Save it Alfred, I'll take your statement later." "Now let's ride before it gets any colder."

Before closing this tragic day. Let's back up a to the point when Alfred tells Nick to get back in the wagon at the Eason place and they proceeded to Vaughan Ranch. It was about 11.30 a.m. when the four horses pulled the wagon back into the Vaughan's barnyard. Part of the following conversations report here came from Nick Rest's testimony that he made at the coming trials. Lee Vaughan, the father and Mr. Tipsword, met Alfred and Charlie as they pulled the wagon to a stop outside the corral.

"What in hell you guys doing back here?"

"We had some trouble with the Litster's."

"What kind of trouble, Alfe?"

Charlie interrupts: "Alfe shot Johnny and Willie."

"You did what?

"They wouldn't let us go through the Gap at the fence."

"Did they shoot at you?"

"No Pa!" "I just got mad" "I can't stand that smart ass Willie."

"Did you kill them?"

"I think so, Johnny for sure."

"What about Willie?"

"He is gut shot and he ain't gonna make it,"

"We left him as he was about to die."

This was about the time Harry too returned to the ranch with a load coal he brought from the Switch. Harry responded: "You dumb assholes" "You don't know how long he'll live." "You left him alive to testify against you."

Alfred answered: "It is our word against theirs and besides I said he was dying."

Later Nick will testify that the family continued to talk about what they should do.

Lee Vaughan told his sons: "You got to let the Sheriff know it was a gunfight and they started it."

Alfred and Charlie will stick to this story throughout all three trials to come

Poor Nick Rest, he must have been wondering what in the hell I am doing here. Nick is not family and his presence during the shooting of Johnny and Willie was not going to make his life easy. It was agreed that they must go to town as Alfe had said back at the Gap. He would tell the Sheriff it was gunfight and Charlie would backup his story. Alfred and Charlie saddled two horses and left for Austin at 2:30 p.m.

Nick said: "I don't want any part of this."

Lee Vaughan told Nick he really doesn't have a choice.

"You are in it the same as Alfe and Charlie."

Lee Vaughan continues to persuade Nick that he must back the boy's story or he too will be swinging at the end of a rope. Nick finally agreed to support Alfe's story. It was about three o'clock when Nick said he would be willing to go to the Sheriff.

Lee Vaughan said: "We can ride to Austin in my wagon."

Lee and Nick arrived at the Sheriff's office at the courthouse just a little after 7:00 p.m. Here they found the Sheriff had arrested both Alfe and Charlie and they were being held in a jail cell at the courthouse.

Sheriff Easton said:

"I understand that Nick was with Alfred and Charlie today."

Lee responds:

"That is why Nick is here to give you his statement."

"I've decided not take any statements till morning, but right now I'm going to place Nick under arrest."

The Sheriff and Jones had already reported to W. H. Bray, the Coroner about the death of at least one of the brothers. They didn't know at this time that both brothers had been killed. Jimmy told the Sheriff, Johnny was dead and Willie was shot. This December 28, 1893 was coming to a close. It was a most tragic day for the Litster's. The days that will follow will only add to the sadness a murder can bring. As for the Vaughan's, they too have been deeply hurt, but in a different way. They must now try to save their son. I have a problem with this and their lack of compassion for what Alfred did. The Vaughan's most tragic day will come in a couple years on April 10, 1896.

The following timeline is the basis of my reconstructed version of this story. I believe the details as presented are closed to the actually happenings. Still, I am the first to say these details have many missing parts. These parts have been lost like much of our history and written records can never fully recapture the reality of the past. As a reader, you can decide whether the timing and occurrences agrees with the testimony that will be given in the following trials.

Timeline: Killed at the Gap, December 28, 1893

5:00 a.m.	Elizabeth is up and the stove is on and coffee started
5:30	Mom now wakes William, Johnny, Willie and Jimmy.
6:00	Brothers get dressed gather eggs, milk and wood.
6:30	Breakfast for parents and big boys.
7:00	Mom now gets Lizzie, George and Louis out of bed.
7:15	Boys start work by finish house chores and start feeding barn animals
7:30	Breakfast for little kids.
7:45 a.m.	Johnny and Willie hitch workhorses to slide and load it with hay.

8:15 a.m.	Jimmy leaves on horse to get mail at the Vaughan Station
8:15	Hay sled brought to house for William.
8:30	Johnny & Willie feed barn horses.
8:30	Vaughan's and Rast start up Boone Canyon.
8:45	Johnny & Willie gather tools for fence repair work.
8:45	Jimmy passes Vaughan wagon and say good morning Nick responds.
9:15	Johnny & Willie ride to the corral to talk to William
9:20	Johnny & Willie: left the corral to work on fence repairs in upper pasture.
9:20	William sees Vaughan wagon about ¾ mile down the canyon.
9:25	Jimmy is coming back and he stops to visit Joe Eason.
9:30	Vaughan Wagon on main road passes Corral area 150 yard to south side of canyon.
9:35	William takes team to barn and unhitches horses
9:45	Alfred stops wagon to walk and lets Charlie drive.
9:55	William and little boys go to house.
10:00	Mother tells William to check on the boys.
10:00	Vaughan wagon arrives the gap, gate has been closed, argument starts.
10:10	William leaves house and walks towards ridge fence line.
10:15	Alfred shoots Willie, then he shoots Johnny.
10:20	Charlie turns wagon around and starts back down the road, horses loping.
10:30	William sees wagon coming back down road.
10:50	Vaughan stops at Eason's Nick said trouble.
10:55	Jimmy rides home from Eason's.
10:55.	William finds boys shot at gate.
11:00	William rides Willie's back to house.
11:15	William arrives at house, tells Mother.
11:20	William and Jimmy hitch buggy.
11:20	Little George to Dunsdon's to get a doctor for Willie.
11:25 a.m.	William, Mother, Jimmy leave house for Willie, Lizzie and Louis sent to Eason's.

11:30 a.m.	Vaughan's arrives back at their ranch.
11:45	Place Willie in the back of buggy.
11:35	Mrs. Eason and her son Joe start for Litster ranch.
11:55	Mrs. Eason and her son, Joe, arrive at house.
12:15 p.m.	Willie is brought into house.
12:20	Willie makes dying declaration to Mrs. Eason.
12:20	George arrives at Dunsdon place.
12:30	William and Jimmy go back for Johnny' body.
12:30	Nate Dunsdon rides 17 miles to Austin for Doctor.
12:45	Tom and Emily Dunsdon with wife with George starts back to Litster Ranch.
1:15	William and Jimmy return with Johnny's body.
1:35	Jimmy rides 6 miles to Watt Ranch.
2:00	Nate arrives in Austin.
2:10	Jimmy and George Watt, Jr. start for Austin.
2:15	Tom and Emily Dunsdon arrive at Litster Ranch.
2:20	Willie makes dying declaration to Tom Dunsdon.
2:25	George Watt, Sr. and Isabella leave for Litster's.
2:30.	Alfred and Charlie leave for Austin.
2:30	Doctor Huntsman leaves Austin.
3.00	Nick Rast agrees to go with Mr. Lee Vaughan.
3:00	Jimmy and George Watt, Jr. meet Sheriff on the road. Jimmy returns to ranch.
3:10	George Watt, Sr. and Isabella arrive at Litster's.
4:20	Willie dies from gunshot wound to stomach, time of death, recorded by Mother.
5:00	Sheriff Easton and George Watt, Jr. leaves for Vaughan Ranch in George's wagon.
5:10	District Attorney W. D. Jones goes to Litster's.
5:30	Sheriff arrests Alfred and Charlie.
5:30	Doctor arrives at Litster Ranch.
7:00	Lee and Nick arrive at Sheriff's office, Nick is arrested.
9:30 p.m.	District Attorney Jones arrives at ranch to get a statement from the Litster's and the others that were there.

Again, I want to say the scenario presented in the second and third chapters for the events of Thursday, December 28, 1893 should be close to the truth of this tragic day. It would be impossible to reach another interpretation after I researching the available records

Hatred within Alfred Vaughan soul was truly the reason why he shot Johnny and Willie.

The cause of Alfred's hatred really doesn't matter.

Yes, Willie said: "You have no mine."

Yes Johnny said : "You can't use this road anymore."

Yes, William said: "Don't ever come back with that pistol."

Nothing the Litster's did or said can justify what Alfred did!

4

INVESTIGATION

What really happened?

Friday, the day after the shooting, the people in Austin were talking about just one thing. The shooting was on everyone's mind. What really happened? Had both brothers been killed? Someone said the doctor was seen driving his wagon back into town about 9 o'clock that morning. Others were saying that Sheriff Easton had Alfred and Charlie Vaughan locked up in jail. Another person said he also has Nick Rast in jail too. The news yesterday generated a lot of excitement following Nate and John Dunsdon's report that Willie Litster had been shot and he needed a doctor. Later this morning they will learn that both Johnny and Willie were killed.

The news really spread last night when Sheriff Easton reported the shooting to the District Attorney, W. D. Jones. The initials stand for William Dudley and to friends he was just called "WD". Before Jones left for the Litster Ranch last night he told the Coroner, W. H. Bray, there was at least one death as the result of the shooting and he must conduct the inquest on Friday. Jones told him Joe Moss went with the Doctor and they both stayed over night at the Litster's. Bray made plans to travel with the other members of the Coroner's Jury, Charlie Polkinghorn, Billy Sciuchetti and Elsie Whaley. The twenty-two mile buggy ride to the ranch meant they would be sitting most of the day going to and from the ranch. They left Austin a little after six o'clock. Bray wanted to be at the Litster's by ten o'clock that morning.

They were about ten mile out of town when they met Dr.

Huntsman coming back to Austin. The Doctor told them to expect a sad scene at the Litster's and both Johnny and Willie had been killed.

When they arrived at the Litster's they saw how right the Doctor was about the sad scene. Members of the family and friends were still crying. They saw all the swollen eyes from the crying and lack of sleep. William Litster took them first to see the bodies of the two brothers. They were each lying on their own beds in the room where the older brothers slept. William told Bray that Dr. Huntsman had examined the bodies last night before going on to the Watt Ranch where he spent the night.

It was very hard for family members to talk when they so tearful and choked up. Mollie and Emily had spent the night helping Elizabeth by never letting her be alone. Bray told William that they would need to get the boys ready for a burial. He also said he would arrange for the church service at one o'clock tomorrow afternoon, if that was all right with William. "That will be fine, we will be there about noon."

Bray then asked William if he would show them the place where the boys were shot. Tom Dunsdon hitched his wagon. Then the two buggies made the short mile ride through the upper pasture. The snow was still covering the rough frozen roadway. When they turned off the main road they could see the opening at the Gap. As you recall, the Vaughan's wagon had to drive through the Gap to turn around without running over Johnny. They could see the evidence in the snow and it told a clear story. Footprints and wagon tracks were seen, as were the horse tracks from the Vaughan's wagon.

It appeared like the Vaughan wagon nearly ran over the boys as they were lying at each edge of the road. The wheels came close to where the boys had lain. They could see that the Vaughan wagon had went through the opening in the fence and made two full circles before coming back through the Gap. Remember, Charlie was having trouble controlling the horses. They obviously were leaving the scene in haste. William said he saw the wagon coming down the road yesterday while he was on the ridge above the road. He added that he knew something was wrong by the way they were making the big horses lope. This was not normal for a big wagon. Clearly everyone's eye had focused on the blood stained marks in the snow left by the bodies of Johnny and Willie after being shot and left for dead. It was especially upsetting to see the blood and vomit left by Willie.

Each of the attending members of the Coroner's Jury made notes of the murder scene. Then they returned to the Litster's house where they questioned Tom Dunsdon and Mollie Eason in private. They were particularly interested in whether Johnny and Willie were carrying guns. Tom and Mollie both said they had not seen any pistols or any other weapons carried by the boys. Bray also asked William and Elizabeth if their sons were carrying any firearms. They said no and that it was not their practice to carry guns. You know Bray must have been thinking about a possible gunfight between these young men. Pistols would not leave any shell casings lying in the snow, as Alfred's rifle would have done when he chambered the second round before shooting Johnny. However, nothing was ever said about finding any shell cases during the coming trials. Mollie's statement was extremely important because she was at the house when both boys were brought to the house and she confirmed the fact that neither boy had a gun when they were carried in the house.

Mollie told Jones and Bray that the Vaughan wagon briefly stopped at her place yesterday and she said:

"Nick Rast told me there has been some bad trouble at the Litster Ranch."

"He also told Jimmy that he better go home fast."

"Nick never said anything about a shooting."

Jimmy was visiting with her son Joe when Nick jumped off the wagon and told Jimmy and Mollie. She said she had her son hitch a wagon so that they could go to the Litster's. On the way up the road they met Lizzie and Louis who had been sent to her house.

"They were both crying." "It was terrible." She said she was horrified when she heard Lizzie say that her brother was dead.

Mollie and Tom both heard Willie say several times that Alfred Vaughan shot Johnny and him. I first thought it strange the Litster's did not hear those two gunshots until the current ranch owner told me that sound does not travel in the canyon. I thought a 44-caliber rifle would have echoed loud and clear down the canyon.

They all reported to Jones and now Bray that Willie said before he died, Alfred shot him first and then he next shot Johnny. Willie said he knew Johnny had been killed as soon as he was hit. He went down and never once moved. He said he knew he too was going to die.

Elizabeth said: "Willie did accept the medicine I gave him, but he was just doing it to please me."

Can you imagine the emotion of Willie's mother on this second day with her two sons lying dead in the bedroom?

It was about 1:30 p.m. when the group from Austin thanked them for the noon meal and they headed back to Austin. They arrived just after sunset. It was agreed they would call it a day and they would continue the investigation at 7 a.m. tomorrow. Before retiring for the evening, Bray went to Sheriff Easton's office where he reported he had been to the murder scene and he told the Sheriff's he wanted statements from Alfred, Charlie and Nick about the shooting. Bray said: "I want to talk to the prisoners, but not until tomorrow morning, say about eight o'clock."

Saturday morning Bray and Moss went to the Sheriff office where they spoke separately with each of the Vaughan brothers and Nick Rast. Alfred and Charlie said it was self-defense, because the Litster's had shot at them first. They were saying it was a gunfight. This is the question Bray was researching: When Nick Rast was questioned he told them that he didn't see anything because he was opening the Gap. However, he did say that he thought boys had pistols. He wasn't sure how many shots were fired. He could recall two, but he said there could have been more. Later that morning the Coroner's Jury after hearing Bray's report, they issued the following statement:

"John and William Litster were brothers and that they had been shot and killed by Alfred Vaughan. This was without any just cause or provocation."

Saturday, December 30, 1893, was the day Johnny and

Willie must now be laid to rest. William and Elizabeth were very fortunate to have dear friends to help them through this sad day. The boy's bodies were taken from their bedroom. Elizabeth insisted boys must have shirts put on for the funeral. Recall the Dr. Huntsman had Joe Moss cut the clothing from the boys body. Bray told William before he left yesterday that he would see to the arrangements. The funeral service would be at one o'clock in the Methodist Church.

Early that morning the bodies were placed side by side in William's big wagon. Tom drove this wagon as Emily sat beside him. William, Elizabeth and Mollie would lead the way on the Litster's buggy. The Steiner's and Duffy's arrived about 8 o'clock to join in the procession. Nate drove the Dunsdon buggy carrying Lizzie and the small children. James and Joe Eason were allowed to ride saddle horses. George Watt, Jr. came over early that morning and he rode ahead to tell his parents to meet the procession at the junction below the Watt Ranch. Miss Stina Wagner, the schoolteacher joined in the procession and just about everybody living in the Silver Creek area was there to make the solemn ride to Austin.

In 1893, you did not have vehicles and all the professional services our present day society takes for granted. Litster's were now over the initial shock of what had happened. They were tired and didn't seem to be aware of everything that was happening. Many of the town's people were good friends and they too were upset about the shooting. They wanted to help in any way possible. The women and young girls could not hold back the tears when they saw the wagon carrying the boy's bodies. Can anyone not share their emotion, by just thinking about what they were feeling on this day? Still the loss, the hurt, the grieving by the family was as much as anyone could bear.

The bodies were placed inside the Methodist Church just prior to noon. The services did commence at one o'clock. This church still stands in Austin today and a picture has been included in the Appendix. The ladies at the church decorated two arches with evergreen limbs cut from pine trees and they made an evergreen cross connecting to the two arches. Each boy's body was placed under an arch. Every seat in the church was taken very early and many of the men stood outside the church. Everybody was there to pay their respects to the boys and the family. Reverent Allen delivered the sermon. The large audience was permitted to view the boy's dead bodies. That was common in those days. We don't like to do that these days, do we?

The twelve pallbearers were: W. H. Bray, Sam Crescenzo, John Dunsdon, Nathan Dunsdon, Joseph Eason, Wm. J. Francis, C. A. Richards, Jr., Issac Solomon, Charles L. Steiner; Chas. Steiner, Jr., Wm. Steiner, J. Timlin.

Following the service at the church the bodies were carried by the pallbearers to a special wagon used only for this purpose. Once the bodies were place in a wagon with six pallbearers walking at each side the procession began the long mile walk. It is nearly a six percent grade down the main street in Austin to flat lands below town. The newspaper reported the procession by these mourners making this trek was nearly three quarter mile in length. The gravesite for the burial is in the Masonic Cemetery west of Austin.

Today you can find this cemetery just past the road to the old Clifton Mill and northwest of the present highway junction of US 50 and State Route 305. A common grave had been freshly dug early that morning in the frozen ground. You know it was not easy digging the hole in frozen ground. A common grave for the bodies was fitting for these two brothers that shared their entire short lives together. The gravesite is near the location of their grand parents, James and Christina Litster's graves.

The bodies were placed side by side in the cold ground. A photo of the stone marker can be seen in the Appendix. The stone marker was added later reads:

Hail Ye Blessed
John G. Litster Aged 19 years
William Litster Aged 16 years

The following newspaper account was also taken from the Reese River Reveille:

"There bodes to return to dust and their souls to await the great resurrection".

"Here the veil is drawn over the first scene in this horrible affair, and we await the next, which the Courts will have to manage. Two homes have been horribly wrecked by the affair and tears, heartaches and a multiplicity of troubles surround them, while the entire country is shrouded in gloom."

The news article also said it was common knowledge that there was a feud between the Litster and Vaughan brothers.

Nick Rast was now finding that it isn't going to be as simple as Alfred's father, Lee Vaughan, had told him. He didn't expect to be arrested or to be in a jail cell. This 43 years old German emigrant was now being charged as an accessory for his part in the act of the two murders. One can only speculate, but how can Nick get out of this mess? His first statement had been less than truthful. And we need to remember, Alfred had threatened him on the day of murders when he asked: "Do you want to be in a dead man's coffin too?" He had heard a lot of talk Thursday by the Vaughan family after they returned to the ranch, including the alibi about a gunfight and self-defense. He heard Harry and Frank cursing the fact that Willie had been left alive to testify. Being locked up in a cell with Alfred and Charlie only made Nick fear a little more for what might happen to him.

He must have wondered how he could only get out of this jail? It sounded so easy when Lee Vaughan explained self-defense to him on Thursday. He would give the Sheriff a statement and that was all he had to do. He didn't think he would be arrested when he agreed to support the gunfight alibi.

Before we get to his story and that of others, remember the Vaughan wagon did go through the gate at the Gap before retreat back to their ranch. They left the both Litster brothers lying in the snow and they also knew Willie was not dead. As far as Alfred was concerned he was left to die. Nick felt terrible and this was probably the reason he jumped off the wagon when he saw Mollie Eason and proceeded to tell her there had been trouble. Nick was afraid of Alfred, but he found enough courage to tell Mollie something bad had happened.

We know that Nick was worried about passing the Litster ranch house because he thought Alfred would kill anyone that might try to stop him as they drove the wagon down the road. I've thought about this too and I think he was right. When you consider the time William left the house with respect to the shooting, yes he could have met the wagon. He even could have arrived at the Gap a few moments after the boy were shot. Life is strange, had William ridden a horse, possibly there would have been a third Litster killed on Thursday. Alfred said as much when told Nick he had plenty of bullets for anyone trying to stop them.

Nick Rast story will change several times prior to the first trial. Still, Nick really doesn't have any reason to lie about what happened at the Gap, unless the Vaughan's had threatened him. Nick didn't know what he should do to extricate himself from the bad situation he then found for himself. The two Vaughan brothers really were not Nick's friends.

Nick as well as Alfred and Charlie did not act in a rational manner following the shooting. Nick first statement was not consistent with any of the testimony given at the coming trials. Why did Nick agree to lie?

The following is a summary of Nick Rast's first statement he made for the Coroner's Inquest. He said Johnny and Willie Litster stopped the Vaughan's wagon at the Gap. This was while he and the Vaughan brothers were traveling to the Vaughan's mining claim. He said Alfred argued with the two Litster boys who were using bad language. He said, he was about to open the gate when four or five shots were fired. He said he had not noticed whether Alfred was carrying the rifle. When he looked up he said he saw Johnny fall to his knees and the same was true for Willie. He said Willie was calling for them to get his father. Nick also said, he told Charlie drive fast to the Litster house so they could tell them what happened. Of course, this did not happen. Why did he say four or five shots were fired?

Recall Alfred told him to finish opening the gate so Charlie could turn the wagon around. They headed back down the road passed the Litster's house. On the way back Nick said: "We saw Mrs. Alex Eason at her house and I told her there had been a shooting up at the Litster's and it was bad trouble." This is a little confusing, why did Alfred let Nick say anything to Mrs. Eason? He didn't let him. Nick just did it.

We will learn from the trial testimony that she was outside and apparently near the road as they came by. Both of the boys, Jimmy Litster and Joe Eason were nearby at a haystack. She may have asked the Vaughan brothers in a friendly way: "Hey didn't I just see you guys going up the road?" Nick must have been determined to tell someone about the trouble. So he jumped off the wagon when he saw her and passed the word about trouble at the Litster's ranch. Alfred told Nick to get back in the wagon and they continued down the road to their ranch.

Why didn't Nick insist that they help Willie? Did he think Willie was near death? Or was it because Alfred was pointing the rifle at him as he told him to get in the wagon? Nick tells another lie as he adds to his statement that he thought the two brothers might have had guns. And that he thought Johnny and Willie might shoot Alfred, Charlie and himself. When asked, Nick said, "He didn't know who did the shooting." Can Nick live with this statement? Shortly, we'll hear the answer is "No"!

The statements by Alfred and Charlie were simple and they would only say to the Sheriff and Bray that it was self-defense. They said Johnny Litster shot first and Alfred had to defend himself. Charlie said Willie charged Alfred with an axe. Can Alfred's alibi of self-defense stand up to the questions that will be asked by the Jones? Can this justify Alfred's reason for shooting the brothers?

The Preliminary Examination was set for the following Wednesday, January 3, 1894, with Justice of the Peace, Weller presiding. The Lander County District Attorney, W. D. Jones, would represent the State's 3rd District Court for the people. Jones lived in Austin and for the last seven years he has been the District Attorney. Battle Mountain's attorney, James F. Dennis, was hired to represent the defendants. Lee Vaughan had telegraphed Dennis last Friday and retained his services to defend his two sons and Nick Rast.

Dennis took the train ride to Austin. He arrived about 1:30 p.m. Tuesday. It was the day after New Years. He really didn't have much time to familiarize himself with case or to instruct Alfred, Charlie or Nick about what they should or should not say at the hearing. The Preliminary Examination on Wednesday was a closed-door affair with the Sheriff present and only one witness at a time before Justice Weller. Nick and Charlie's testimony regarding the shooting produced conflicting statements and Alfred refused to testify.

It was reported in Thursday's newspaper, January 4, 1894; on the following day that Nick Rast was examined first. Nick has now changed his statement. The substance of his testimony was as follows: He said that he and the two Vaughan brothers left the ranch to go to work the mining claim above the Litster Ranch. They went in a four horse drawn wagon. Charlie had asked Alfe whether to take a shotgun or rifle. Alfe said a rifle would be best. Alfe drive the wagon and Charlie carried the rifle. Then Charlie drove and Alfe carried the rifle.

He said the distance to the Litster Ranch is not far; about four miles and it only took a little more than a half hour to get to the Litster's. Nick said, when we got up the canyon close to the Litster's corral we saw Johnny and Willie ride away from the corral towards their home. As the wagon came closer to the corral we saw Mr. Litster and his two younger boys, George and Louis. They were feeding the cattle. Nick then said they drove on into the mouth of the Water Canyon where they turned off the main road to the road that went up the Water Canyon.

Nick continues by saying: "We found the two older Litster brothers standing in the road." He said, the Litster boys were using bad language and told the Vaughan brothers they cannot go through here. Nick said, "Maybe they said they could not go through alive, but I'm not sure of that." Nick must have thought that if he told this story like Lee Vaughan said, he would be released from jail. He said he and Alfe went to the front of the wagon ahead of the lead horses, to the gate where the Litster boys stood in front of the closed Gap.

Tough words were spoken. Nick said Alfe was holding the rifle with the stock on the ground and his hand over the muzzle.

This is just the opposite of what Charlie is going to say. He said Alfe and Willie continued to quarrel. Willie was being very quarrelsome and he was using bad language. Nick said, Johnny was not arguing. Then he said he told the Litster boys that they must let them go through the gate and finally Johnny consented.

The shooting that follows doesn't seem to fit Nick's story. He said he had to step between Alfe and Willie a time or two to keep them from fighting. Nick was asked about seeing Willie's hands. He said he saw nothing in them. Nick said the gate was stapled to the post. Nick said he went to the wagon to get an axe and an iron spike to take the staples when the shots were fired. Nick continues to lie as he now starts to add some color to his story. He said he heard Willie say, "take that" Bang, Bang, as the first shots were fired. Nick said, he jumped 10 to 12 feet over the fence and when he whirled around he saw Johnny had halfway fallen and he said Willie was also on his knees. He stated that he ran to Willie, then to Johnny. Johnny was dead. He went back to Willie and asked him if he was bad hurt and Willie said, "Yes." "Go and tell my father." You might be asking what are the Vaughan's doing at this time?

Nick said Charlie drove the wagon through the gate opening and proceeded to turning around. This would mean after the shooting Nick had to unfasten the remaining wire to open the gate. There were two bodies on this side of the gate and they were in the way of a turning wagon so the wagon needed to go through the opening in order to turn around. Willie was not dead. He was on his knees and vomiting in the snow as his brother lay dead about twenty feet away on the opposite side of the road.

As the wagon came about Nick said he got on and he told the Charlie to drive fast so he could tell the Litster's. It appears from Nick's story they were leaving Willie to die in the cold snow. Nick doesn't say anything about wanting to put Willie in the wagon. No, they just left both boys lying on the snow-covered ground. Why didn't Nick say what Alfred was doing during this time after all Alfred was the boss? Also, he doesn't mention Alfred pointing the rifle at him.

The accounts given by Nick and Charlie at this examination

fail say anything about what Alfred might have said. This must have seemed strange to Justice Weller.

Nick said when they got to the Litster corral, they don't see Mr. Litster, and so they drove on. Why didn't they go to the house that was less than 100 yards from the main road and they could have taken Silver Creek road right to the house. Nick doesn't explain, but he said they did stop the wagon at the Eason place where he told Mrs. Alex Eason that there had been shooting up there and she asked if bad and he said, "too bad". He said they continued on the road to the Vaughan Ranch.

Nick said the Vaughan boys told their father what had happened. Lee Vaughan said they must tell the Sheriff. Then Alfe and Charlie got on horses and rode to town. Notice Nick does not says much about the conversation that took place at the ranch when they told what had happened. Nick said: "Later Mr. Vaughan and I went to town to give my statement to the Sheriff". Nick recants and he now says in his best judgment only two shots were fired. Nick has changed his story about four or five shots being fired. He must have felt safe, as he knew Alfe and Charlie were not able to hear him make this statement about only two shots.

Before the Preliminary Examination, Nick's brother, John Rast came to visit him in jail. His brother told him that he was in big trouble and he must tell the truth. Later Nick will tell his brother he was afraid of the Vaughan's.

It is very obvious that Dennis didn't have time to influence what these three men should say at this hearing. After Nick's testimony, Dennis tried to prevent Charlie from testifying, but the magistrate ruled against him. Charlie was then given an opportunity to explain what happened and he stated they left home between 8 and 9 a.m. to go the mine. He says nothing about taking a gun. Charlie said when they saw the Litster's corral they saw the two brothers jumped on their horses and they rode ahead up the road. He said they found Johnny and Willie at the Gap. He said Alfe asked the boys to please let them go through. The boys refused. He said Willie was standing behind some brush so he could only see his head and feet. He says nothing about Willie swearing or Nick coming between

Willie and Alfe. Why does Charlie want to say that Willie is behind the brush?

He then said Alfe stood near Willie with the muzzle of his rifle pointed to the ground. Charlie said: "The boys told them, your not going through except over our dead bodies". Charlie adds that while Nick was opening the fence, Johnny said: "You bastard son of bitch take that and he fired at Alfe with a small pistol and then fired several more shots quickly, probably four or five shots." He said he didn't see any shots except the first one by Johnny". Charlie's story would have some merit if Johnny and Willie were armed. Charlie's gunfight story will become the foundation for claiming self-defense in the coming murder trial.

Charlie said he drove through fence opening, Alfe got on and he turned around and as he drove by Rast got on. They drove off leaving Willie to die there in the snow beside his dead brother. Nothing was ever said about why they decided not to carry Willie back to the Litster house. Charlie said they drove in a slow trot and only to stopped when they saw Mrs. Alex Eason. He said Nick told her that there has been trouble at the Litster Ranch and then they continued to the Vaughan Ranch. Charlie doesn't say anything about Willie's requesting help from his father. Have you noticed the gunman, Alfred Vaughan from these two stories has been totally quiet? I think we should all have our doubts.

Also appearing at this Preliminary Examination was the Coroner, W. H. Bray and Doctor Huntsman. Bray described the ground where the bodies were found. The doctor described the wounds. Willie being shot from left to right though the stomach and his arm had been grazed. How was this possible if he had his arms over his head? This question was never asked during the three trials. Johnny was shot through right nipple and the bullet passed through his heart before exited out of the body on the left side.

Alpheus Vaughan was called but he absolutely refused to testify at this hearing. The newspaper accounts and court records have used many different names for Alfred. They've called him Alpha, Alfa, Alfe, Alfred and now Alpheus. You would think that Alfred was his correct name and the others were perhaps nicknames. However, I do have one document with Alfred's signature, he signs his name as Alpheus Vaughan. When his father testified at the coming trials, he calls his son Alfe. The State of Nevada calls him Alfred.

What was happening by Alfred refusing to testify? I think his attorney; Dennis told him they are just loading evidence against you. So don't help them, wait and you can tell your story at the trial.

The testimony submitted against Alfred, Charlie and Nick was enough for Justice Weller to rule that all three would be held without bail and charged with the two murders. They were remanded to Sheriff Easton and the case was turned over to the Grand Jury for their action. Two month will pass with these three men confined to in jail while the town's people anxiously waited for the Grand Jury to indict these men.

Dennis voiced his objection to the seventeen new empanelled members of the Grand Jury by charging to many were from Austin and this produced prejudice to his three clients. On March 3, 1894, the Grand Jury called three people to testify behind closed doors before issuing the indictments. This too was a closed-door hearing and the public was not privileged to hear what was said. Testifying before the Grand Jury was William Litster, Dr. Huntsman and Nick Rast. Why did they call Nick Rast? It could be because his story at the Preliminary Examination appeared to have more elements of truth and it was not Charlie's simple gunfight story. The newspaper reported on March 3, 1894:

"A great deal of curiosity was manifested by the citizens last Thursday as to the action of the Grand Jury in the case of the Vaughan brothers and Nick Rast who were now charged with the killing of the Litster boys in December."

The newspaper also reported that there has been much interest in this case:

When it was known that the Grand Jury had reported the excitement was intense, but very little was said by anyone about the decision. They verified that two indictments for murder found against each of the accused and that seemed to give the people in Austin a sense of general satisfaction." The trial was set for April 3, 1894.

Another month would pass and the weather had turned from winter to spring. The days were now getting warmer in this high plateau country. Had these young men adjusted to the jail life at the courthouse? I think not. This is hard to believe but the Vaughan's were allowed to have their pocketknives and they were busy making quirts while sitting in the outer jail room. Nick continued to have conversations with his brother but he only had brief moments to talk in private. Dennis came several times to the jail and he explained what might happen at the coming trial. They learned that the District Attorney was planning to try each of them separately and that Alfred would be the first.

The old Sheriff's Office at the Courthouse was on the first floor at the east front corner of the building. The jail has four cells; one cell has a solid door with only air holes near the bottom of the door. The other three cells have a bar covered window in the door. These cells are approximately 8 by 10 feet. There is a hallway in front of these cells adjacent to the outer courthouse wall with barred windows. Nick refers to this hall as the "gangway". The gangway connects to the outer jail room approximately 14 by 14 feet. This room was next to the Sheriff's Office. The outer cell room was where the prisoners on good behavior were allowed to sit and pass the time during the day and where they eat their meals. This is the room where Alfred, Charlie and Nick made quirts with their pocketknives. These facilities are not longer use.

The courtroom is upstairs and it is a must for historic preservation. It has been well maintained. The bench seating provides space for about 100 spectators. The twelve juror seats are placed in two rows and each row has a brass rail for a boot rest. An old antique wood stove is located at the rear of the courtroom. There is one large table that would have been shared by both the prosecution and the defense.

The fact that these men would be tried separately should have made Charlie and Nick feel better. Still it is hard to pass time in jail. The people in Austin were looking with anticipation to the April trial.

There was some concern about the lack of accommodations. Austin's two hotels, the International and the Magnolia did not have rooms for all those that would be coming to Austin. The County Clerk was in charge of finding space in private residences for the trial participants. Sixty witnesses were subpoenaed and that the jury pool would be much larger.

Alfred's trial did start on a Tuesday morning at 10 a.m. April 3, 1894. State of Nevada vs. Alfred Vaughan, charged with the murder of Willie Litster. District Attorney W. D. Jones and D. S. Truman, Associate Counsel, to represent the State. J. F. Dennis of Battle Mountain and J. H. MacMillan of Ogden, Utah represented the Defendant.

Times have changed in Austin; just a few years prior to this killing there was a situation where the following took place. While lynching was not as common as Hollywood would have us believe, Austin did have at least one such occurrence in 1881. A Richard Jennings connected with this type of justice. He got into an argument with a respected citizen named John A. Barrett at the bar in the International Hotel. Jennings suddenly drew a revolver and shot Barrett three times. He was subdued by the bar patrons and taken to jail.

The local citizens contemplated the shooting that had taken place the next day, the group decided to save Austin the expense of a trial. So at about 1:30 a.m. that night twenty-five mask men broke into the sheriff's office and took the prisoner and place rawhide around his neck. The rawhide lariat was thrown over the cornice on the front porch of the courthouse and Jennings was strung up, as the saying goes. The same cornice is still available at the courthouse today. The next morning members of the coroner's inquest concluded:

"Death was at the hands of parties unknown to us."

Letting Judge Lynch handle the case did save tax dollars. Jennings was a bad apple and it is surprising his life had lasted as long as it did. He started a life of crime at the age of ten as a horse thief at Grass Valley, California, but he managed to live some thirty years before having this necktie party.

You might conclude somewhere between 1881 and 1894 the old west ended. The last confrontation the American Indians had with the US Army was in 1890 at Wounded Knee, and this was 14 years after General Custer exercised such poor judgment at the Little Big Horn.

There is more similarity with Alfred Vaughan's coming trials to our present day criminal justice system than those of the old west. When did our leaders, attorney and judges really take over the West? I don't know, but they did. Since then many rules have been added to the Criminal Justice System. These rules must be adhered to regardless of what a common citizen may think about justice. They call this "the rule of law". Then as now the system seems more concerned about following rules than bring justice for the victim's.

5

TRIAL NO. 1

Can We Claim Self Defense?

The trial got underway as scheduled on April 3, 1894. Tuesday morning was the start of a beautiful spring day here in Austin. Three months have lapsed from that December 28, 1893, the day Alfred shot and killed the two brothers. Today's justice system could never start a trial this soon after a criminal charge of murder. It often takes years for a person these days to have a trial following a murder. No, this was not the lawless Old West either where a mob might hold a Hollywood cowboy type trial at the local saloon. Does three months seem reasonable and better than our present stalling practice? Still three months was a very long time for Alfred, Charlie and Nick, and it was the longest three months in their lives. They were being held in a jail without bail.

W. D. Jones, decided to pursue the first and most obvious act of murder by having Alfred Vaughan tried first for the murder of Willie Litster. Jones felt very confident because he had witnesses that could testify to Willie's dying declaration. The case, State of Nevada vs. Alfred Vaughan was going to be heard in Third District Court. The Honorable Judge L. A. Fitzgerald would preside.

Two of the three transcript volumes from the first trial were found, but one has been lost. Book No, 1 containing the examination of the prospective jurors and Book No. 3 contains the last half of the trial testimony. Book No. 2 probably was lost or misplaced during the relocation of the County Seat from Austin to Battle Mountain in May 1979. Consequently, the

Reese River Reveille, the two volumes of the transcript and the written opinions by the State Supreme Court are the records available. The local newspaper stated that there was a great deal of interest and emotion surrounding the coming trial.

At this time in our nation's history, only men were summoned for jury duty It would have been unthinkable for women to leave homes and perhaps travel many miles on the western frontier to perform jury duty. Civilization must wait until 1920 and the 19th Amendment to the U.S. Constitution for women to serve on juries. Yes, ladies did not have to vote either in those days. We often like to be critical of the past and today we call this discrimination. However, today most people fail to understand the conditions of the past for our developing nation. It certainly would not have been safe for women to travel alone for a jury summons. Think about it? Today modern women vote and work like men, but in 1894 that was not the case. Don't misunderstand, women work even harder. The job of being homemaker in those days was not easy. Women today may have the same job as man and many mothers must rush their kids off each workday to daycare. We call this equal opportunity and parents today are puzzled when they are told their children should be put on a drug called "Ritalin".

Over a hundred citizens were summoned for jury duty and they came from all over Lander County. A few were from Battle Mountain. Still others came from the ranches and places like Cortez. Cortez is about 65 miles northeast of Austin. The people here most likely traveled north and caught the train to Battle Mountain and then the short line to Austin. This would have been a two-day journey. Just think, we complain now days when we have to make a half-hour drive to the courthouse. It is amazing that Austin could provide sleeping quarters for all the people involved in this trial.

The examination of the prospective jurors started at 10 a.m. Seventy-five of those summoned for jury duty were examined before settling on the selection of the twelve jurors. The attorney's on both sides had their standard boilerplate questions. The defense attorney typically started the questioning and then prosecuting attorney would follow with his questions. The questions by these attorneys varied and they would either pass the juror; challenged on the ground of implied bias; deny the challenge; traverse the challenge; and at times the judge had to rule on the qualification of the prospective juror when neither attorney were able to make the decision. This process was followed by the peremptory excuses. The defense used all eight of their peremptory challenges while the State used six. Forty-nine potential jurors were dismissed for cause.

The defense was particularly concern that a juror might be unacceptable because of the local sentiment for the Litster's loss of their two sons. Dennis asked each person the following questions, however he would vary the timing and phasing:

"Do you stand in relation of guardian or ward, master or servant, landlord of tenant, attorney or client to any of the parties?"

"Do you have any bias or prejudice for or against the defendant, or any member of his family?

"Have you ever formed or expressed an unqualified opinion or belief with regard to the guilt or innocence of the defendant"

Many of those being examined did not understand the difference between an unqualified and a qualified opinion. This question was difficult and did cause many to be excused. On the other hand the State had their concerns too. Jones also had three questions that he asked as he examined each person:

"If the offense charged were punishable with death, do you entertain such conscientious scruples as would prevent you from finding the defendant of guilty?"

"What degree of proof, if you were taken as a juror to try this case, would you require before you would find a verdict of guilty?"

"Would you require the charge to be proven beyond all possible doubt, or simply beyond all reasonable doubt?"

Several people were dismissed because of their position regarding the death penalty. While others wanted the proof to be beyond all doubt. It appeared that several did not understand the difference between beyond all doubt and the meaning of reasonable doubt.

Three and a half days were consumed with selection of the

following jurors: (1) M. E. Ryan; (2) A. P. Mastretti; (3) E. Deringer; (4) James Roberts; (5) John Thorpe; (6) William Walsh; (7) A. Layton, served as foreman; (8) E. Trescott; (9) E. M. Bingham; (10) J. C. Dulin; (11) Peter Shay and (12) James Lovey. At eleven o'clock Friday morning the clerk swore the jurors. The indictment found against the prisoner by the Grand Jury was read and the jury was told the defendant has pleaded not guilty.

Judge Fitzgerald asked Jones to makes his opening statement to the jury. Jones listed all the facts the State will rely on for the conviction of said defendant for the crime charged in the indictment. The courtroom was a packed to hear his opening statement and this included a large number of ladies. They took most of the seats as the gentlemen opted to stand. There had been considerable debate prior to the processing's regarding the matter of ladies attending this trial out respect for the language that might be used by the witnesses. Judge Fitzgerald said he would be alert to any unnecessary bad language and it was agreed that the ladies would be allowed to attend.

Dennis asked the court to allow him to reserve his opening statement until after the plaintiff had rested. The court was then recessed till 1:30 p.m. on Friday afternoon and at that time the State would call the first witness.

Daily travel to and from Austin was also out of the question for both the Vaughan's and the Litster's. William and Elizabeth could stay with their eldest daughter, Mary, as she and her husband, William Christian, were now living in Austin. Recall they had been temporarily living at Cortez where they were running the store at the mining camp. Or they may stay in the house that George Watt owned in Austin. Jones told the Litster's that he expected to call them as well as Jimmy to be early witnesses. Anyhow a daily travel of 44 miles to and from Austin by the Litster's as well as the Vaughan's was out of the question. William had made arrangements with George Watt to see that the stock on the Litster Ranch was cared for during their absence.

Dennis told the Vaughan's that they didn't have to attend

first part of the trial, but he wanted them to be in town just the same and that he had made arrangements for them to stay at the Magnolia Hotel. Frank and Harry could look after the ranch while they were in town. He told them that they would be called later and the boys needed to check the mail at the Vaughan Switch everyday.

William, Elizabeth and Lizzie rode on spring wagon as they traveled the Silver Creek road by Dunsdon's ranch and on to the Watt's. The boys, Jimmy, George and Louis rode ahead on horseback. The little boys rode double. Three of the children would stay with their aunt and uncle at the Watt Ranch while their parents and Jimmy were in Austin.

The follow list shows the order that the witnesses did testify at this trial: You can see that most of these witnesses were called to the stand at least twice.

1. Dr. A. J. Huntsman	2. William Litster
3. Dennis Scully	4. William Litster
5. Mrs. Alex Eason	6. Thomas Dunsdon
7. James Litster	8 Mrs. Elizabeth Litster
9. William Easton	10. Joseph Moss
11. William Litster	12. Joseph Moss
13. William Litster	14. James Litster
15. E. Craine	16. Charles Vaughan
17. Nick Rast	18. Lee S. Vaughan
19. Mrs. E. Vaughan	20. Albert Tipsword
21. Frank Vaughan	21. W. D. Jones
22. D. S. Truman	23. W. D. Jones
24. Nick Rast	25. Lee S. Vaughan
26. Harry Vaughan	27. Charles Thompson
28. Thomas Smith	29. L. A. Weller
30. Phillip Duffy	31. Frank Vaughan
32. Albert Tipsword	33. E, Craine
34. James Earles	35. J. E. Cox
36. Mrs. E. Vaughan	37. Charles Vaughan
38. Joseph Moss	39. Alpheus Vaughan
40. Thomas Dunsdon	41. Frank J. Whaley
42. J. B. Eagan	43. James Earles
44. Camillio Sanchez	45. Joseph Eason

46. T. J. Perkins
47. Sam Puryear
48. Nels Haydon
49. William Litster
50. G. Polkinghorn
51. T. J. Perkins
52. William Shinn
53. George Watt
54. William Daugherty
55. Joseph Moss
56. Nick Rast
57. Dr. J. A. Huntsman
58 Dr. W. H. Hood

The first witness to be called was Dr. Huntsman. He described the wounds he found on William Litster, Jr. He stated that he arrived at the Litster Ranch shortly after Willie had died on the afternoon of December 28, 1893. He said Willie had a fatal wound and nothing could have been done to save the boy's life. The doctor then described the path of the bullet that struck Willie. That bullet did not exit Willie's body and it could be felt near the surface of his skin on the left side of his abdomen. The shot in the stomach caused internally bleeding into the stomach. Recall it was reported that he vomited blood throughout the day until he died. Dennis had no questions for the Doctor.

The second witness was Dennis Scully. He was a Civil Engineer and he was asked to describe the maps that he had made of the Litster Ranch.

The third witness was William Litster, Sr. Jones started by asking what Willie had been able to tell him before he died. Mr. MacMillan, a Co-Defense Attorney objected strongly to the question and the attempted answer by Mr. Litster. His contention was that this testimony pertaining to the boy's dying declaration to his father was hearsay. The judge overruled the objection and William was allowed to continue where he described the events of the day, including what Willie had told him and his mother. Dennis briefly cross-examined Mr. Litster and the newspaper reported that this did not produce any new facts:

"The testimony given by Mr. Litster was heart rendering and the strong man that he is, he fought back tears that would come to his eyes, and many spectators openly wept."

A recess was called for the weekend and the trial resumed on Monday, April 9, 1894, and at that time Mrs. Alex Eason was called to the stand for the prosecution. She testified in substance to that sworn by William Litster. She said she was present when Willie made his dying declarations. She was then followed by the Thomas Dunsdon. His testimony was in substance the same as William and Mollie regarding Willie dying declaration. James Litster was called to the stand and he too collaborates the three prior witnesses testimony.

After the lunch recess the jury would hear the testimony by Elizabeth Litster. Here we can imagine the emotion she brought to the stand. The newspaper said she bore up bravely under the ordeal of answering questions from both the prosecution and the defense until she was excused. Many of the ladies present wept openly as she testified about trying to get her son to take some medicine as he was lying in bed waiting for death. As she left the stand Jones was able to keep her from falling to the floor as she collapsed.

Monday afternoon Sheriff Easton testified that he had obtained the rifle Alfred Vaughan used to shoot the boys on the 28th day of December 1893. He said he found Alfred and Charlie coming to Austin that same day. He said he placed them both under arrest and brought them to jail. He said he also arrested Nick Rest later that evening when he came to town with Lee Vaughan.

Joe Moss was called to represent the Coroner's jury. He testified about the inquest for the deceased. He had gone with the doctor to the Litster's house on the day the boys were shot. They arrived a little after five o'clock. . He said he help the doctor cut away the boy's clothing to the examination of the bodies. He identified Willie's bloodstained vest. It clearly showed a bullet hole. He then described the events that took place on the day after the shooting. Jones called a few more witnesses before saying:

"The State Rests."

It was now the Defense's turn. Dennis quickly summarized his opening statement to the jury by saying his defendant was just defending himself. Dennis said the Litster brothers refused to let the Vaughan wagon pass through the Gap on the road to the Water Canyon. This was the road they always used. He said the Vaughan brothers told Johnny and Willie they had to go up the road because they could not even turn the wagon around at this location. And when they started to open the gate Johnny pulled a pistol and fired several shots missing Alfred. Then Alfred fired his rifle shooting Johnny. He then turned quickly and shot Willie as he charging him with an axe raised above his head.

Dennis called Charlie Vaughan to the stand. His testimony was contradictory to the State's witnesses. Charlie did make some changes from his testimony he had given at the preliminary examination. Charlie told a story about the Litster boys shooting in the direction of the Water Canyon while he and half brother Frank were there one-day last summer. He does not repeat this story at the second trial. He said they did not talk to Nick after leaving the Gap or anything else about the shooting as they drove back down the canyon to tell Mr. Litster about the shooting. They assumed he would still be at the haystack in the lower corral. He wasn't there so they continued down to the Eason Ranch. Charlie also maintained they never talked about their testimony while they were in jail.

Seven day have lapsed since the trial began, it is now Tuesday morning, April 10,1894. Charlie was still on the stand and would remain here all of Tuesday and until till mid morning on Wednesday when the Jones concluded his cross-examination. The Reese River Reveille reported:

"Charlie's testimony did not hold together and that he became badly tangled up in his story."

Nick Rast was the next witness called by the defense. He was going to Dennis' principal witness. The defense obviously felt Nick was going to back Charlie's testimony and this would refute the so-called dying declaration by Willie. After being sworn, Attorney MacMillan began by asking the usual general questions. Nick was a German emigrant. He gave a brief history of his life up to the time of December 28, 1893. Judge Fitzgerald then called a lunch recess.

After the lunch MacMillan started to resume his questioning as to what transpired on the morning of the shooting. Nick turned to the Judge and asked if he could make a statement because he did not thoroughly understand the attorney's questions. The Judge grants Nick request following the strong objection from the defense. You can just imagine what Messrs Dennis and MacMillan were thinking. Then in a straightforward manner Nick told how they left the ranch that morning and arrived at the Gap where the homicide took place. It was reported that Nick's words fell on the ears of those in the courtroom, like a bombshell had exploded and the excitement could not have been more intense. Dennis and MacMillan tried desperately to stop the witness by interrupting his statement. The Judge overruled the objections time after time as he restored order in the courtroom. Still the defense attorney's both continued unsuccessful to stop Nick's statement. Was Nick telling the true story about what really happened?

After Nick concluded his statement, MacMillan notifies the Court that the defense was withdrawing Mr. Rast as witness for the defense on the grounds that they had be deceived by Mr. Rast.

Jones then asked Judge Fitzgerald to have Nick's quarters at the jail moved so that he in no way would have any communications with the Vaughan brothers. This motion was granted. His testimony and cross-examination would have been extremely interesting and it is a shame that this was in the only lost transcript volume for these trials.

The news of Nick's testimony spread around Austin like wildfire. As expected Thursday, a large crowd jammed the courtroom hoping Jones would call Nick Rast back to the stand. This is exactly what he did. He moved that the State be allowed to reopen their case with more testimony for the State. The objections by the defense were overruled. The judge granted the motion and he ordered the jury out of the courtroom until order could be restored by the defense. Nick Rast was then put back on the stand and the jurors returned. Both defense attorneys resumed their continued argument. They were now demanding a dismissal for this trial. The Judge continued to overrule each outburst from the defense.

As a witnesses for the State, Nick remained on the stand for the rest of Thursday and Friday. The court was then adjourned for the weekend. The following Monday, April 16, 1894, Nick returned to the stand. During the cross-examination as quoted from the third transcript volume, MacMillan stated to Nick:

"And on two other occasions, you swore before the court and before the committing magistrate that there were from two to four shots fired."

"I did."

"You were sure there were from two to four shots fired because of what?"

"Because Mr. MacMillan, I was threatened and my excitement, even Mr. MacMillan I thought of the Fifth Commandment of God, what says to save your own life and health and you are not to injure any man."

"That is the Fifth Commandment."

"Yes."

"Do you find that in the Bible, or where do you get that commandment?"

"When my father and my mother send me to school I learn it in church"

Is this a new Nick Rast Commandment? Nick was finally excused. It was just before the noon recess. Nick had been on the stand since a little before the noon recess last Wednesday until the noon break here on Monday.

At this time Jones says: "The State Rests."

Can the defense recover from this unforeseen turn in their case for the defendant? Nick Rast's testimony was unexpected and completely caught the defense off guard. Now W. D. Jones had more than just Willie's dying declaration. I doubt that anything like this would not happen in a modern criminal trial.

Dennis didn't have a choice really except to continue his case by attempting to refute everything Nick said. Dennis resumed by calling Lee Vaughan. He was follwed by Harry Vaughan. Harry did present a totally different story about the Litster heifer that got into their pasture. He also told about the Vaughan's having three pistols and one rifle at the ranch. Harry said he wasn't at the ranch when the wagon returned. Also, he said the Litster brothers like to shoot at their mail box.

Dennis then called Thomas Smith. This elderly man was the Jailor and he told about Nick having more privileges and testified that Nick said he was not afraid of the Vaughan's. The Jailer is the only person I found during the research that referred to W. D. Jones as "Billy".

Phillip Duffy, a rancher in Iowa Canyon since 1868 said he stopped by the Vaughan's just before Lee and Nick went to Austin. He was asked:

"What was the custom of the Vaqueros carrying firearms when riding after stock in the hills?"

"Some of them carry firearms and some didn't, but I do carry a sidearm myself."

Alfred had worked for Mr. Duffy at various times.

Elizabeth Vaughan was brought back to the stand. She said her reaction was:

"Oh! Alfred what a terrible things this is when he told her he had to shoot the two Litster boys." "Alfred said he had to do it to save his own life."

She was asked about visiting the jail last March 21st where Nick said she admonished the boys to read the Bible and they would find worse murders.

She was asked:

"If it was not done in self-defense, do you feel that he ought to be punished?"

"Yes, as much as I love him, if it was not done in self-defense and if he committed a cold blooded murder, I believe he ought to be punished."

A statement by the Supreme Court's during the appeal they commented about Lizzie hearing Alfred's mother tell their neighbor Mrs. Eason that her boys were going to the mine tomorrow. This would imply that Mrs. Vaughan was at Mollie Eason's house? Mrs. Vaughan's testimony was suggesting that Litster boys knew her boys were coming and they had planned to keep them from going to the mine. Dennis wanted the jury to think about a planned confrontation. However, Judge Fitzgerald did not allow this statement by Mrs. Vaughan. The Supreme Court also noted another statement not reported by the newspaper. This was about the Litster's dog being poisoned. Presumably by the Vaughan's and it too was not allowed by Judge Fitzgerald. Neither of these stories was repeated during the second trial.

Can Alfred's testimony offset what Nick said? Alfred must explain why he had to shoot the two brothers. MacMillan had him describe the events going to the Gap and then he asked Alfred to tell the jury what happened when they found the brothers standing in front of a closed gate. Alfred's story was very different from both Charlie and Nick. You would think Alfred and Charlie's testimony would have been more complimentary.

The newspaper reported Alfred readily answered the questions put to him by the defense, but it was another matter when he was cross-examined and he either could not or would not answer Jones' questions.

Alfred remained on the witness stand until Wednesday, April 18, 1894. Several times during Alfred testimony his language become foul. Alfred did not hold back from repeating any foul language. I found the newspaper amusing when it was explained that his words drove all the ladies from the courtroom on more than one occasion. Didn't Judge Fitzgerald say he could handle the bad language? Times were different then. Words that wouldn't even cause a lady today to bat an eyebrow sent these women fleeing from the courtroom.

Alfred said he and Nick were walking behind the wagon as it turned from the main road and crossed the bridge toward the fence where Johnny and Willie were standing.

He was asked:

"Do you know how far the bridge is from the fence?

"I should think it was 65 to 70 feet."

"It is a short distance?"

"Yes, Sir."

Alfred followed by giving his account of what happened at the Gap. Alfred maintain that he was just defending himself because Johnny shot at him and Willie charged him with an axe. He was asked to explain why he was not on good terms with Willie. He said it was because Willie owes him money. The Judge sustained Jones objection. Alfred said Willie had fired two shots at him on December 4, 1892, when he was at the lower gate to the Litster Ranch. The Judge rules the statement inadmissible. Alfred said Willie was always threatening him.

Dennis asks:

"Do you remember a threat that Willie made about getting his crowd together and cleaning your crowd out?"

"Yes, Sir.

"Tell us about that?"

"That was at the same time at the hay corral; Litster's three boys were there, Willie, Jimmy and Johnny and they called us bastardly sons of bitches and squaw fucking sons of bitches, and they said they would get their crowd together and clean us out."
"And that was on the 4th day of December, 1892, at their corral."

I am sure the last statement by Alfred sent the ladies fleeing the courtroom.

The Judge then allowed the statement about Willie shooting at Alfred. During the cross examination Jones must have made Alfred sound silly by him contending he was afraid of Willie. He said the reason he packed a gun was because of Willie's threats. Jones also brought the jurors attention to the fact that Alfred could have withdrawn for the confrontation at the Gap. No one was forcing him to stay there.

Alfred responded by saying: "We went there to go through to our mine and we had to go through."

Jones added: "Nothing else would satisfy you, you were bound to go through."

Alfred claims he was afraid to turn his back on Willie. He also claimed it was impossible to turn the wagon around without going through. He was right because the body's of Johnny and Willie were in the way, but he doesn't say anything about that as he states the ground was to soft the turn the wagon on this side of the gate.

Trials were still pending for Charlie and Nick at this time. Later the charges will be dropped against these two men. Accordingly, the local newspaper acting responsibly and did not report the details of Alfred's testimony. Jones pressured hard during the cross examination. Apart from Alfred story being completely different, Jones drove home the point that Alfred could have withdrawn from the conflict at the Gap. No one was forcing him to stay there after permission to pass was denied.

Again Alfred said he was afraid of Willie. Jones produced additional testimony to verify that they could have gone to the mine by using two alternate routes. However, they were much longer than the road up the Water Canyon.

All old trial records prior to 1911 in Nevada are stored at the various District Courts for each County. I feel it was fortunate to have been able to obtain the complete record of the second trial that began in April of 1895. It was quite by accident even to find the records for these trials. They had not yet been microfilmed. These dust-covered binders were found on top of a bookcase where the old records of the County were being stored at Battle Mountain. The County was most helpful and agreed to complete microfilming process and instead of the practice of destroying the old documents after microfilming it was agreed that I could have them.

As the trial was drawing to a close Jones stated to the Court:

"I hold in my hand the Catechism of Christian Doctrine prepared and enjoined by the order of the Third Plenary Council of Baltimore, which I desire to introduce in evidence, or at least so much of which I shall read to go into the record. I offer it on account of the slurs of counsel with regard to the testimony of the witness Nicholas Rast, who they seem to intimate, has introduced a new Commandment."

Dennis objected:

"We object to this introduction of the matter on the ground that it is incompetent, irrelevant and immaterial, and not rebuttal, and upon a collateral matter, but we do not object upon the ground that it is not the best evidence, we waive that ground."

"The objection will be overruled."

Jones proceeded to read:

"I will read that which I desire embodied in the record."

"What is the Fifth Commandment?"

"The Fifth Commandment is Thou shalt not kill."

"What are we commended by the Fifth Commandment?"

"We are commanded by the Fifth Commandment to live in peace and union with our neighbor, to respect his rights, to seek his spiritual and bodily welfare, and to take proper care of our own life and health."

"What is forbidden by the Fifth Commandment?"

"The Fifth Commandment forbids all willful murder, fighting, anger, hatred, revenge and bad example."

The record Jones introduced seemed to surprise everyone. I too thought Nick had created a new commandment.

Wednesday, the defense introduced their last witness, Dr. Hood of Battle Mountain. He was called as an expert witness to testify in regards to the path of the bullet through the body of Johnny. The reason for his testimony will become apparent during the next trial.

Thursday morning was spent preparing instructions for the jury. The court was convened that afternoon at 3:30 p.m. The court was crowded with spectators, many of which were the same ladies that could not bear to hear the foul language that said the day before. Judge Fitzgerald collected the instruction from the attorney's that they wanted to have him include in his instructions to the jury. He then announced court would adjourn till Friday 9:30 a.m. at which time the closing arguments will begin.

Friday morning found the courtroom crowded again with the ladies, as they must have found this trial entertaining. The newspaper reported that these spectators dressed in their Sunday fineness and they arrived early, nearly a hundred ladies being present. It was standing room only for the men. Jones commenced his closing argument that lasted nearly two hours. He gave a general review of the testimony. His graphic description had to have had an affect on the jury when he told how William Litster found his two boys lying in the snow. The newspaper reported that a number of the ladies and even gentlemen present were again moved to tears.

After the lunch recess, Dennis, the attorney for the defense followed and he spoke for an hour and a half. Truman, the associate council for the State spoke for a bit more than two hours. He was basically outlining the instructions that the State felt the jury should have. Those in the courtroom thought he did a good job. Court was adjourned at 5 p.m. till Saturday at 9:30 a.m. and at that time Truman could resume his argument.

MacMillan closed the case for the defense Saturday April 21, 1894, that afternoon and was followed again by Jones to close for the State. Two days were used for these closing arguments. The trial used fifteen day to reach this point. Notice in those days court was held on weekend as well as evening time. I didn't find anything about taking any afternoon off to go to the club or to play golf. Yes, our criminal justice system has progressed. Still here in 1894 you can find many similarity to the present day courts.

Judge Fitzgerald now instructed the jury and then adjourns court as the jury retired to deliberate. The Judge finished reading his instruction at 5:00 p.m. that Saturday afternoon. The fate of Alfred rested with the twelve jurors.

It was reported that the jury's first vote was ten for murder in the first degree, while two thought it should be murder in the second degree. At eight o'clock the jury asked Judge Fitzgerald to instruct them as to the penalty for first and second-degree murder. The Judge declined to add further instruction to those that he had already given the jury. This would prove to be one of the reasons the Nevada Supreme Court overturned this verdict. Just a little after nine o'clock the jury retired for the night.

Sunday morning the jury took another ballot. This time it was eleven for the first and only one for second-degree murder. At two o'clock that afternoon the jury reached a unanimous decision. The Foreman informed the court by notifying Sheriff. Order was called at 2:30 p.m. and each juror answered the roll call. The courtroom was still as death itself waiting for the Judge to speak:

"Do you the jury have an agreed verdict?"

Foreman Layton answered: "Yes Your Honor." He then handed the verdict to the County Clerk and to be passed to the Judge. He read the verdict and handed back Mr. Layton. The Judge then asked Mr. Layton to read it aloud to the court.

"State of Nevada vs. Alfred Vaughan, We the jury in the above entitled case find the defendant guilty of murder in the first degree. Signed and dated, April 22, 1894, A. Layton, Foreman".

The judge directed the Clerk to record the verdict and afterward read it again to the jury and ask if it was their verdict. Dennis then asked that the jury be polled and so that each member could say it was his verdict. Lee Vaughan sat beside his son as the verdict was read. News spread rapidly through Austin that afternoon. The general sentiment was that the verdict was proper.

The conviction of Alfred Vaughan at this trial was just for killing Willie. The indictment for killing Johnny still stands against the defendant. Alfred had turned 21 nine months ago. He was born at the ranch in Lander County. His father was in his 70th year and his mother in her 60th year. If only Alfred had got off the wagon without that loaded rifle how different things might have been.

Can anyone understand why he shot the brothers except for his obvious hatred of the Litster's? People are responsible for their actions and should bear the consequences of those actions. Alfred was convicted for killing an unarmed boy. Was it just because he got mad? We all get mad, but we know that does not justify killing someone. Alfred had killed two boys. He was not being tried for shooting Johnny. Remember he was the boy backing down the road with his hands over his head pleading for his life when Alfred shot him. There was no indication that Alfred was mentally unstable or intellectually handicapped.

Yes, we are different from that time, a little more than a century ago. Perhaps, Defense Attorney's had not yet honed their skills for a plea of "Temporary Insanity". I wonder if by today's standards could Alfred have been convicted of murder in the first degree? Do you think they were wrong by doing so? I don't. I think we're wrong today. Just look at our criminal justice system and our overflowing prisons. Then try to convince me that we are doing things right.

The following Monday morning, April 23, 1894, Judge Fitzgerald reconvened the court and dismissed the jurors. Jones then moved that the court dismiss charges against Nick Rast and Charlie Vaughan who had been held as accessory to the killing of the two brothers. Looking back at Nick's first testimony for the Preliminary Examination shows that he must have been afraid of the Vaughan's. His fear may have saved his life.

Mr. Jones didn't have sufficient evidence to put Charlie on

trial even though he knew Charlie's testimony during this trial was obviously a complete lie and that he was just trying to save his brother. The Court granted W. D. Jones' motion and charges against Charlie, as well as Nick were dismissed. Most should agree nothing has been said to indicate that Charlie knew what his brother was about to do on that cold December morning.

The Judge gave Messrs. Dennis and MacMillan time to present their motion for retrial and the courts was in recess till seven o'clock. At that hour the court was reconvened and the defense requested additional time to obtain and review the record of the short hand court reporter prior entering a their motion for a new trial. After considerable discussion the Judge set June 11th as the time for the argument of the motion for a new trial.

Time passes fast except for Alfred. He was now in jail by himself. He had family visitors, but not often as it was a long ride from the ranch to town and if they came by train they would have to stay overnight for the return trip.

June 11, 1894, fell on Monday. This was the day the Honorable; A. L. Fitzgerald would again convene court during the afternoon to hear the defense's motion for new trial. The time was running late and the matter was continued to Tuesday morning. Dennis filed the motion for a new trial based on the five grounds. After listening to this lawyer talk throughout day and the next day till 2:30 p.m. on Wednesday, the Judge ruled on the motion. You don't have to be a rocket scientist to know how this Judge was going to rule. He denied the motion and said he was ready to pass judgment on Alfred Vaughan.

The Judge did show some emotion by saying that he hoped he would never have to do this again when he pronounced sentence. The newspaper said, Alfred was asked to stand as the sentence was read. Lee Vaughan and Alfred's brother, Frank both withdrew from the courtroom just before the sentence was pronounced. Alfred seemed to show less emotion than the Judge Fitzgerald. He seem to be smiling, but others said it more like a nervous twitching, as he braced himself by spreading his feet while the Judge spoke:

"It is therefore ordered, adjudged, decreed and considered, that you Alfred Vaughan, as punishment for the crime of which you have been found guilty, be, and you are hereby remaindered to the custody of the Sheriff of Lander County, State of Nevada, to be by him safely confined and kept until a day and time to be fixed by warrant of the Judge this court in accordance with the law, and that on that day and time so to be appointed and fixed in and by warrant you, the said Alfred Vaughan, be taken by the Sheriff to a place of execution to be prepared for that purpose within the enclosed limits of the jail in said Lander County, and if such an enclosure does not exist, so as to screen the execution from public gaze, a suitable and sufficient enclosure for the purpose shall be provided by the County Commissioners of said County in which this execution is to take place, and that, then and there by said Sheriff, you Alfred Vaughan be hanged by the neck until you are dead."

Alfred dropped back into his chair after the sentence was read. Deputy Sheriff Smith was then told to remove the prisoner. Alfred told the deputy that if he had to be hung he was going to take it like a man.

Dennis did appeal this decision to the State Supreme Court after all papers were properly filed for their review. The high court must confirm the execution or grant a new trial. Here we see that justice had more in common with present than any Hollywood version of the Old West. There would be no public hanging. And the hanging had to wait on the State's high court to rule on the appeal and if the conviction were upheld then a date would be set for the hanging.

The details of the second trial will be presented in a different format to reduce the repetition of the history of this case, but next you can read the opinions by the Supreme Court Justices.

6

APPEAL NO. 1

How Did The High Court Rule?

Eight months has lapsed since Alfred Vaughan's conviction. The Nevada State Supreme Court set February 4, 1895 to hear the argument for the appeal. The hearing was scheduled at Carson City. This was the first time for Jones to appear before the high court. He would need help from the State's Attorney General, Robert. M. Beatty. Messrs Dennis and MacMillan would present the argument for the appellant.

The Reese River Reveille reported January 30, 1895:

"The trial elicited more interest than any case that has been tried in Lander County".

The newspaper also said the courthouse was crowded during the entire twenty days for the trial and the verdict satisfied the community because Jones had shown that the killing was without any mitigating circumstance. Now again there is anxiety regarding the final decision for this matter. The Supreme Court's decision would be known within a few weeks following the hearing.

Listed below are the eleven complaints for Alfred Vaughan's appeal. Dennis added a description for each of the complaints. I have not included them, because they will be restated in the following text. The record of this court action was taken from the Court's book that shows the Supreme Court's decisions for 1895. This record can be found in the Reports of Cases on page 287, State v. Vaughan. I have omitted many of the legal references recorded for this appeal.

The Court's decision certainly complicated the case. You

already know the outcome of the Supreme Court's decision and perhaps you don't want read this following record. However, there are a few good reasons to read what the court said about this case.

1. You will learn how the court viewed the testimony from the trial.

2. You will have a better understanding why the court did overturn the verdict.

3. You will recognize a lot of work was done for this appeal and many hours were spent in preparation.

The case was costing Lander County's taxpayers far more than anyone imagined. After studying the record, I question Justice Bigelow regarding his understanding of the location of the murder scene. And I don't understand why the Justices felt the evidence relating to the feud between these families was immaterial. Additionally, why was the issue of trespass considered prejudicial to the defendant?

The STATE OF NEVADA, Plaintiff and Respondent.
ALPHEUS VAUGHAN, Defendant and Appellant.

Eleven complaints for Alfred Vaughan's appeal:

1. Juror Challenges for "implied bias," insufficient.
2. Challenge, Allowed, no ground for exception,
3. Dying Declarations, when admissible
4. Evidence, Error, How Cured
5. Same. Assault Upon Others by Deceased
6. Same Reputation of Deceased
7. Same Presumption
8. Malice Aforethought How Established
9. Instruction, Irrelevant when prejudicial
10. Improper Instruction,
11. Evidence of Collateral, Occurrences, Material of

ARGUMENT FOR APPELLANT BY: James F. Dennis and J. H. MacMillan:

The first point relied on by the appellant is: That the

challenges to the jurors C. W. Hilkey, John Tallack, D. McCloud, George Schutes, 0. J. Heath and John Thorpe should have been allowed, and to deny either one was a fatal error.

There are but two cases which we deem it necessary to cite in support of this contention: State v. McClear, and the State v. Murphy. The case of State v. Murphy was rendered by Dunbar, and concurred in by a full bench of the supreme court of Washington, D.C. It is useless to quote from these cases, as they are full of the doctrine. The record shows that defendant asked for and was denied the privilege of an extra peremptory challenge, when in fact he was entitled by reason of the court denying his challenges to six extra peremptory challenges.

The second point is that juror Rapley was a qualified juror in every way. We acknowledge that it seldom is error to excuse a juror, but in this case, we desire the attention of the court to the fact that when the State interposed a challenge, very little grounds were needed to have the challenge sustained; but when the defendant interposed a challenge no opinion, however strong; was sufficient to support the challenge.

The third point is that the dying declaration of Willie Litster was not admissible under the defendant's (*appellant's*) objections. It was not made to appear that Willie Litster had a prospect of "almost immediate dissolution," and that is the test.

The only foundation for the introduction of this evidence is at the time it was introduced, "He said he was going to die, and he knowed (sic) he was going to die." Is it not a fact that we are all going to die, and that we all know we are going to die? But we do not know when, where, or of what cause. There never was a dying declaration admitted on such a foundation. *Remember this is Alfred's attorney's argument.*

It was error for the court to strike out the latter part of the sheriff's testimony. If any part of the statement was admissible, then it was all admissible. The jury was the ones to judge of its truth and weight. It was an admission, and all of it, or none of it, should have gone to the jury. "Where the verbal admission of a person charged with crime is offered in evidence, the whole of the admission must be taken together."

The question asked Charles Vaughan, about defendant's

(*appellant's*) intention with regard to the shooting, was a proper question, and that, therefore, the court erred in ruling it out; right at the time the shooting transpired what was said was competent and part of the res' gestae. (*This has to do with the rule where remarks are made spontaneously.*) Charles Vaughan should have been permitted to answer the question: "Were you in the habit of shutting these gates or not?"

The answers of Charles Vaughan were made under duress at the coroner's jury, and he should not have been compelled to answer on or about them. (Fifth Amendment to Const. U. S.)

The question: "What religious denomination do you belong to?" This should never have been answered. It was sectarian. The question asked by the defense was general and touched the old common law qualifications of the witness' reliability, but whether he was protestant or catholic, or how he worshiped God, has never been admissible. "Do you believe in God, the immortality of the soul, the reward and punishment for deeds done in this life?" They are always pertinent and admissible.

"State, from your observation of Willie Litster, what his general disposition was?" This question should have been allowed, to show how the defendant regarded him. The jury is the judge of the defendant's theory of self-defense, and in order to do so the defendant should have been allowed to testify what feelings operated upon his mind and the cause, which produced such effect. Whether it was reliable or the truth, the jury was to judge of its reliability and weight, and the same rule applies to the threats and shot.

The testimony about Lizzie Litster hearing that the Vaughan boys were going to mine the next day should have been left in the case. A girl 12 years of age knowing of the feelings which existed between the families would be sure to go home and tell it, and at any rate, the jury should have been left to judge of it.

The testimony as to Willie Litster's character for peace and quiet should never have been allowed in the case. It had never been attacked.

The court takes out of the case the doctrine of self-defense by instruction No. 2, and does not say that the indictment might include justifiable homicide.

The court takes out of the case the doctrine of self-defense by instruction. No. 1, and says that the presumption that the killing is malicious unless the same proof that establishes the killing shows mitigation, to the exclusion of any other proof, which, under the law, would be sufficient, no matter from whence it comes.

By instruction No. 5, the jury was told that they must find the defendant did voluntarily and unlawfully kill Willie Litster, or that he was not guilty. No intermediate course was left to them. We say such an instruction is not law and misled the jury and prohibited them from bringing in any verdict but murder in the first degree, or that the killing was justifiable.

Instruction No. 6 misstates the law and tells the jury that it must appear that the circumstances were sufficient to excite the fears of a reasonable person. We say that it must have appeared to the defendant as a reasonable person that the circumstances were sufficient to excite his fears as a reasonable person, placed as he was at the time.

Instruction No. 8 is misleading in not going far enough and giving the whole section 4582, Com. Laws of Nevada.

Instruction No. 11 takes the doctrine of self-defense out of the case entirely and says: “that a killing which is intentional is willful, if the intention to kill has been formed, etc., etc., will be murder in the first degree.” Now, everyone who shoots in self-defense has the intention to kill formed before he shoots, and yet no one will say it is murder if done in self-defense.

Instruction No. 14 is in the teeth of the statute, and should not have been given, because the statute says no other definition of a reasonable doubt is to be given but the statute.

Instruction No. 16 draws the attention of the jury to the testimony of the defendant and so does No. 13, and presents to the jury his testimony alone and not in conjunction with others, and, therefore, was not correct.

Instruction No. 17, also, takes out of the case the doctrine of self-defense and says that there need be only the intention to kill and never mentions the words: “and not in necessary self-defense.”

Instruction No. 18, also, eliminates the doctrine of self-defense and says that: "malice aforethought means the intention to kill; and when such means are used as are likely to produce death, the legal presumption is that death was intended." This language conveys the idea that the intention to kill manifests malice no matter how much danger the slayer was in, at the time, from the person killed, and is not law.

Instruction No. 19 is not applicable to the case and is not the law. On the contrary it is unlawful to fence up the public domain by settlers.

Instruction No. 21 again picks out the defendant and his witnesses to the jury, and says if he or any witness for him have sworn falsely, you may disbelieve them. Such picking out of the defendant and his witnesses, and constantly holding him or them up to the jury takes the place of bold assertion; that the defendant is not to be believed, nor are his witnesses to be relied upon.

The court tells the jury Rast may be believed, although he acknowledged to perjuring himself before the coroner's jury, the committing magistrate and the grand jury, and that, he lied in the district attorney's office. Yet the court tells the jury they may believe him, but does not say if you believe he has lied or sworn falsely, you may reject his testimony.

Instruction No. 24 totally ignores all kind of provocation which might reduce it to murder in the second degree, or manslaughter, and just says: "If he did the killing not in necessary self-defense, it would constitute murder in the first degree."

These instructions are biased, one-sided and misleading, and no instruction, which is misleading, is cured by an instruction, which gives the law correctly afterwards. This rule is clearly set forth in the case of People v. Berlin, and authorities therein cited in the dissenting opinion of Smith, J., and on rehearing concurred in by Merritt, C. J., and made the opinion of the court. "The rule that when a charge is erroneous in one part, and injurious to a defendant, the mere stating of a correct rule in another part does not cure it." Every authority entitled to respect establishes this.

We believe that there are many errors in the case, which is

noticed in our bill of exceptions-in fact, the record bristles with them--but feel confident that each of the many we have herein pointed out, would in itself, be sufficient error to reverse the case.

FOR RESPONDENT: Robert. M. Beatty, Attorney General and W. D. Jones, District Attorney of Lander County.

The first point relied upon by appellant is that the challenges to the jurors Hilkey, Tallack, Thorpe and others should have been allowed. They fail to show that John Thorpe was the only juror named who served on the jury. This is true, however, for Thorpe is the only one of the jurors complained of that served upon appellant's jury, Hilkey, Tallack and others having been peremptorily challenged by appellant. Thorpe was challenged by appellant for "implied bias," which was overruled by the court. After this proceeding as to Thorpe, and before the jury was sworn, appellant exercised three peremptory challenges, being: apparently satisfied with Thorpe .as a juror. The challenge to Thorpe, Hilkey, Tallack and others complained of were all challenges for "implied bias." The statutes of this state (Gen. State. 4220, amended 1889, 83) permit a challenge for one or more of nine causes. In the challenge to Thorpe appellant failed to name any one of the statutory causes. In State v. Gray, this court said: "If the challenge be considered as made for implied bias it was properly overruled, because it does not set forth any ground upon which a challenge for implied bias may be made."

These authorities are ample to dispose of the challenges; they are conclusive, but on the principle that the last should be the strongest and to clinch the point we cite Gen. Stats. 4222: "In a challenge for implied bias, one or more of the causes stated in section three hundred and forty (4220) not be alleged." The defendant had the power and the right to use his peremptory challenges as he pleased; he was free to use or not to use them, as he thought proper, but having resorted to them they must be followed out to all their legitimate consequences. He thereby voluntarily blots out all error, if any occurred, in overruling the challenges for cause, and cannot be heard to allege any exception as to those jurors.

In accepting Thorpe while the accused had unused peremptory challenges he is estopped from complaining that Thorpe was not impartial.

As to juror Schutes, his case was doubly cured, for before he was peremptorily challenged he was challenged for actual bias. Triers were appointed who found the challenge untrue, which was final as to his qualifications as a juror in the case.

The second point made by appellant is: "that the juror Rapley was a qualified juror in every way." Counsel: "admit that it is seldom error to excuse a juror on challenge." The supreme court of California in People v. Murphy says: "The action of a trial court in allowing a challenge to a juror for implied bias is not open to review."

The defendant peremptorily challenged Schutes. "The decision of the tiers is final and it is not subject to exception or review upon appeals." The juror Thorpe was a qualified juror under State v. Millian.

Where a juror states that he has an opinion that it would take evidence to remove, yet, if it appears that he could discard that opinion, and render an impartial verdict without being influenced by the opinion, he is not disqualified. Chief Justice Marshall has laid down the sound doctrine.

Before a juror is disqualified his opinion must be a fixed, absolute, positive, definite, decided, substantial, deliberate, unconditional one. The rule is almost universally laid down by these words or words of similar import. A conditional, hypothetical, contingent, intermediate, floating, indefinite, uncertain opinion will not do.

The case of State v. Murphy cited by appellant is not in point here. In that case, when appellant was forced to take juror Kile, defendant's peremptory challenges were all exhausted. State v. McClear, does not support the contention of appellant.

The dying declarations of Willie Litster, the deceased, were clearly admissible. The foundation for the dying declarations of deceased was fully laid.

In-State v. Streeter, this court held: "Objections to

questions asked a witness and ruled out by the court become immaterial and will not be considered in the appellate court where it affirmatively appears that the witness was afterward allowed to answer questions of the same import."

It was not error to ask Nick Rast the question: "What religious denomination do you belong to?" The defendant brought it out.

We notice that in copying the instructions into the bill of exceptions counsel have made a few errors and omissions. We suggest that the court use the instructions in the record that were copied by the clerk, as they are free from error. In No. 14 counsel for appellant omit the word "mathematical" entirely. The appellant alleges error in each of the twenty-seven instructions given on behalf of the state, but argue only fifteen, and we take it that they waive objection to those they do not argue.

We are unable to find any error in any of the instructions. From Nos. 1 to 11, inclusive, were given by Judge Beatty in State v. Anderson, and by that judge in every murder case tried before him until he left the nisi prius bench, and after that these same instructions were given by Judges Boalt and MlcKenney for all the years they were judges, and not one of those fourteen instructions have ever been unfavorably criticized by this court, although presented to it on appeal times without number. Instruction 15, immediately following 14, gives the statutory definition of reasonable doubt verbatim, and this was the only definition of reasonable doubt given in the case. No. 16 is statutory; it is a copy of our statutes of 1889. Nos. 17 and 18 each state the law of this State. No. 11 is statutory. No. 20 is not argued. No. 21 states the law correctly, and so does No. 11. No. 21 is not argued. There is no error in No. 14; it clearly says: "If from the evidence you believe that Alfred Vaughan killed Willie Litster, not in necessary self-defense, but with malice aforethought, willfully, deliberately and premeditatedly, then such killing would constitute murder in the first degree, and you should find this defendant guilty thereof."

We ask the court to read the instructions given on behalf of defendant. There are twenty-nine of them and they are each fair and favorable to him. His counsel sought and obtained every legal principle and definition known to the law to avoid to him the awful consequences of his premeditated, willful and deliberate act of feloniously slaying Willie Litster.

If the evidence in this case does not justify the verdict, this court will never be called upon to review a case where it does.

The law in its majesty demands that just punishment be meted out to Alfred Vaughan for the killing of Willie Litster. He, who shall, without authority of law, and with malice aforethought, either express or implied, kill a human being, shall be deemed guilty of murder in the first degree. Alfred Vaughan so killed Willie Litster; he has been duly convicted of that crime.

OPINION OF THE COURT, By: C. T. Bigelow

The by following Syllabus was written Justice Bigelow. He states that the facts are sufficiently stated in the opinion.

The defendant was convicted of murder in the first degree for the killing of William Litster, Jr. At the time of the homicide the defendant was 21 years of age, and the deceased 16. For some time prior to the killing, there had been trouble between the family of defendant and the family of deceased. This seems to have been greater between defendant and deceased than between the other members of the families, and was principally concerning the right to free passage through a ranch owned and possessed by the father of deceased, situated in Boone Canyon, some four or five miles above the ranch owned by the father of defendant. The Litster ranch was enclosed with a wire fence, which crossed the road running up the canyon, gates being put in at the crossings. The Vaughan's claimed this to be a public road, and sometimes, when passing along it, they left these gates open.

On the morning of the day of the homicide, the defendant, his brother Charles, and a hired man started, with a team loaded with supplies, to go to a mining claim owned by them in the hills or mountains above the Litster place, which they intended working. They passed into the Litster ranch through the lower gate, and up through it, nearly to the upper side, where they turned off the main road for the purpose of taking a road up a side canyon known as "Water Canyon," which ran in the direction of the mine. A few rods from where they turned off they came to a division fence crossing the road, and through which it was necessary for them to pass. There was no gate in this fence, but there was a place where the wires had been previously taken apart by people passing through, though the gap was then closed. At this point they met the deceased and an elder brother, who objected to their passing through the fence. In the difficulty, which ensued, both the Litster's were killed by the defendant with a Winchester rifle, the brother dying immediately, and William living but a few hours. As to this difficulty the testimony differs widely; that of the state tending to show a willful and unprovoked murder by the defendant, and that upon the part of the defendant that the Litster's were making a violent assault upon him, one with a pistol, and the other with an axe, and that, to save his own life, he was compelled to shoot them.

1. Several errors are assigned upon the court's rulings denying the defendant's challenges to trial jurors who were challenged on the ground of "implied bias." This is not such a challenge, as the statute requires. The term "implied bias" covers nine different grounds of challenge. Section 340 of the act regulating criminal proceedings provides that, “in a challenge for an implied bias, one or more of the causes stated in section 340 must be alleged.” This was not done, and consequently the challenge was insufficient to raise any point for the consideration of this court.

2. It is claimed that the evidence shows the juror Rapley to have been a qualified juror, and, consequently, that the court erred in excusing him upon a challenge by the State. But the right to reject does not include the right to select jurors. If the defendant was tried by an impartial jury, that is all he has the right to demand; he has no vested right to be tried by some particular juror. Besides, the action of the court in allowing challenges is not made the subject of an exception.

3. The third point is that the dying declarations of the deceased were not admissible, for the reason that no sufficient

foundation had been laid; that it did not appear that they were made under a prospect of "almost immediate dissolution." The evidence shows that the boy was shot about 11 o'clock in the forenoon; that he fell at the place where shot, or very near it, and lay there until carried to the house, where he died about 4 o'clock that afternoon; that he suffered greatly from the wound, and stated that "he was going to die, and he knew he was going to die right away;" that he refused to take medicine, saying there was no use to take it; there was nothing could do him any good. A physician had been sent for, but he said he would be dead before the doctor could see him, and, in fact, did die before his arrival. This evidence was uncontradicted, and, if not sufficient foundation for the admission of the declarations, we are unable to see what would be. The fact that these statements that he expected to die were not all made prior to his first relation of the circumstances of the homicide is immaterial. The circumstances were told several times after they were made, and, in fact, the only figure these statements cut is to show that his relation of the circumstances was made under the expectation of impending death. They show that from the first he had no hopes of recovering, and that is sufficient.

4. The officer who arrested the defendant, testifying in the case, was asked what the defendant said at the time of the arrest, and replied: Alpheus Vaughan said, “I shot Willie Litster; I think it was in self-defense.” The prosecution moved to strike out the latter part of this answer, presumably the part stating that the shooting had been done in self-defense, and the motion was granted. Subsequently, however, on the same day, the prosecution asked to withdraw the motion, and that the whole answer be permitted to stand. The court thereupon informed the jury that the objection to the testimony had been withdrawn, and that the entire answer was before them as evidence in the case. We see no reason to doubt that this cured the error in the first ruling, and it is unnecessary to consider it further.

5. Charles Vaughan testified that about a year prior to the homicide, while he and another brother, Frank Vaughan, were working at the mine, the two Litster boys had shot at them twice, apparently either wantonly or for the purpose of driving

them away. This evidence was, upon motion by the prosecution, stricken out. While the practice of admitting testimony without objection, and then moving to' strike it out, is one not to be commended, particularly when done by the State in a criminal case, where about the only effect of striking it out is the additional chance of making an error, we do not think that the court erred in the ruling here. Evidence of collateral matters should only be admitted when it has some tendency to throw light upon the circumstances surrounding the killing. This is the principle upon which threats, previous attacks, etc., made by deceased upon the defendant, are admitted. Ordinarily, assaults made upon a third person by deceased could only bear upon his general character or disposition, and as to that it is only evidence of general reputation, and not of particular actions, that is admissible. We do not think the evidence shows such a feeling by deceased against Charles and Frank Vaughan and the defendant jointly as should alter this rule.

6. The prosecution was permitted in rebuttal, over the defendant's objections, to introduce testimony to prove that the character of deceased for peace and quietness was good. It is argued that this was error, because his character had not been attacked. But there may be such attacks made as will authorize the admission of evidence of good character without any witness having testified directly that the reputation of the attacked party was bad, and that seems to be the case here. The defendant, and others in his behalf, had testified to many facts tending to show that the deceased possessed a quarrelsome, turbulent and violent disposition; that he was in the habit of using very bad language towards the defendant and his family; that lie had frequently made threats against them, including defendant; that upon one occasion he had wantonly shot at him, and at the time of the homicide was making a murderous assault upon him. We think this was equivalent to proving his character as a quarrelsome, turbulent, and violent boy, and fully justified the admission of the evidence of good character in rebuttal.

7. The mother of defendant testified that, the day before the homicide, she had been at a neighbor's house, and there stated,

in the presence of a sister of deceased, about 10 years of age, that her sons were going to the mine the next day. No objection was made to this testimony when offered, except that the attorneys for the state stated that they reserved the right to move to strike it out if not properly connected. At the close of defendant's case, they made this motion, upon the ground that it did not appear that the girl had told her brothers of what she had heard, and the evidence was stricken out. It is now contended that this ruling was wrong, because the jury might have inferred that she had done so. But, before evidence of one fact should be admitted as presumptive evidence of another fact, there should be some usual and recognized connection between them. This does not exist here. The information may have been communicated, or it may not. There is as much probability one-way as the other. At the best, the deduction would be a "mere guess", which is not permissible.

8. The "Catechism of the Christian Doctrine" was improperly admitted in evidence, but it was so entirely immaterial that it could not have influenced the verdict in any way, and consequently the error was harmless to the defendant.

9. As already stated, the defendant admitted the killing by shooting with a rifle, but claimed it had been done in self-defense. Under these circumstances, the issues before the jury was (1) whether this defense had been made out; (2) if not, of what degree of crime the defendant was guilty. It was in the power of the jury to find him guilty of murder in the first degree, murder in the second degree, or of manslaughter. It consequently became highly important that correct instructions defining the distinctions between these different degrees should be given. In the second instruction the court informed the jury that murder is the unlawful killing of a human being with malice aforethought, either express or implied, which is correct. But in the eighteenth instruction, in attempting a definition of malice aforethought, this language was used. The use of a dangerous weapon under a provocation by words only, or under no provocation, is always evidence of malice aforethought. To constitute malice aforethought, it is only necessary that there be a formed intention to kill. Malice aforethought means the

intention to kill and, where such means are used as are likely to produce death, the legal presumption is that death was intended. This, we think, was error. The fact that a killing was intentional does not necessarily prove that it was done with malice; for an intentional killing may be entirely justifiable, as where it is done in necessary self defense, or it may be only manslaughter, as where it is done in the heat of passion caused by a sufficient provocation. What it is must depend upon the manner of the killing and the surrounding circumstances.

The instruction was highly prejudicial to the defendant, for, if guided by the law there laid down, the jury must have reasoned thus: (1) The defendant admits the use of such means as were likely to produce death, and that did produce death; therefore, the presumption is that death was intended. (2) An intention to kill constitutes malice aforethought. (3) A killing with malice aforethought is murder. Therefore, upon the defendant's own admission, without regard to anything else, he is guilty of murder. We say without regard to anything else, because, although the law concerning self-defense and manslaughter is correctly laid down in the instructions, they contain nothing, and, indeed, scarcely could contain anything to correct the error made here.

In the twenty-fifth instruction the law concerning malice is correctly stated, and, as it clearly demonstrates the error of the eighteenth instruction, we quote from it: "The existence or non-existence of malice is an inference to be drawn from all the facts in the case. If malice is found, it must be drawn as an inference from everything that is proved taken together as a whole. Every fact, no matter .how small, every circumstance, no matter how trivial, which bears upon the question of malice, should be considered by the jury at the same time that they consider the use of the deadly weapon, to wit, the gun with which the defendant here admits that he shot, the deceased, Willie Litster; and it is only as a conclusion from all these facts and circumstances that malice is to he inferred." But, of course, the giving of it correct instruction does not cure an incorrect one, because it is impossible to determine which the jury followed. That an intention to kill does not constitute malice is well settled by the authorities. In Dennison v. State, the trial court had instructed the jury that, "if there be evidence of express malice that is, a positive intention to kill existing in the mind of the slayer at the time of inflicting the wound, the killing is murder in the second degree." Commenting upon this, the court said: "This latter instruction contains an error which may have misled the jury. It informs them that intention to kill, existing at the commission of the act, constitutes express malice." This is entirely wrong. In justifiable homicide there is intention to kill, but not necessarily malice or premeditation.

In murder in the first degree there is intention to kill, accompanied with premeditated malice, except in certain cases in which certain acts are made murder by statute. In murder in the second degree there is intention to kill, accompanied by malice, but without premeditation. In manslaughter there may be intention to kill arising from the sudden transport of passion, but it may, and must in this grade of offense, be unaccompanied by both premeditation and malice. In Trumble v. Territory, the following instruction was held to be erroneous: "Where the fact of killing purposely by the use of a deadly weapon is proved, malice is to be presumed, unless it appears from all the evidence in the case that the killing was without malice, or was justifiable or excusable." The court saying: "The jury should be directed that it was their duty to decide from all the facts of the case, many or few, whether the killing was malicious." In People v. Barry, where the instruction was in case of a mutual combat, "When one uses superior weapons to those possessed by the party slain, malice may be inferred, and the killing amounts to murder." The court said: "If A should make an assault upon B with a deadly weapon, by the use of which he might readily accomplish his manifested purpose, to kill B, and the latter, having no other means of saving his own life except by killing his assailant, should in necessary self defense, slay him, could it be seriously contended that the act done in such necessary self-defense was done with malice, and that the killing was murder, because it happened that the weapon so used in self-defense was superior to that in the hands of the assailant? No one, we apprehend, would deliberately undertake to support such a proposition."

10. The jury was also instructed that any person passing through gates in fences inclosing fields, and not shutting and fastening the same, shall be deemed guilty of a misdemeanor. While this was substantially copied from the statute, we cannot but regard it as erroneous and prejudicial to the defendant, under the circumstances existing here. In the first place, it is, at least, doubtful whether the statute would apply to the case of a gate placed across a public road, as it appears the Vaughan's claimed this to be. But, disregarding that, the instruction was upon a point that cut no legitimate figure in the case. As we have seen, the main question for the jury to decide was whether the defendant, in killing William Litster, had acted in self-defense. It was proper and necessary for them, in determining this question, to consider everything admitted in evidence that would assist in coming to a correct conclusion as to what occurred at the fence that fatal morning. That was the central point, and evidence of collateral occurrences was only material in so far as it tended to throw light upon what took place there. Did the defendant kill the deceased without cause or excuse, or did the Litster's first make such a murderous attack upon him that he was justified in killing in self-defense, as he claims?

As reflecting upon this, as well as upon the question of malice, it was proper to show the state of feeling existing between the parties. There was a conflict in the testimony as to what occurred when they met. If the defendant had such feeling against the deceased as might prompt him to attack and murder him without cause, this would strengthen the case of the prosecution. On the other hand, if the feelings of the deceased toward the defendant were such as might have caused him to make the first murderous assault, its tendency would be to strengthen the defense. In showing this, evidence concerning the gates was, necessarily admitted, because this was the matter, or one of the matters, about which the feeling had arisen; but the fact that, in leaving them open, the defendant had committed a misdemeanor, had no tendency to show an increase or diminution of his animosity, nor, indeed, that he had any animosity whatever. The defendant was not being tried for leaving gates open, and the instruction was no more relevant to the issue before the jury than would have been an instruction that taking another's horse amounted to larceny had there been evidence that at some time the defendant had taken some other person's horse. It was calculated to create prejudice against the defendant, by showing that he had committed a crime in another matter, and to divert the minds of the jurors from the real issue in the case.

11. In regard to the fourteenth instruction concerning reasonable doubt, in view of the fact that the case must be retried, it is only necessary to call attention to what was said by this court in State v. Potts, concerning the advisability of adhering strictly to the statutory definition.

This is sufficient to dispose of the appeal; but, in view of the fact that the case will have to be retried, it is proper for us to notice other rulings that, although they have not been particularly called to our attention, were, some of them at least, objected to by the defendant, and, if repeated, may be urged as error upon another appeal. As already stated, the only evidence properly admissible is that which in some manner tends to throw light upon the killing. Upon the opening, it was necessary for the state to introduce its evidence tending to establish the commission of the homicide by the defendant, and such as tended to prove that it was malicious, willful, deliberate, and premeditated. In defense, the defendant could introduce his evidence tending to show that it was done in self-defense, including such as might tend to prove that the feelings of deceased towards the defendant were such as might have caused him to begin the deadly affray, or to make the first attack. Rebuttal evidence would then be all that tended to establish that the killing was not done in self-defense. Perhaps this general statement will not assist very materially upon a retrial; but in the face of such a voluminous record, unassisted by argument upon the points, it is difficult to draw the line as to all that was properly admitted and what was not. Without attempting this, it is safe to say there was much evidence on both sides that could have no legitimate influence upon the verdict.

In our judgment, as the case is now presented, the evidence as to whether there was any other road that the Vaughan's might have taken in going to their mine, whether the road up Water Canyon was good or bad, whether they had any mine, whether a team that had been driven up to the fence could be turned around without passing through the gap, whether the elder Vaughan had ever asked permission of William Litster, Sr., to pass through the fence, of the conversation between them concerning the poisoning of the dog, of what title Litster had to his ranch, was all irrelevant, could only tend to distract the attention of the jury from the real issue, and, so far as objected to, should have been excluded.

Of course, nothing we have said must be construed as in any way reflecting upon the defendant's guilt or innocence. That is a question for a jury, and is one that we have not at all considered. **However guilty he may be, he is entitled to a trial in accordance with the rules of law;** and, as we find that in some respects he has not had this, the judgment must be reversed.

Judgment reversed, and cause remanded for a new trial.

Reese River Reveille, March 23, 1895:

On Thursday morning District Attorney Jones received a telegram from Attorney General Beatty announcing the reversal of the judgment of the District Court in the Vaughan case, by the Supreme Court, for, the error in the instructions of the trial court. The action of the Supreme Court necessitates a new trial of Alfred Vaughan, for the murder of Willie Litster, on the 28th of December 1893, the same as, if no trial had ever been had. District Attorney Jones will press the time for the new trial for as early a date as possible. He desires it for some date in April, and will do all he can to have the trial come off then. This is costing the taxpayers of the County, the sooner the trial takes place the less expense to the County, besides there having been a trial heretofore that attorneys can be ready on much shorter notice than if it was to be the first trial.

We have no doubt, but that a jury can be obtained in Lander County for the trial. Some give their opinion that another jury cannot be had here, but there seems to be no good reason for this conclusion. There are many jurors in the County who are not disqualified, and it would be much cheaper to try the case here than elsewhere.

The result of the decision is that Alfred Vaughan has another chance with a new jury. The Attorneys and other Court officers now must repeat their work while the County must pay the additional expense of a second trial. It seemed certain to everyone that a second trial would not be as lengthy or as costly as the first trial.

The defense had claimed many errors were made during the trial among which were the unlawful grand jury; the disqualification of Juror John Thorpe; no foundation for the dying declarations of Willie: Litster was laid; that Jurors Hilkey, Tallack, Heath, McLeod, and Schultes should have been excused by the Court; that Juror Rapley should not have been excused by the Court; the testimony as to Lizzie Litster overhearing a conversation should not have been stricken; the Litster should not have been permitted to testify about the poisoning of their dog; Nick Rast should not have been permitted to answer as to his religious belief; the Court should have told the jury what the penalty for murder in the second degree is; and it was not shown that Willie Litster was under a sense of impending death when he made the dying declaration. The Supreme Court held that there was no error on any of these points.

The verdict was overturned on the language in instruction No.18, given by the Court stating: "Malice aforethought means the intention to kill." Also, the instruction given to the jury, “that any person opening and passing through gates when said gates are in fences enclosing fields and not shutting and fastening the same, shall be deemed guilty of a "misdemeanor," was held prejudicial.

Reese River Reveille, March 27, 1895:

The Carson Appeal says: The Supreme Court has reversed the case of Alpheus Vaughan sentenced to be hung at Austin for the killing of William Litster. The Supreme Court held that the lower Court had erred in, instructing the jury that the use of dangerous weapon under provocation is always evidence of malice aforethought. The Supreme Court held that the intention to kill does not necessarily indicate malice as the killing may lave been justifiable. The trouble occurred over the right of two families to use a certain gate as a free passageway between fields. The lower Court held that the passing of the defendant through the gate was a misdemeanor. While this was correct as a matter of law, it tended to create a prejudice in the minds of the jury regarding the defendant, as he was being tried for murder and not for the passing through the gate. On these two points the case was reversed and a new trial granted.

Author's Summary:

Dennis only needed the High Court to agree with one of his claimed errors for them to find in his favor and he would get a new trial for Alfred. Yes, you can tell the attorneys and judges were very concerned about the "Rule of Law" in 1894.

The High Court's decision was based on the errors made in the instructions by Judge Fitzgerald regarding "malice" and a "misdemeanor trespass". Therefore, Alfred got a new trial. Also, it was the Justice's opinion that Judge Fitzgerald didn't allow the defendant's claim of self-protection to be heard without prejudice. They felt by the judge allowing testimony regarding possible misdemeanors by the defendant that this caused prejudice for the jury.

The Justice's seemed to think the issue of the feud between these young men was irrelevant and this was a cause of distraction from the real issue of murder. The only way these Justices could rule this way was because of the obvious failure by Judge Fitzgerald's instructions. Perhaps justice was sacrificed to the rule of law.

7

TRIAL NO. 2

Is This A Second Chance?

Disappointment certainly would understate the Litster's feelings when they received the news about the Supreme Court ordering a new trial. Of course they wanted this matter over and done with. On the other hand, the Vaughan's had renewed hope for Alfred. Nearly ten months had lapsed from the trial last April.

The Litster's were aware that Jones and Truman as well as Alfred's attorney's had traveled to Carson City during the month of February to argue the case before the high court. Jones told them when he returned it would take about month for the court to have their written opinion ready and at that time they would announce their decision.

A telegram from the Supreme Court was dated March 20, 1895. The message reads:

"Supreme Courts overturns the Alfred Vaughan conviction and orders a new trial. Copies of the court's opinion will be mailed tomorrow."

The Third District Court in Austin could now schedule the date for a new trial. The Supreme Court's annual publication, "Report of Cases", dated January 1895, records all court actions taken for the year 1894. This publication was not issued until midyear in 1895. Notice the difference from that time to the present. Appeals take years these days for cases like this to be heard.

Life was never the same for either of the families following the murder of Johnny and Willie. It was especially hard on

William; he no longer had his sons to help with the work at the ranch. Jimmy was now 15 years old and he tried to fill the void but that was too much to expect. William had to hire help handling the hay crop last summer. While the first trial was behind them, no one could forget for a moment that Johnny and Willie were gone. As they say, "life goes on" but that does not say it will be easy. It was very sad during the evening when Elizabeth would read the Bible to the family. She liked to read the Psalms and she tried to help the children to understand they needed to trust the Lord and thank Him even now for taking care of Johnny and Willie. Elizabeth too felt the suffering of her husband. He seemed to be taking the loss harder than anyone else. Reading the Bible may have helped the children, but Elizabeth could see the sadness it brought in her husband's eyes.

Jimmy was looking more like his older brother's. He was big for his age and was a handsome young man. He was an excellent horseman like Johnny and Willie, well not as good as Willie. It would be a few more years before George and Louis could help with breaking the wild mustangs. They were eager to learn and they did get a big kick out of watching Jimmy land on his backside as he attempted to let one of those horses know that it was normal for a man to sit on them.

Jimmy had to forego school that year to help his father with the work at the ranch. George and Louis continued with their schooling last fall, but it would be George's last year too. After finishing the fifth grade, he too had to work full time at the ranch. The Litster family had less income this year and William attributed it to the loss of his two boys. It was necessary to supplement the income, so he hired John Mitchell to be a full time woodcutter last October. John had worked steady during the last seven-months and the sale of firewood proved to be a good source of income.

Jones announced a new trial would start in May. The decision by the Supreme Court was not well received by most of the people in Austin. Now they would have to relive the events of the first trial. The family again was forced to think about a new trial. No one wanted to talk about it, but it was impossible not talk about it as their thoughts continually drifted back to the day Johnny and Willie were shot and the prior trial. William must have thought many times about why he didn't stop the Vaughan wagon as it passed the corral. He could have explained to Alfred that the boys were closing the fence at the Gap. Alfred could tell the boys that their father said it was all right for them to pass through the Gap. And if they were not at the Gap just be sure to close the gate.

William should have filed a complaint to the Sheriff long before about the Vaughan's disrespectful neglect regarding the ranch gates. Perhaps if he had ridden a horse to the Gap after his wife insisted that he check on the boys. Maybe he could have prevented the shooting. However, I think Alfred's attitude on that morning, may well have seen William's name added to his list of victims if he had confronted the Vaughan's.

The winter of 1894-95 was harder in many ways than the previous year's winter, however the Vaughan's never came through the ranch again. The Litster's too made sure that they did everything to avoid the Vaughan's. It was very difficult for Jimmy to ride down to the mouth of the canyon for the mail at the Switch. The Vaughan's reputation in Austin was very bad among those that knew and liked the Litster brothers. Yet, Lee Vaughan was still respected by his few friends. He was now an old man at 71 years.

The Vaughan's came to Lander County in 1867 from La Porte, Sierra County, California. That place is even more remote than the Reese River Valley. His wife gave birth to three of the five sons at the Vaughan Ranch. Frank Vaughan was a half brother and Will Jackson was a stepbrother to the three younger sons. The Vaughan's pretty much isolated themselves from the community. Still one of the family members usually made the weekly trip to Austin to see Alfred. Life in a small jail cell for this 22-year-old man probably seemed worse than death itself. Now with the high courts ruling for new trial, his family had hope again and may be this time Alfred would be released.

It is impossible to put yourself in Alfred's mind. Could he have been evil or was he just unstable? Did he ever feel bad about what had happened? There was never any expression of guilt or remorse on his part. Did he feeling sorry for himself? Of course he did, but Alfred was a tough young man, just maybe a little too tough. Hopefully, his lawyers will be able to convince the new jury that he shot the brothers in self-defense. Dennis told him several times they were sure all charges would be drop if the jury finds in his favor. Dennis could only continue the strategy of self-defense. The dye was cast during the Coroner's Inquest and they must continue this argument as presented at the Preliminary Examination and the First Trial.

The transcript of the second trial was complete. Records from more than a century ago are not like what we have today. I would venture to say this is the major difference from that time to the present. The court reporters using shorthand did an outstanding job. They would type the transcript after the trial ended.

The events I have extracted from the second trial transcript were compared to the newspaper articles. The transcript for the second trail allows a closer look and it provides a word picture for the witness's testimony about what took place in the courtroom. You might glean a better understanding of what really happened on December 28, 1893. Perhaps, you might conclude that Willie really was a hotheaded young teenager. Maybe, you'll learn why the Vaughan's felt they could freely trespass anywhere on the Litster's Ranch. How long had this feud by these brothers from the two families been raging? Were the Vaughan's willfully leaving gates open at the Litster Ranch? Can William Litster explain why he did not confront the Vaughan's about their free roaming through his ranch?

Spring in 1895 arrived at Austin right on time, but not on time for Alfred's retrial as far as the Litster's were concerned. The trial date was set for May 21, 1895. Again, families had to make arrangements to attend the trial. The Vaughan's grown sons were running their ranch. Dennis planned to call Charlie and Harry to testify. Frank Vaughan was not going to be called. Dennis anticipated that jury selection would take a few days. It was hard for Alfred's mother and father to be in Austin when there was so much emotion among the town's people. The Litster's again could rely on George and Isabella Watt to see that their ranch was cared for as well as Lizzie, George and

Louis. The kids always liked going to their Aunt and Uncle's ranch at Silver Creek. Here they didn't have any chores.

The trial started on a Tuesday morning. Alfred has been held in jail at Austin now for nearly seventeen months. Does he have a new sense of hope? The same two attorneys would represent him, James F. Dennis of Battle Mountain and J. H. MacMillan of Ogden, Utah. This time they must convince the jury that Willie was shot in self-defense. The Honorable C. E. Mack was going to be the judge for the retrial of Alfred Vaughan. Jones and Truman would again represent the State. William Christian had become the new County Clerk and the Court Reporters were: Mrs. A. M. Warren and Mrs. J. D. Fisher.

The details of the Second Trial are covered in this and the following four Chapters. The following timeline shows dates for primary trial events. It is recommend that you skip over this summary and only use it when you have a question regarding timing.

TIMELINE SECOND TRIAL 1895

May 21, Tuesday, Case No. 592, Presiding Hon. Charles E. Mack, Appealing for the State: W. D. Jones and D. S. Truman; for the Defendant: James F. Dennis; Clerk, W. W. Christian. Start Jury Examination.

May 22, Wednesday, Jury Examination.

May 23, Thursday, Jury Examination.

May 24, Friday, Jury Examination. Motion is made by Dennis to change the venue. He withdraws motion.

May 25, Saturday, Court admonishes jury not to converse with anyone. No other business or motions.

May 26, Sunday

May 27, Monday, Court orders the Clerk to call the roll, asks for any motions, none. Adjourn till next day.

May 28, Tuesday, Jury Examination. State accepts jury, Dennis peremptorily challenge. Jury is selected. Clerk reads indictment at 2:15 p.m. Some witnesses for State and Defense are sworn. Witnesses examined today: Mr. Scully, Surveyor, Maps-Exhibit No. 1 and Dr. Huntsman.

May 29, Wednesday, Dennis asks court to summons Harry

Vaughan. Wm Litster and Thos. Dunsdon examined for plaintiff before noon recess. More witnesses are sworn. Mrs. Alex Eason and James Litster examined. Vest-Exhibit No. 2; Sheriff Easton examined, Rifle and cartridges-Exhibit No. 3; Nick Rast examine started.

May 30, Thursday, Memorial Day

May 31, Friday, Jones asks court to excuse Rast. Jones asks for juror Flint to be dismissed. Dennis objects. Court orders witness to be heard. Moss, Kessell and Dunham are examined. This took place with the jury in the box. Court noon recess. After recess Court orders A. A. Flint was excused. Court orders more juror names to be drawn. Motion by Dennis to excused the defendant from courtroom till June 5th. Court is adjourned till June 1, 1895.

June 1, Saturday, roll is called, jury admonished, no business, recess till Monday.

June 2, Sunday

June 3, Monday, roll is called, jury admonished, no business, this case is being continued until this time.

June 4, Tuesday, roll is called, jury admonished, Court meet in chambers to discuss State of Nevada vs. A. A. Flint. Hearing is set for 1:30 p.m. for Flint. Flint declines to make a statement.

June 5, Wednesday, Mr. Flint is order to appear at 2 p.m. Court meet in chambers with Kessel, Moss, Dunham, Recend and Finegan so that they could sign testimony given yesterday. Court binds Flint over on charge of perjury, fixing bail at $750. At 3:30 p.m. Court orders jurors to be called. Dennis objects to filling the panel with new juror and that it is illegal. Court overrules. John Savage is selected as the twelfth juror. Court recesses till 8:15 p.m. Court orders the trial to once again start from the beginning, Jones makes opening statement; Dennis declines; Dr. Huntsman is examined.

June 6, Thursday, Sculley examined, Map-Exhibit No. 1; Wm. Litster, Mrs. Alex Eason, James Litster are examined. Wm. Litster recalled. Noon Recess. Mrs. Wm. Litster and Thos. Dunsdon examined. Mrs. Wm Litster recalled, Vest-Exhibit

No. 2; Sheriff Easton examined, Rifle and Cartridges Exhibit No. 3. Nick Rast is called as witness for the State.

June 7, Friday, Court orders Sheriff to produce pistol taken from Charlie Vaughan because it was evidence in the first trial as Exhibit No. 4. State Rests. Court orders now for the Defense to proceed. Dennis wants court to instruct jury regarding former jeopardy, Jones objects, Court sustains. Dennis now enters the record prior to discharge of Flint as Exhibit A. Dennis makes statement to jury. Noon Recess. Alfred Vaughan and Charlie Vaughan examined.

June 8, Saturday, Cross-Examine for Charlie resumed. Harry Vaughan examined; Noon Recess; Indian Muncey and L. S. Vaughan examined, Defense Rests. State calls Rebuttal Witnesses: Sheriff Easton; George Steiner; testimony of Frank Whaley from first trial; Jas. B. Egan; George Watt, Jr.; Stina Wagner; John Mullen; Thos. Dunsdon; George Watt, Sr.; Mrs. Wm. Christian; Dugal McGregor; Matt Edwards; John Mullen and James Litster. Defendant declines to take the stand again. State Rests; Defendant Rests. Court notifies that attorneys that that must submit immediately all instructions they wish to have given to the jury. Court recess till 8:30 p.m. Jones commences with the argument for the State. The court now will recess till 10 o'clock Monday.

June 9, Sunday

June 10, Monday, Jones resumes argument for State and concludes at 11 a.m. Dennis opens argument for the defense; Court calls recess. Dennis resumes argument till 2:20 p.m. Truman follows with the added argument for the State and concludes at 4:30 p.m. Truman was reading the instruction that would be given by the State; Dennis's objection is overruled. The court now reads the instruction to the jury. A recess is now called until the Jury has a verdict. Jury Verdict was swift. Court reconvened at 7 p.m. Verdict given to Court. Judge asks Clerk to read it. "State of Nevada vs. Alfred Vaughan: We the jury in the above entitled cause do find the defendant guilty of murder in the first degree. Dated June 10, 1895, John B. Paul, Forman."

The following article was copied from the Reese River Reveille, May 22, 1895, as it welcomes Judge Mack to the community. No details were given but logic tells us that the Second Trial of Alfred could not have Judge Fitzgerald again to hear the case.

Hon. C. E. Mack, District Judge of the First Judicial District of Nevada is presiding at this session of court. Judge Mack is a very able man and bears the distinction of being one of the best jurists in the State. His defeat of Judge Rising, who had been in office for 30 years at the late election show esteem in which he is held by his constituents in the first district. The Judge has succeeded in making himself very popular with our citizens during the short time he has been among us.

Judge Mack was ready to call for order in the Court for Alfred Vaughan's second trial. After order was called, Dennis asks to have James Egan, Esq. entered as an attorney for the defense. Jones objects on the grounds that Egan has been a witness for the prosecution at the first trial and he would be called again by the State. Judge Mack tells Egan:

"You really need to think about this because it could cost you your license." "I want you to let me know your decision by tomorrow."

The next day he did tell the Judge that he would not assist the defense.

William Christian had returned from Cortez and he was running a store in Austin before being elected to County Clerk. He was Willie Litster's uncle by marriage. Dennis was aware of this relationship to the Litster family and he was rather suspicious about the names that had been selected for jury duty. It was the County Commissioner job and he was aware that Commissioner's Hogan, Welch and Kelly had used members from the County staff to assist in the process. They had placed 266 names in the box for the drawing. They planned to draw out 150 names; however they drew 166 names as potential jurors.

Dennis was really smarting because he did not get a copy of the list of jurors until the day before the trial. Dennis states that he was now objecting to the list of people summoned for jury duty. Dennis demanded that the County Clerk be sworn so he could ask questions for the record. The Court allows his motion. The newspaper had published list of names of those being called for jury duty even before Dennis got a copy. The Judge said the procedure used by the County Commissioner did not place the defendant in jeopardy.

The examination of the jurors for this trial should have been simpler than it was for the first trial. The attorney's were able to excuse many jurors faster on the ground of implied bias. Even with the slow start caused by Dennis's challenge regarding jury pool selection process, ten jurors were passed to the peremptory challenge by the 5 p.m. adjournment on the first day.

Wednesday morning the courtroom was crowed. The jury selection process consumed the entire day and by 4:30 p.m. 134 names have been exhausted from the panels. The first trial was able to obtain a jury after the examination from a venire of 75 potential jurors. Sixteen possible jurors had passed and the State challenged two and the defense challenged three, which left eleven men in the jury box, subject to peremptory challenge. Jones was finding that obtaining a jury was not going to be as easy as he had hoped. Therefore, he asks the Court to order another venire to be issued. He was sure more people would be needed for jury panels. Dennis counters by saying that he would offer a motion on Thursday morning for a change of venue. Judge Mack then instructed the Clerk to draw an additional venire of 69 jurors and made the venire returnable by next Tuesday morning.

When the court met Thursday, Dennis asks the court to set a time to hear the argument for a change of venue to be moved to Friday at 10 o'clock, and this request was granted. The Judge then order the Clerk to notify the County Commissioners to meet for the purpose of placing additional names in the jury box. Friday morning Dennis formerly presented his application for a change of venue. Jones stated the State neither favored or opposed the change, but asks the Court to hold the application in abeyance until 100 jurors from outside districts of the County, that had been summoned by the Sheriff and were examined first. He sighted several authorities stating the change of venue was in the sole discretion of the Judge and that he had the right to hold the application in abeyance.

Judge Mack then permitted Dennis to show the proof in support of his application, and he put E. Craine, and L. A. Weller on the stand to prove that there was such a bias and prejudice against Alfred that he could not get a fair trial in this County. According to the newspaper, on cross-examination by Jones made it clear that neither witness knew anything about the sentiment of the people outside their circle of friends, which included the Vaughan family. As the noon recess approached, Dennis asked for time so he could summon witnesses from the street. The Court was reconvened at two o'clock and Dennis announced Alfred was ill and could he be allowed to retire. The Court granted his request. He also withdrew his application but did reserve the right to renew it at any time. You can assume he didn't find anyone on the street that suited his purpose. The jury selection process now resumed.

The attorney's returned to examining the jurors as to their voir dire (vwar dir). This is a French word used by lawyers for many years; it basically means a juror is ordered to speak the truth. Most jurors were just simply excused when Dennis asked the following question: "Have you ever formed or expressed an unqualified opinion as to the guilt or innocence of the defendant?"

Dennis continued to beat the drums with his question about expressing an unqualified opinion. While Jones was busy trying to think of a new way to ask if their conscientious scruples would preventing them from finding verdict of murder in the first degree if penalty were death. That is another difference to our present day courts and with a separate penalty trial phase. It was simpler then and there wasn't variety of sentences that could hand down. Where did we go wrong, they had it right?

There was one juror, J. B. Paul that did answer Dennis's question that yes he had expressed or formed an unqualified opinion. I think Dennis and MacMillan both forgot to excuse him. I thought surely they would later use a peremptory to excuse him, but he did not.

Another juror Dennis challenged was named J. W. Adkins.

Dennis asked where he lived? "Out in the range woods, in the mountains." Jones traversed the challenge; Dennis says that he can prove his challenge. The Court allows this and he called Lee Vaughan to the stand. Mr. Vaughan uses the nickname name Alphe for his son. He then proceeds to tell about hearing Adkins while drunk saying:

"Well, Alphe ought to be hung."

The Judges excuses Mr. Adkins for implied bias.

Another two and one half days was used before the jury is sworn. The final make up of the jury had four members from Battle Mountain; one from Yankee Blade; one from Argenta; three from Austin and three others that were not identified as to where they resided, but it was probable they too were Austin residents.

The idea about jury selection being easier for this trial was proving to be painfully wrong, as each panel of twelve were called and examined. Only two jurors, Heflin and Dobbs that had been selected on this first day remained in the box. The examination of those summoned would continue into Saturday. Finally, after examining 153 men twelve jurors were agreed to sit on this jury just before noon. The Defense had used seven of eight peremptory challenges while the State only used but one. After the noon recess at 2:15 p.m. the County Clerk swore the following 12 jurors. These jurors were as follows: (1) Heflin; (2) E. Gifford; (3) G. Austin; (4). J. Gunser; (5) G. Middleton; (6) C. Kearns; (7) A. Flint; (8) P. Brennan; (9) J. Morgan; (10) W. Dobbs; (11) J. Paul, (12) J. Jones.

The Judge asks Mr. Christian to read the indictment to the jury and the defendant's plea of not guilty. The Clerk was also asking to swear several witnesses for the State and for the defendant. The courthouse was still packed with people anxious to hear the testimony.

Jones began with his opening statement. Again, Dennis asks that he be allowed to reserve his opening statement and said he would wait until the plaintiff rests its case. There was a big surprise waiting for those involved in this trial. I'll get to that in a moment. But right now Dennis is not making the Judge pleased with his conduct. Jones was ready to call the first witness.

The follow list shows the order these witnesses testified at the second trial: Here there are 42 calls for individuals to testify as compared to 58 at the first trial. Again, you can see that most of these witnesses were called to the stand at least twice.

1. Dennis Scully
2. Dr. A. J. Huntsman
3. William Litster
4. Thomas Dunsdon
5. Mrs. Alex Eason
6. James Litster
7. Elizabeth Litster
8. William Easton
9. Nicholas Rast
10. Flint Proceedings
11. Dr. A. J. Huntsman
12. Dennis Scully
13. William Litster
14. Mrs. Alex Eason
15. James Litster
16. William Litster
17. Elizabeth Litster
18. Thomas Dunsdon
19. William Litster
20. William Easton
21. Nicholas Rast
22. William Easton
23. Alfred Vaughan
24. Charles Vaughan
25. Harry Vaughan
26. Indian Munsey
27. Lee Vaughan
28. James Ryan
29. William Easton
30. George W. Steiner
31. Frank J. Whaley
32. James B. Egan
33. George Watt, Jr.
34. Miss S. Wagner
35. John Mullen
36. Thomas Dunsdon
37. George Watt, Sr.
38. Mrs. W. W. Christian
39. Dougal McGregor
40. Matt Edwards
41. James Litster
42. Dr. A. J. Huntsman

Dennis Scully, the local Civil Engineer, describes the maps he made of the Litster Ranch and the crime scene. The maps were entered as the Exhibit A. He was followed by Doctor Huntsman and William Litster followed him. The hour was getting late when the Judge called a recess till 10 o'clock Wednesday morning, May 29, 1895. William was again on the stand. Thomas Dunsdon; Mrs. Alex Eason; James Litster; Elizabeth Litster; Sheriff Easton and Nick Rast would follow him. Notice that I've skipped over their testimony. The reason will shortly become obvious

The jury has now heard the testimony of those named above

and while Nick Rast is on the stand the Judge calls a recess until Friday morning. The Judge didn't say so, but May 30th was Memorial Day and it was a holiday. I first thought the Judge might have had a golf date, but that practice came later with the modern criminal law. I am sure a judge today would have taken a four-day weekend. Here this Judge not only works on Friday, but Saturday too and including an evening session called for 8:15 p.m. Saturday night. This is hard to imagine, right?

Now comes the surprise? As order was called and before Nick was brought back to the stand, Jones makes the following statement:

"If your Honor please, since court last adjourned I have been informed, and have what I believe to be reliable information, that there is a member of this jury who is entirely disqualified to sit in this case."

"We have the witnesses present to establish the fact of the information that we have received" "I now ask leave to present the testimony in support of the disqualification of the juror and after that is done I will take such further proceeding to present the matter to the Court as I may deem proper".

"I would like to have James Kessell called as a witness."

Jim Kessell was a sixty-year-old man and one of Austin's old miners; he came to Nevada in 1875. And like many miners he spent a good deal of his time at Harry King's Saloon when he wasn't working.

Dennis responds: "Your Honor please, we have jury here impaneled under the law and sworn to try this case."

"I now object to the proceedings going to the disqualification of any juror upon this panel."

Dennis continues to argue and the Judge finally overrules the objection. Here we find the difference in trial procedure of that time to the present. They did not have juror alternates. I don't know how the practice of the criminal justice evolved pertaining to this problem, but this may well have been a case used to show the need for jury alternates. Dennis continued to object to everything that was taking place regarding this matter, to, which the Judge would rule: "Objection overruled, you may have an exception."

Jones stated Mr. James Kessell has been called to testify as to the qualifications of Juror, A. A. Flint.

"State to the Court, Mr. Kessell, whether or not before the commencement of this trial, you at any time or place heard Mr. Flint"

Dennis objects: "I want to add a further objection that there is no issue before the Court, from the fact that Mr. Flint has not denied the charge, or been called upon."

The Judge tells Dennis that it is not necessary to deny the charge. However, Flint speaks up and states:

"You Honor, I deny the charge."

Under the direct examination by Jones, Kessell was finally able to relate a conversation he had heard a few months ago down at Harry King's Saloon.

"Mr. Flint and Mr. Moss were there arguing one way or another and the Alfred Vaughan trial came up and he said, if he was on the jury that he wouldn't hang him."

"Joe Moss was swearing at him and called him bad names and he said, he ought to be run out of town, when he found a man guilty he wouldn't hang him after he listened to the evidence."

"Mr. Flint argued and he said the reason was he didn't believe in capital punishment, and he wouldn't hang him for no consideration."

Mr. Kessell continues to describe their heated argument. Dennis refuses to cross-examine this witness.

Jones now calls Joe Moss to testify. Joe was also a long time resident of Austin. He had lived here 32 years, that would make him part of the Silver Rush in 1863. Joe says he has known Mr. Flint for twenty or twenty-five years. Joe proceeds to relate to the details of the argument he had with Flint at the saloon. He quotes Flint as saying:

"If I was on the Vaughan's jury, I wouldn't hang him." Joe said he asked why not and he said,

"I wouldn't." "I am opposed to capital punishment." Joe said, "I felt so contemptible mad at the way he talked, I said, you god damned son of a bitch of a fool you ought to be took out of town and killed."

"Mr. Kessell heard all of this and so did Harry King who was behind the bar." He said, "Dick Burroughs and Ned Dunham were there too."

Dennis again refuses to cross-examine this witness.

Jones now calls Edward "Ned" Dunham to testify. Ned also came during the Silver Rush.

"When you heard he was on the jury you made the remark that you didn't think he could sit on the jury?"

"Yes."

"Why?"

"Because I had heard him talk so much about it."

"Have you heard him, at any times, express an opinion, as to the guilt or innocence of Alfred Vaughan?"

"Well, Yes, he said he was guilty; I often heard him say he was guilty." "I don't recall when I heard Mr. Flint talking about capital punishment, but he and Joe Moss talked about the case many times."

Again it was Dennis turn and he said: "No questions."

Flint now asked Ned a question about hard feelings between Joe and himself? And if he heard the language that Joe used about him being a SOB?

"I heard you both talk in that kind of language several times."

The Judge asks: "Mr. Dennis have you anything further to say?" "The testimony here proves that this man claimed your client was guilty." "Do you desire to proceed with him on the jury?"

"Your Honor please, I object to the discharge at this time."

Flint now asks the Judge to have the questions regarding his qualification as a juror read. The judge so orders. W. D. Jones then read the evidence given by Flint. Remember the question about having formed an opinion, which was the very first question Dennis asked:

"Mr. Flint, have you formed or expressed an unqualified opinion or belief as to the guilt or innocence of the defendant here? Mr. Flint you answered, I have not."

Dennis now responds: "Your Honor please, I now ask the

District Attorney to be sworn."

What is Dennis trying to do with this matter? The Judge grants the request. Dennis wants Jones to explain how he came by this information and when.

Jones says: "I just heard about it, but didn't learn any of the facts, until yesterday morning about eleven o'clock."

"When did you first inform the Court of what you had heard?" "Last night as to the facts, yesterday in the forenoon as to the rumor."

"Can you state why you didn't inform me of it?" "I didn't consider it was any of your business until I found out whether there was any truth in it or not?"

Jones said he and Mr. Truman made an investigation and that it wasn't until late last night at about 2 a.m. that he felt the evidence was true.

Dennis asks: "Mr. Flint did you ever talk to me about this case at any time?" "I never did."

Dennis was covering his own backside. "Did you ever talk to any member of the Vaughan family at any time about this case?" "Yes I talked to Frank Vaughan one time."

It is now Jones turn and he asks to have Mr. Dennis sworn.

Jones wants Dennis to admit that he has been canvassing the to community to find the state of mind for possible jurors. Dennis will only admit that he was being diligent. Jones says that is not an answer.

Judge now asks: "Do you decline to answer it or not?" Dennis says again that he only wanted to know the mind of the community.

Jones asks: "You had no intimation of knowledge of the condition of the mind of Mr. Flint when you took him on the jury?"

"Not in the least."

By examining the voir dire of Flint, he did answer all question put to him in such a way that made him appear to be a qualified juror.

Dennis states he too first learned about this at 4 p.m. yesterday, but it was after the jury had been sworn.

Judge Mack states: "I am convinced from the testimony,

that Mr. Flint has expressed an opinion that the defendant is guilty; with that expression of opinion he is disqualified and cannot give the defendant a fair and impartial trial". "He is clearly unfit to sit upon this or any other jury"

The Clerk is asked to remove Mr. Flint's name from the box. The process of selecting the 12th juror would once again commence. The newspaper reported a short time after Mr. Flint left the courthouse a warrant was issued by the Judge and Deputy Pollock made the arrest.

I wonder did Dennis know about Flint's feelings regarding his client and his feeling about capital punishment? However, he said he did not. This situation seems to give the Defense an argument, but why would it help Dennis in his defense of Alfred? Remember, Alfred was guilty in Flint's opinion. He would no doubt have argued during the jury deliberations for something less than first-degree murder. Even so, this would not have freed Alfred. So what or how would this issue impact the trial and how will Dennis conducts himself? You can bet Judge Mack is not going to be happy about his conduct.

So we have a trial in progress following the selection of the jurors. And these jurors have heard two days of testimony from the witnesses for the State. Now the Judges is going to order the Clerk to draw names for other potential jurors to fill the vacancy left by Flint. The Judge is going to restart the trial. This would be especially hard on the Litster's. It means they will have to go back on the stand and testify all over again and Dennis's conduct was not making it any easier.

Dennis says he now wants the entire jury dismissed and they should start fresh. Judge Mack said he sees no good reason to dismiss the other qualified jurors. Dennis argues it is not the same because eleven members will have heard testimony twice and for the new juror it will be just once. Judge Mack doesn't agree and thinks it will not have a bearing on the outcome of the jury's verdict.

Jones moves:

"I feel the Court should proceed by telling the jury that so far as the trial of case is concerned, the matter is placed in status quo, and that your Honor are under law to draw a sufficient number of jurors to fill the vacancy."

Truman asks Judge Mack:

"We will ask your Honor to instruct this jury in regard to the evidence already given; that they will not consider or have anything to do with the evidence heretofore given."

Dennis objects. The Judge now instructs jury not to allow any of the proceedings of this day affect their minds in any way whatever.

The Sheriff is sworn to take charge of the jury and a recess is taken until 10 o'clock Saturday morning, June 1, 1895. You can see there was history behind the modern practice of selecting juror alternates.

Dennis continues his badgering, as he tells the Judge:

"I should be allowed another eight peremptory challenges and I wants to re-examine the jurors already sworn to determine their state of mind after the replacement of Flint."

Judge Mack concludes by saying:

"This is a new question to be determined whether we should impanel another juror and proceed with the case or discharge the eleven jurors." "As far as discharging the eleven jurors are concerned, that has been clearly determined. "The Supreme Court has not decided what course to pursue."

Jones told the Judge that he would bring charges against Flint for his false testimony.

On this Saturday, it is early evening and the Judge declares a recess till 8:15 p.m. After the court is called to order, Judge Mack starts by saying:

"I am not able to say just what position the Supreme Court will take, but it strikes me that the eleven jurors were called and examined and were qualified and passed and they should be allowed to stay, Mr. Dennis your objection will be overruled."

To that Dennis adds:

"I wish to state an exception to your Honor's ruling." Dennis again asks the privilege of a peremptory challenge against the new jury.

Judge Mack responds:

"State your position and I will rule; do not keep me in the dark." The Judge is getting very tired of Dennis and he reminds him that he only has one peremptory challenge remaining and it will not be used to discharge the jury as a whole.

Time was needed to summon the additional prospective jurors, so while the Court has been interrupted by the Flint perjury. The State proceeds to charge Flint with his crime of perjury. Judge Mack will use the first three days of the next week to hear Flint's case before resuming the Vaughan trial. Bail was set at $750 for Mr. Flint. He was costing the County much more and more to come.

As the Vaughan case resumed, names had to been drawn from the box and the new prospective jurors were summoned. It was 10 a.m. Thursday, June 6, 1895 when they started to examine a replacement for A. A. Flint. Another fifteen jurors were called before the new juror was selected. This brings the total number on men examined to 168. Dennis continued to object during this time and he refused to examine any of fifteen jurors.

Personally, I think Judge Mack should have held Dennis in contempt when he refused to examine any of those called to replace Flint.

Finally, the Judge agreed with Jones that Mr. J. Savage was a qualified juror.

Savage was a foreman at the Manhattan Mill. He had come to Austin in 1873 but he had been away the last few years to Alaska before returning.

Jones now asks:

"You Honor please, I submit the juror is a competent juror and we pass him and ask to have him sworn."

Dennis states:

"I desire to interpose the same objection."

Dennis now enters a plea of former jeopardy on behalf of the defendant.

The Judge says:

"Let it be filed and become a part of the record."

"Mr. Christian, you will now swear the Juror, Mr. Savage." "Gentlemen of the jury, the evidence that has been introduced before you heretofore, you will entirely disregard that and not allow it to influence your mind whatever."

"You will be governed solely by the evidence introduced from this time on, in the case." "Are there any other objections, or exceptions at this time?"

Dennis now says:

"I desire to say that I except to the swearing of the juror, Savage." "You may have the benefit of the exception."

Perhaps, I should clarify what the attorney's and judge means when they use the term "except or exception. They are formally objecting to the order or ruling by the court. Under their rules of practice it is my understanding the attorney by claiming an exception to the evidence or ruling they are preserving the appellate rights.

"Mr. Christian, you may read the Indictment."

Monday June 3, 1895, has been a long day and it wasn't until the evening session that Mr. Jones again was asked to make his second opening statement before calling Dr. Huntsman as the State's first witness. Nothing new is found here as the doctor tells his story about going to the Litster Ranch and examining the bodies. Court was adjourned at 9:30 p.m. till Thursday, June 6, 1895.

You might be wondering what happened to Tuesday and Wednesday. Judge Mack had set those days aside to hear the case against our perjured juror, Mr. Flint. I didn't bother to see what Mr. Flint's judgment amounted to.

The State's second witness on Thursday morning was Dennis Scully, and he again describes the maps he made.

Dennis states: "No cross-examination, Your Honor."

William Litster returns to the stand and is sworn as the third witness. He was probably thinking about the fact that I've already done this. Can Jones bring out anything new with his testimony? They've already had a rehearsal and Dennis knows the exact line and timing for his objections and exception to the Courts rulings. William's testimony was again the sad story as Jones asked all these questions again about how he found Johnny and Willie and how Willie was brought back to the house. He described the declaration Willie made while knowing the he was dying and who heard him speak before he died.

Dennis cross-examinations stoops to a lower level by asking

William to admit the he hated Alfred

"Do you or do you not entertain considerable feeling of hatred or malice at this time."

"I do not see how it could be otherwise."

"You do entertain such feeling, don't you at this present time?"

"Yes".

"Did you not, on or about the 21st day of the last month in this building, or in the hallway of the building near the recorder's office, attempt to shoot this defendant with a deadly weapon?"

Jones quickly objects. The Judge tells William that he doesn't have to answer that question.

What had happened at the Courthouse took place when William was walking down the hallway while a deputy was bringing Alfred in the opposite direction. Words were exchanged and William apparently took a swing at Alfred.

William continues his testimony by saying that the Vaughan wagon passed him at the corral about 10 to 15 minutes after his boys rode up the canyon.

Mrs. Alex "Mollie" Eason was the fourth witness. She said she has been a neighbor for 13 years. Nothing has been said, but Alexander Eason, Mollie husband who died in 1891 was Christina Litster's nephew. Christina's maiden name was Eason. Aunt Mollie tells how she came to the ranch that December 28, 1893, and how she helped bring Willie into the house. She also testifies to hearing Willie's declaration.

Dennis declines to cross-examine.

Jimmy Litster was next to be called. He was at the Eason place when the Vaughan wagon came by and he testifies that Nick Rast said there was trouble up at his family's ranch. Dennis tries to show that Willie had hostile feelings resulting from the cow that got in the Vaughan pasture 10 days prior to the shooting.

Jones recalls William Litster the stand. He forgot to establish in evidence the fact the boys were not armed.

"Mr. Litster, did Willie tell you at any time after you found him and before he died, as to whether he or Johnny had any weapons of any kind on the day you found him up there?"

"Yes, sir."

"What did he say?"

"I asked him distinctly if he any and he told me no, he did not; we have no weapons on the ranch."

I find the last part of William's answer very interesting. Only a person that truly did not have firearms would volunteer such a statement. I really can't understand not having weapons for self-defense at the ranch, but that is what he said. The Judge now calls for a noon recess.

Elizabeth Litster will be called as the sixth witness. Again she will tells how she helped bring Willie home and how painful the wagon ride was for Willie as she and Jimmy held him while blood continue to come out of his body. She said that she heard Willie tell Jimmy that Alfred shot him.

Dennis declines to cross-examine.

The seventh witness was Thomas Dunsdon, he confirms what the others have said after he arrived at the house.

"Well, when I went over there, Mr. Litster was crying over the boys of course and he said to me, Tom this is pretty tough." He mentions seeing the bullet that was lodged just under the skin. He said he told Willie the doctor would be able to take it out. He said Willie told him that he knew he was going to die.

Under cross-examination, Mr. Dennis gets Tom to admit he made a misstatement when he said Willie said, Nick told him that we are going through even if your father was here. It was Alfred that said this. Why did Dennis want this clarified?

Jones again realizes he forgot to enter Willie's vest in evidence. So he recalls Elizabeth and asks her about the vest with the bullet hole?

"It is Willie's vest."

Sheriff Easton was then called and he tells about George Watt, Jr. and him arresting Alfred and Charlie. They met them coming to town down by the bridge over the Reese River. The Sheriff said he asked to see Alfred's rifle. It was a Winchester, 44 caliber. It had 13 cartridges when he took the rifle. Jones offers the rifle in evidence. The Sheriff said he allowed Alfred to carry the rifle back to the jail after unloading it. Strange law enforcement procedure, wouldn't you say?

The German fellow, Nick Rast will be the next witness. Because he has become the State's star witness a chapter will be used for his testimony. Two additional chapters will be used for the testimony of Charlie and Alfred so you can compare the conflicting testimony.

8

NICK REST

Was He Afraid Of Alfred?

The State's prosecution team of Jones and Truman called Nicolas Rast for their ninth and star witness. It was Thursday, June 6, 1895. Nick was not a young man like the others. He was now 44 years old. He told the Court that he came to Lander County in 1880 and that he has worked most of his life as a miner. Nick lived at his brother John's home near the Silver Creek School between the Litster and the Watt ranches. Nick said he was born in Loraine when it was under the French flag and that is was now part of Germany. Nick like many older European emigrates had a very strong ascent. German was his native tongue. There was no mention about his education, but you can picture in your mind that he was a strong hard workingman. Perhaps, a little slow in understanding, but he was a gentleman.

With the help of his brother he came to his senses. He had no reason to lie about what happened. Except for the fear factor that Alfred made so clear to him when he pointed that rifle in his direction. It was a real shock to the defense when he stopped himself from being used as a witness for the defendant during the first trial. This was most unfortunate for Alfred Vaughan. Alfred's plea of self-defense no longer hinged on debunking Willie's dying declaration. Without Nick Rast backing Alfred's story, the fundamental question for the jury has been reduced to a matter of who is telling the truth? Recall, the Vaughan's hired Nick the day before the shooting. He had spent the night at their ranch in anticipation of going to the mining claim with the

Vaughan brothers. History shows nothing ever came of that mining claim up in the Water Canyon. Willie was really right when he said, "You got no mine."

The testimony given at the first trial and now repeated here shows that it was his testimony that led to dropping the charge of murder for Nick Rast. The Sheriff had Alfred, Charlie and Nick under arrest by the evening of December 28, 1893. They were sharing the same outer cell room. Police procedure today would not allow this for obvious reasons, but that was not the case then. Nick was in a very awkward position. He knew what Alfred and Charlie were going to say about the Litster brothers attacking Alfred and that Alfred was just defending himself. Nick stayed during the day light hours in this outer cell with the Vaughan brothers until that day during the first trial when he said he must now tell the truth. Jones had him moved to another room at the courthouse where there could be no contact with the Vaughan brothers.

The testimony shows that Nick never felt right about what happened when the Litster brothers were killed. Dennis tried hard to show that Nick must have made a deal with the District Attorney to save himself. Nick was not that clever. His brother, John Rast finally learned what Nick's problem was by him being in the same cell room with the others. It was difficult to find privacy and when John did he told Nick you can get out of this jail only if you tell the truth. John went to see Weller; the Justice of the Peace at Austin and Weller said he would make the arrangements.

Again, I am sure the transcript from the first trial would have been most interesting when Nick dropped the bombshell. Jones will make it very clear that he did not promise Nick anything to get him to change his testimony from that given at the Coroner's Inquest and the Preliminary Examination. Jones knew Nick's early stories were not truthful or there would have been more agreement with the Vaughan's.

They were all lying and that is what Jones told Nick:

"You have not told the truth have you?"

Justice Weller asked Jones, Truman, Sheriff Easton and Mr. Chartz the former County Clerk to hear privately Nick's statement about what really happened. Nick was not moved to a separate place at the courthouse until he found the courage to correct his early statements. Later the charges were dropped against him as well as against Charlie Vaughan. They were then set free.

The direct examination for Nick began with Jones asking questions. Please bear with Nick's testimony. It is real and as accurate as the court reporter could copy by following his oral testimony. You will only be able to get the word description at times when the witness is referring to map exhibits. Nick often pointed to them while explaining what took place. It is difficult to understand him. I've added comments to his testimony by using italics.

Jones now states:

"Then the difficulty took place between these two boys on December 28, 1893?"

"Yes Sir."

"Where?"

"At Boone Canyon, about three quarters of a mile above the Litster's house."

"Tell the jury, Mr. Rast, all you know about the matter from the time you started from the Vaughan's house, if you did start from the Vaughan's house all the way there, just explain now so you can be heard."

"Now Gentlemen of the jury, I tell you on the 28th day of December 1893, we left the Vaughan Ranch."

"I was hired to go to work for them in the mine and I went there the evening before, the 27th, and we prepared everything and on the 28th we got the wagon loaded and started between eight and nine o'clock, the time I don't know because I had no time."

"Then we came to about three quarters or a mile above the Vaughan Ranch and met the Litster boy, the third Litster, I believe his name is Jimmy, and I says, 'good morning Jimmy' and he says good morning Nick', but the Vaughan boys never spoke to him."

Jimmy was going to down to the Switch for mail that morning and this testimony shows that Nick did recognize

Jimmy.

"So we went on down to Mrs. Alex Eason's and Charlie got off the wagon and he takes the rifle and he shoots at a cottontail rabbit three times and missed him."

"So we went on up by Mrs. Alex Eason's through the Litster gate into Litster's ranch."

"I opened that gate and shutting it and when we was come distance of two or three hundred yards above the Litster gate the road makes a turn and strikes a straight line; and when we made this turn the Vaughan boys say,

"There is Litster feeding his cattle and I said he has to feed them already." "The cows were eating the hay."

"We saw two riders go away from the lower hay corral." "When I saw them they might have been fifteen yards above the corral on the road going to Litster's house, and then these riders went on and the Vaughan's say:

"It is some of the Litster boys at the corral."

"So then I say, that cannot be, the Litster's, I say, Mr. Litster and his wife went to visit Mrs. Christian in Cortez."

This does not sound right; didn't Nick just say he had said good morning to Jimmy?

"Then they said, then it must be the Watt's."

"So we went on down to the corral and there was two horses hitched to a sled they were standing each side of the tongue of the shed and two little Litster boys stood in front of these horses."

"Describe those boys?"

"They were just that high *(showing)* little bits of fellows." "I believe one is named Lou and the other I don't know, I have forgotten."

The other boy's name is George.

"There are two corrals there, the upper and the lower; the lower one is where he keeps his hay and the other he keeps his cattle; he was in the lower corral, and he had a pole in his hand tamping posts when we went by, so we went on up until we came to the road what turns this side of the Litster house so you can go by the Litster house."

"So we took this road what goes around the Litster house

and when we came about the middle of that road, Charlie Vaughan got off the wagon."

"Charlie had a rifle in his hand and we took the road that goes up Boone Canyon." "Alfe drove the wagon to there and; then Alfe says to Charlie, I got cold you had better drive this wagon."

"So Charlie got off and Alfred gets on." "Charlie had the rifle and Alfe had the pistol and now they change so Charlie has the pistol and Alfe has the rifle."

"We went on up the road and they said, there are the Litster boys."

"Who said that?"

"Vaughan boys."

"So we drove up and to the Gap and there was the Litster boys, and Vaughan boy say, you son of a bitch open this Gap." "And the Litster boys repeated, we are not more sons of bitches than you are."

"Then Alfe goes on one side of the wagon and I take the other." "He ran with the rifle in his hand and the Litster boys had each a willow in their hands. "They were small about the size of a candle, two and a half may be three feet long." " I didn't measure, but that is my judgment."

"We had some pick handles so I got one out of the wagon just in case these boys got in a ruckus."

Was Nick planning to use a pick handle to break up any fight that might start?

"Where was Charlie then?"

"He was sitting on the wagon."

"Now you can describe this thing better?" "Now take this opening in the railing here and show us where the wagon was?"

"Now you see this place, this is the wagon, and Alfe went in on this side and I on this side." (Showing with the map).

"Alfe stood here and the Litster boys stood here, I stood between."

Jones knows that Nick's positioning of the boys conflicts with what Alfred and Charlie will say.

"I said to the Litster boys; you better let us go through this time, then we will never bother you anymore."

"I talked to the Litster boys nicely and told Johnny this make no sense."

"Johnny Litster says, alright, Nick but this is the last time we are going to let you go through."

"The willow stick was still in his hand and he throwed it down in front of him."

"Willie was keeping his stick in his hand and Willie moved his position toward the house." "This is his position (showing) and I stood there."

This would be on the right side of the road looking up Water Canyon. Nick is on the left side of road by the lead horses about 8 feet from the fence talking to Johnny and Alfe is on the right side arguing with Willie.

"And Alfred Vaughan stood in front of Willie and I still stood there talking to Johnny Litster and then I went to Willie to see if I could open the gate,"

"Willie told me the wire was spliced in the middle, then I went to open the wire." Johnny was standing on the upper side and along side of me."

"I throwed down one half of the wire towards the Litster house and Johnny throwed the other end."

"I went around to the other side of the gate where he told me the lower wire was spliced."

Nick had stepped over the lower wire and was looking for the splice.

"You went over where?"

"On this side of the gate where he said there was a short splice at the other end,

Jones asks: "That is the upper end?"

"Yes."

Meaning the left side of the road.

"While Johnny and I were talking and I took my tobacco out of my pocket and filled my pipe."

"Johnny was saying, Nick we wouldn't mind the Vaughan's going through our ranch if only they would shut the gates."

"We have stock in our fields, and we can't watch them everyday, when they leave the gates open."

"I said, Johnny, I always shut them when we go through."

"And he says, Nick I know that."

"I then asked him if he was go to school when school opened and he asked me if Hubert was going back too, that is my brother's boy."

"I started to open the wire and I had stoop down when the first shot was fired."

Jones asks: "Where was Johnny?"

"He stood along side of me and was close enough to hold his hand." "Johnny was facing this way, and I was facing this way and Willie stood here and Alfe stood here." (showing)

I stooped down and the shot was fired, and it scare me." "I ran about fifteen feet up Water Canyon road."

"Johnny stood this way and he ran by the wagon." "I will say about here from the horses." (showing)

"Alfe moved from here and pointed the gun at Johnny Litster."

"I hollered at him not to shoot and ran at him and I came so close to him as I stand to this gentleman."

"Bang, the gun went off again as Johnny turned around and he dropped dead."

"He was begging for his life and when I ran he waved his hands over his head."

"Charlie did beg Alfe not to shoot but he did shoot him all the same."

Jones asks: "Show the jury how he did that?"

"Johnny was standing side ways flapping his hands." "I don't exactly know, but that is what he looks to me." (showing) "He had his hands that way and waving his hands, and when he was shot he made a kind of a turn, and fall down".

Obviously there was more than what Nick has said, yet we can picture what he was trying to describe, as the acts of murder was committed. Alfred and Willie were on the right side of the road when Alfred suddenly shot from the hip a bullet into Willie's gut. What was said that caused Alfred to shoot the rifle? Did Alfred realize the impact of what the Litster's were saying? This is the last time they could use the Gap going to the Water Canyon. Did Alfred feel the Litster's had just taken their mining claim away by denying the use of this access road?

As Nick described Alfred walked across in front of the lead horses to the left side of the road after shooting Willie. Johnny who had been at the gate helping Nick undo the spliced wires then backed towards the rear of the wagon towards the wood bridge. Nick said he ran a short way up the road looking for cover after the first shot was fired. Charlie must have had his hands full holding the horses following the first shot. Next Alfred had the rifle shouldered and he was pointing it at Johnny. Johnny was waving his hands and pleading with Alfred not to shoot. As Johnny turned and starts to run, Alfred fires the second fatal shot.

Jones asks: "Where was Willie?"

"He was down, he dropped about eight feet from the post where I was standing; and still kept on rolling over."

"He rolled over; was he down on the ground?"

"Yes, he was on the ground."

"Did Willie still keep the willow in his hand when he dropped?"

"No, as he was standing there, he told me there was a short splice and he had the willow in his hand and he then throwed it over his shoulder on the other side of the fence."

"Describe to the jury what took place after that?"

"Then Gentlemen of the jury, when I did come to him." "I first went to Alfe Vaughan as quick as I could." "I say, Alfe for Christ's sake what did you shot these two boys for?"

"He says, the sons of bitches did said we have no mine."

"I never heard them say those words." "I never did hear that."

Nick may have not heard Willie say this, but Alfred did. Alfred just told Nick what pushed him over the edge and this caused Alfred to commit murder.

Jones asks: "What do you mean; you never did hear the Litster boys say they didn't have a mine?"

"No, I never did."

"But you did hear the Vaughan boy say so?"

"He said, the sons of bitches did say we have no mine."

"I said, Alfe, I am sorry you have done that." "And he says, the sons of bitches they ought to have that a long time ago and what do they amount to?" "He says, I am going to town and he told Charlie to turn the wagon around." "He said I will go to town and give myself up."

Has Alfe already made his plan to claim self-defense?

"Willie Litster was calling me and I went to him and I say, Willie ain't you bad hurt?"

"He put his hand on my breast and says, Nick, Oh, by God, go and get my father."

This is a sad scene; think of the pain Willie is now experiencing. It is a little after 10 o'clock and it will be another six hours before he bleeds internally to death.

"And I said, I will go and see Johnny first."

"And the wagon had started and I went around the wagon to see Johnny; and he was lying with his feet away from the road about six inches on his back."

"I hollered out to him, Oh Johnny, and all I could hear he had his mouth wide open, and all he did say was u-g-h."

"I saw I could do nothing for him and Willie was still calling me and I went back over to Willie, and again he asked me to go and get his father."

"I said Willie, are you bad hurt? And he again put his hand on his breast and he says, oh, by God, Nick, go and get my father." "I started on a beeline for the Litster Ranch."

"But Alfred Vaughan stood there with his rifle in his hand, and he said, Nick where are you going?"

"And I said Alfe, I go to give the alarm of what happened." "He had a gun and he said, you had better come and get on the wagon."

"I was afraid to go any further, and I got on the wagon."

"We started down the canyon, and when we came to the road going around the Litster house, I asked Alfe have he had any more cartridges?" "And he says, lots of them."

"He says, ain't you afraid?"

"I say, yes and he says, well you must be afraid I will kill anyone what comes to bothers us." "I felt I had better stay on the wagon."

"When we come to the Eason house I say, boys we better give the alarm." "And Alfred said, Nick you stay on the wagon, and I will give the alarm, and I said, no, I will give the alarm."

I said to Mrs. Eason there was a hellish row up there."

"She says is anyone bad hurt?"

"And I say, only too bad, and she cried, and I got back in the wagon and we went on to the Vaughan ranch." "While going down the road I said, Charlie, I feel awful sorry, by God this thing has happened."

"And he said, I don't feel sorry, by God."

Nick must have felt safe when they were in view of Mrs. Eason or he would not have gotten off the wagon when he was told to stay put.

Dennis: responses to his last statement:

"I move to strike that out on the grounds that it is hearsay."

Judge Mack asks: "Are these people present?"

"Yes Sir."

"Strike out the portion relative to what Charlie said that Mrs. Eason said."

Jones asks Charlie to continue:

"So we went on down to the Vaughan ranch and Mrs. Vaughan was stand along side of the milk house when we came and she says, what is the matter, why have you come back?" "The boys jumped off the wagon and Charlie still had the pistol and Alfe had the rifle." "They both went into the house."

"Mr. Tipsword and I unhitched the horses." "I could see that Mr. and Mrs. Vaughan were well pleased."

This is a strange comment by Charlie. How could he see that Mr. and Mrs. Vaughan were pleased or what did he mean by this statement?

Jones now asks Nick some questions about the axe that he had when he was off the wagon at the Gap. Jones knew Alfred was going claim Willie came at him with an axe after he said that he had shot Johnny. Nick confirms the axe had been placed on the oppose side of the road from Willie and about twenty-seven feet from him. Jones asks Nick to explain more about the conversation that took place at the gate.

"I tell you they were calling each other for several minutes each about being sons of bitches."

"I walked between them, and I settled it and the Litster boys said to alright and took my advice."

Jones asks: "And they gave you permission to go through, and Johnny was helping you to go through and Willie was standing there saying nothing when the shot went off?"

"Yes, Sir."

"How long had it been before the first shot went off, since Willie had said anything?"

"You can measure it by what you think in minutes or whatever you can fix it."

"Seventeen or eighteen minutes."

Nick doesn't understand the question.

Jones asks: "That Willie had not said anything?"

"Yes, It might be twenty, it might be twenty-five."

Nick still doesn't understand the question."

How long before Johnny was shot had it been since he, Johnny had said anything to Alfred?"

"About the same time."

"Or to Charlie?"

"About the same time, about fifteen or twenty minutes."

Jones asks: "Then all the conversation that took place there, after you pacified the boys and got consent to go through was what Johnny had to say to you?"

"Yes, and I to him."

If Nick is being truthful, then we must believe that after the initial outburst, Willie and Alfe just stood there facing each other while Charlie sat on the wagon holding the reins. Or that Nick was not paying attention to Willie and Alfred as he talked to Johnny. Also, it appears that Nick does not have a good sense of time. I think Nick was thinking about the lapse of time from their arrival.

Jones asks: "Did you see the first shot fired?"

"No."

Jones continued by asking Nick questions about hearing the shots and the position of the boys and a couple of other minor questions and he closed his direct examinations by asking if they had seen Mr. Litster while traveling back down the road by the Litster's house.

Nick answered: "No."

Dennis begins his Cross Examination by asking questions about what Nick had testified to during the Coroner's Inquest and the Preliminary Examination. He asked him many questions that required Nick to say what part was true and what part was false. Recall Nick had lied during those early statements. Dennis questions did allow Nick to add some additional conversation that he had with Alfred. I don't think Dennis was helping his client with these questions and I'm sure Mr. Jones was more than happy to have Nick provide the additional testimony.

Dennis asks: "When did you first give a true statement of the shooting?"

"Well, I tell you Mr. Dennis, I gave a true statement when the other time of court."

"The other trial of this case?"

"Yes, in this court." "I will tell you Mr. Dennis what I done as I was afraid for my life for the things that had been done to me and what they did say to me." "I was afraid of them when I saw what they did." "I saw those two innocent boys shot like a hunter would go out and kill wild beasts for nothing." "That made me afraid to say anything I was put in jail." "I was afraid of them". "They made threats that I could be looking for my coffin." "They said they would put me into it."

Dennis asks: "Then you testified falsely at the Coroner's Inquest?"

"Yes, for that cause."

Dennis goes through a series of questions in an attempt to show that Nick should not have been afraid. This was a mistake on Dennis part. Remember he was in the same cell with the Vaughan's.

Dennis asks: "Is it not a fact Nick, that you had plenty of opportunities and that there were a number of times when you could have asked the Sheriff to separate you, and take you away from the place where the Vaughan boys were, and tell him that you wanted to tell the truth about the matter and that you were afraid of the Vaughan boys?"

"Mr. Dennis, my brother comes to jail and he says, you see the judge." "And he came and asks me and he says, Nick how is this?" "And I said, brother, you never see anything on paper, you never did hear of a crime like this happened." "He says he goes to the judge, and he goes, so he went to see the judge, and that was three or four days before I come in this chair, then I thought I stayed so long there, then I think to myself, then I could stand this two or three days longer; then I come here in this chair." "Mr. Jones asks to get all fellows separated."

Nick is referring to his testimony at the first trial.

Dennis asks about Nick's testimony at the Preliminary Examination. Again he makes Nick tell what part of his testimony was true and what part was false. Nick is going to provide answers with some very emotional comments.

Dennis said let me read it again as you said (reading):

"Then I and Alfe went into the wagon and then when we went so far as the road turns off going to Water Canyon, one of the Vaughan boys said, there they are waiting for us."

"It was false when you swore to it, and it is false now?"

"Yes."

"You knew it was false?"

"I tell you the reason; I was afraid, I was afraid for my life when I saw them boys killed like coyotes, so it made me still worse by all these records as told in the jail." "Even Mrs. Vaughan comes in the jail and says you boys got to tell lies if to get out of this trouble, and they say, mother we will tell lies, and will stack Bibles to the top of the church to get out of it."

Dennis states: "And your fear, Nick, made you swear to falsehoods like that?"

I cannot believe Dennis would want the jury to hear these comments from Nick?

Dennis continued asking true false questions about Nick prior testimony.

Dennis again reads: "And when the Litster boys said Nick, we have nothing against you, and I said boys I have nothing against you neither."

Dennis asks: "Did you swear to that Nick?"

"I did."

"Was it true or false?"

"Partly true and partly false."

"What part is true and what part is false?"

"I said when their father would be here he would let us go through."

"It was false then and false now?"

"Yes, because I was afraid for my life, when they said you have got to look for your coffin and so on and was talking in jail nothing else as killing and so on, that was still keeping me afraid." "Even Charlie was saying when he was in jail how killing would happen if he was carrying the gun and Alfe says, you know very well I have that gun and Mr. Dennis that would look to me most like that any man would be afraid of such people." "I had reason Mr. Dennis to be afraid, and I think if you saw what I see, you would be afraid yourself."

Dennis continued asking questions and Nick continued to answer by expressing his fear of the Vaughan's.

Dennis reads: "While I rose up I heard a voice saying, take that- and then in the same time the shooting commenced, to be." "And I made a jump and made between ten and twelve feet, might be more or less and then the shooting was done and all the damage." "Did you swear to that Nick?"

"I did."

"Was it true or false?"

"It was partly true."

"Describe what part is true and what part is false."

"When I run and turned back one half the damage was done then, he was laying there, Johnny was waving his hands over his head and begging for his life."

"Then it is true or false?"

"False."

"It was false then and it is false now?"

"Yes." "All except half of the shooting was done when you turned around?" "What I done Mr. Dennis when they came and threaten me with tough talk and what they would do." "Frank would come and say, why did you not finish Willie so you would have no witness." "Charlie says to his brother Frank, he was vomiting blood and grub and he can never be a witness."

Dennis asks: "Now explain to the jury why you were not afraid of the Vaughan's when you swore to what you claimed to be the truth, can you?"

"I tell you Mr. Dennis, I never could go any further, I could not live with it in there, I never could live, I had to say it." "I remember the fifth commandment; it says to keep care of your own self and health, just so you injure no other man."

Recall Nick referred to this commandment in the first trial and Jones gave the source to the Christian Doctrine. I must add that the commandments are not numbered in the Bible. There is a difference between the tradition of the Protestants and the Catholics separation of the 5th commandment. "You shall not murder." And for the Protestants it is: "Honor thy father and thy mother, so that you may live long in the land the Lord your God is giving you." Nick was Catholic.

"And I told my brother when he came to the jail and I was crying like a child." "I told John (his brother), you would never hear anything like that, no man ever lives that heard such crime; then he burst out crying and he left the jail and went home." "He came in afterwards and a day or so he says Nick, I went to see the judge and want you to see him." "He told the judge what I said."

It was a few days after Nick's brother visited him that it was arranged for Nick to make a statement to the District Attorney.

Dennis asks: "Then you were turned out of jail were you not that evening before you testified?"

"No, I testified before Mr. Jones, Mr. Truman and Mr. Chartz."

"But before you went on this stand here you were turned loose out of jail."

"I was that is true."

"Up to the time you made the statement to Mr. Jones, you were in jail were you not?"

"That is right."

You can see where Dennis is going now. He has just added that Nick not only has lied in the past, but he will say any thing to get himself out of jail. At least that is what Dennis would like the jury to believe.

"But when you made the statement to Mr. Jones, you were turned out of jail before you came to testify on the stand?"

Dennis is referring to the first trial.

"I was turned out some time the next day or so after."

"Were you not turned out before you came here to testify on the stand?"

"I was come I believe two or three times."

"I mean the last time; the first time you came before the jury after you made the statement to Mr. Jones."

"Not the first time."

"Not the first time after you made this statement to Mr. Jones?"

It looks like we are having a communication problem. Nick does not appear to understand Dennis's questions.

"I say Mr. Easton did come and took me down there and he said to come to the courthouse and I took this chair and he was turned me loose."

Now Judge Mack is confused.

Judge Mack asks: "You mean to say in response to Mr. Dennis, that if your conscience brother you and you couldn't stand it any longer?" "You had to tell the truth?"

"I do."

"What do you mean when you say you couldn't live any longer?"

Bad question, Dennis.

"I remember now it was soon after the Court was called and Frank Vaughan was coming into the jail and he saying why we not kill Willie entirely, then we would had no witness, I hardly could speak and everything did boil inside me."

"Then they said, what is the matter with Nick?" "They said we will have Mr. Easton chain him up, he is crazy." "That is enough to make any man crazy, Mr. Dennis, I wasn't crazy, I was by God, sensible." "I wasn't crazy, only I was afraid."

"But when you were turned out of jail, you were not afraid?" "Yes, Mr. Dennis one man on the outside has so much show as another." "On the outside I am not afraid; but lots of people tell me, friend of mine, to keep my eyes open, so I tell them I would."

Nick has got more than one person confused by now and it'll be up to Jones to straighten things out. You need to remember this is real testimony and it is hard reading and hard to understand at times. You really must fault the Sheriff or the District Attorney for not seeing that these men were kept in separate cells and were not allowed to be together in that outer cell room where they had their meals and made quirts.

The following is the re-direct examination by Jones:

"Then during all the time, Mr. Rast covered by your testifying at the Coroner's Inquest, the Preliminary Examination and the Grand Jury, you were in jail charged with the murder of Willie Litster and Johnny Litster, were you not?"

"I don't know what I was charged, but I was innocent."

"You were in jail all that time?"

"Yes Sir."

"Inside of the iron doors, were you not with Alfred and Charlie Vaughan?"

"Yes Sir."

"During all that time from the first time you were put in jail until you were taken from the jail you were with Alfred Vaughan, the defendant here, and his brother Charlie?"

"Yes Sir."

Jones continued: "And did any other members of the Vaughan family come in, at any time and talk to you if they wanted to?"

"Yes Sir."

"They came frequently did they not?"

"Did they come a good many times?"

"Mr. and Mrs. Vaughan were stopping when they did come into town, they come in; sometimes the Deputy Sheriff was with them, sometimes not."

Jones asks: "Did ever I, at any time during your life, offer you any consideration of any kind to testify to the truth in this case?"

Dennis states: "I object to the question upon the ground that it is not re-direct examination; that such a thing has not been intimated."

Judge Mack responds: "Yes, it has been intimated." "The natural inference was from the question you put to Rast that he was turned loose just prior to the time he gave his testimony; that naturally led him to believe that your position was that was consideration for which he gave his testimony."

Dennis states: "I disclaim any such intention, and I now here admit that I had no such intention or ever thought of it." "I only aimed to show the fact that he was discharged."

Judge Mack answers: "I think it is a proper question, and will allow it."

Jones asks: "Did I ever at any time offer you any kind of inducement to tell me the truth in this case?"

"Well Mr. Jones, you told me, you wanted nothing else but the truth."

"That is not what I asked you, did I ever offer you anything to tell the truth in this case?"

"No Sir."

Jones continues to drive home the point that no consideration was ever offered to Nick prior to his voluntary statement during the first trial. He claimed he was afraid to tell truth while he was in the same jail cell with the Vaughan brothers. It appears the Jones has out witted Dennis. Dennis pushed his cross-examination to far because it afforded to many opportunities for Nick to make statements very damning to the defendant and his family. It appears Dennis just wanted to plant a seed of doubt in the juries mind, but he over did it.

Jones asks: "Did I ever promise you anything to tell the truth?"

"No, Sir."

"Did I ever intimate that the defendant Alfred Vaughan told the truth?"

"No, Sir."

"Did I ever claim that what you told me was the truth?"

"No, Sir."

"Did I ever intimate to you that you would be turned loose?"

"No, Sir."

"Did I the night you told the truth?"

"No, Sir."

"Didn't I three or four times, from the time Johnny and Willie were killed until you came upon this stand and told the truth, say to you Nick, you have not told me the truth so far?" "Did I not say that to you?"

"Yes, Sir."

"Now Mr. Rast, hadn't you been put on the stand to testify in the former trial of this case a year ago last April by Mr. Dennis and Mr. MacMillan before you made this statement to Mr. Truman and myself that night in Mr. Truman's office?" "Had you not been brought up from the jail?"

"Yes, Sir."

"Had I ever gone to the jail to see you?

No, Sir."

You have to go back to the first trial to understand what Jones is saying. Nick was called as a witness just before the noon recess and he answered a few questions. After the recess he was back on the stand and as MacMillan starts to ask a question, Nick asked the Judge if he could talk without any questions being asked. The Judge allowed this. This was the unexpected bombshell dropped on the defense during the first trial.

Jones asks: "Is it not a fact, Mr. Rast, that wherein all your statements you say you made false statements, that it was done to conceal the truth in favor of Alfred Vaughan because of your fear of them?"

"Only Fear."

"You concealed these facts in favor because you were afraid of them?"

"Yes, that is right."

"Did I know anything about your going to change your testimony when you were on the stand a year ago April?"

"No, nobody knew but myself, Mr. Jones."

"You didn't tell me or anyone who would tell me?"

"No one knew but myself"

"You made it known for the first time on the witness stand in this Court, when this case was tried before?"

"Yes, Sir."

Dennis tied to undermine the honesty on Nick Rast because of the many falsehood he did admit by his prior testimony to the Coroner' Inquest and the Preliminary Examination. Dennis was saying if he lied then for a reason, he could be lying again for another reason. However he erred because he gave Nick many opportunities to say things very negative regarding to the overall character of the Vaughan family and their effort to save Alfred. He should have asked Jones the details about Rast's statement, instead of intimating a favor for his testimony.

The Court now instructs the jury and a recess was taken until Friday, June 7, 1895 at ten o'clock.

After the Court is called to order Friday morning Jones commences by telling the Judge that a search has been made but they have been unable to find the two large, buckhorn pocketknives that were taken from Alfred and Charlie. These knives were used as exhibits in the former trial. Apparently, all the trial documents and exhibits were sent to Carson City and somehow these have come up missing. Jones wants the Court to allow him more time to introduce these items.

Dennis asks: "What is the object of their introduction?"

Jones replies, "We propose to corroborate the testimony of Mr. Rast wherein he was afraid of those men when he was confined with them, because of the fact that he knew they had dangerous weapons upon their person."

I can't believe what I'm hearing. Do you understand these guys had knives while they were in jail? You got that right, they did. Why? Remember, they were allowed to make quirts to pass the time in jail and the Sheriff allowed them to keep their knives to do this work. That would not be done today.

Dennis states: "Your Honor please, I submit that if the knives be admitted at all in evidence, it would be a matter of rebuttal, in as much as I understand the rule to be, that unless the witness's testimony is attacked or an attempt made to impeach it, there is no necessity for such evidence; then your Honor, that would be a matter of rebuttal; then it could be introduced."

Judge Mack states: "I see no reason for delaying the matter." "Let it come out of order, do you have an objection to that?"

Dennis answers: "I submit I will not object to its being introduced as rebuttal testimony."

Judge Mack asks: "That is you mean you will not object to its being introduced out of order?"

Truman states: "We won't offer it as rebuttal testimony, we

will offer it as corroborative testimony. Dennis knew this was what the DA had planned and he now says he may object. The judge told them that they can offer them later and he will rule then, but not now.

Jones recalls the Sheriff Easton for his last direct witness.

"Did you obtained a pistol from Charlie when he was arrested."

Dennis objects and the Judge overrules.

Jones asks if that pistol was submitted in evidence for the first trial and the Sheriff says it was. He stated that he returned it to Charlie after the trial.

"Have you made an effort to obtain it?"

Dennis object and says that it hearsay and said that Charlie was present and can be called.

Judge Mack asks: "What steps have you taken to obtain the pistol?"

The Sheriff said Charlie told him that he traded it to a man going to Mexico.

Jones said he would like to offer the Sheriff's pistol as evidence because it is identical to the one Charlie had.

Dennis's objection is overruled, and he claims an exception.

The Sheriff answered a few more questions about obtaining the pistol.

Jones then stated:

"Your Honor please, the State Rests."

9

ALFRED

Why Did He Hate Willie?

It was just before the Friday noon recess when Jones said "Your Honor please, the State Rests." How is Dennis going to proceed with this case? He seems to have been working hard to have a mistrial declared. Judge Mack asks Dennis if he want to make his opening statement? Dennis says the he will reserve his opening statement, but right now he wants to introduce the testimony by the former juror, A. A. Flint. He asks to have the Clerk read it. Truman objects and Judge Mack overrules. Jones also objects to anyone other than Dennis reading the testimony to the jury. This objection was sustained and Dennis proceeds to read Flint's testimony. Why does Dennis want this as evidence to be part of the trial?

Truman states: "We object on the ground that it neither proves nor tends to prove former jeopardy." Jones adds to the objection.

Judge Mack answers: "It is simply this; the evidence is to go to the jury, I shall instruct them as to the law; I shall instruct against the plea."

Jones tries to get the Judge to rule on his objection now. Dennis also wants the Judge to provide the instruction now for jury about Flint. Judge Mack asks Dennis to provide him with the law that allows such a procedure?

Judge Mack states: "I will say I have no authority, no stature, permitting me to do to that, and that being the case I shall have to follow the regular course, that is when you have submitted your case and rested, I shall give such instructions as you may present and which I deem proper."

Dennis continues his argument and Jones asks that the record to show exactly what Dennis has requested.

Judge Mack now informs Dennis: "You have just waived your opening statement." "The statute says that Counsel shall make his statement and then introduce testimony." "Proceed with your case."

Dennis was about to come unglued as he begs the Court's indulgence. It would appear that the Judge was teasing, well perhaps. He does relent and Dennis is allowed to make his opening statement, to which Jones asks for an exception. After Dennis' statement the Judge called recess for lunch till 2 p.m.

Dennis had planned to have Justice of the Peace, L. A. Weller come to the stand first. He presided over the Preliminary Examination. Dennis opened the afternoon session by saying that he had excused Mr. Weller and would call his first witness, Alfred Vaughan.

Today, it would be very rare for the defendant to be called first if at all. However, the defense doesn't really have many people to testify.

Dennis asks the usual introductory questions. He asked: "Alfred how old are you?"

"Twenty-two years, ten months, and 28 days."

That answer tells a lot about Alfred, he is very bored.

Dennis asks Alfred to tell what they did that morning on December 28, 1893. "After your wagon was loaded up what did you do?"

"Father and Harry hitched up the team and after we had hitched up I got on the seat." "Charlie and Nick Rast went back to the house and after they came back Charlie had a rifle, and that was the first I knew the rifle was going up or that it would be taken along."

Strange the way Alfred mentions the rifle.

"After that what did you do?"

"We drove up the canyon toward Water Canyon and the mine." Alfred tells about Charlie shooting at the rabbit, but he doesn't say anything about seeing Jimmy.

Dennis asked: "What was the first thing pertinent to this

case that you observed after you got into the Litster field?"

"We drove in 200 yards when we saw Litster and the four boys; then we saw Johnny and Willie Litster get on their horses and ride up the canyon ahead of us."

I really doubt Alfred could tell from that a distance of more than a half mile. Perhaps they were closer. But as I recall, Mr. Litster said the boys were gone about 10 or 15 minutes before the wagon came to the corral. Conclusion: He did not know who they were and they could have been the Watt boys as Nick said earlier.

"You saw Mr. Litster and the four boys first?"

"Yes."

"Name the boys?"

"I don't know the little ones names; they were Johnny and Willie Litster and the two smaller boys."

Alfred tells Dennis that the boys rode up the main road and Dennis asks Alfred to describe the roads.

"Did you continue to drive up the canyon?"

"Yes, I drove on up the canyon; as we came to the side road Charlie and Nick Rast got off and went on foot, and Charlie was packing the rifle and him and Nick Rast were on foot on above the house until we came into the main road and we saw two horse tracks and they continued on ahead of us on the main road and we went up the back road."

Dennis asks: "Then you saw two horse tracks, when you came into the main road?"

"Yes, Sir."

I understand the side road that Alfred refers to as the road that connects to the main road in Boone Canyon. This side road seems to passes between the barn and the Litster house. It could be the road you would take if you were going to Silver Creek or Austin. Alfred says Charlie and Nick got off the wagon and went on foot. He doesn't say, but they should have had to open a gate here. Without the exhibits used for the trial it is impossible to understand Alfred's description. I think Mr. Dennis's question was misleading, because the Vaughan wagon was on the main road. It was Johnny and Willie that came to the main road at this point and this is where Alfred saw the horse tracks.

Dennis asks: "Did you continue to drive on up the canyon?"

"I drove on up the canyon, about 100 yards above that and then I told Charlie to get up and take the team that my hands were cold." "He gave me the gun and he got on and I got off and walked along behind the wagon with Nick."

"Did you get upon the wagon again?"

"No, Sir." "I walked from there to the Gap."

"Did you exchange anything else with your brother Charlie when you got off the wagon?"

"No, Sir."

"I never had anything else." "We had no other gun only the rifle."

Dennis asks: "When you got to the Gap that you have described, you can describe whether you left the main road or not, that is before you arrived at the Gap?"

"After we got this side of the Gap a ways, we took the right hand road going up Water Canyon."

"Describe Water Canyon as it appears to your mind with reference to the vicinity of Boone Canyon?" "Start where it branches off, I don't care about your going further up the canyon."

"Boone Canyon runs up the main canyon."

"The Water Canyon goes up on the right hand side."

"This canyon branches off the right hand side of Boone Canyon?"

"Yes."

"Now how far is it approximately, where you left the main road to the Gap, that you have mentioned?"

"You mean the main road that runs up Boone Canyon to the other road to Water Canyon?"

"From where the main road branches off to the Gap?"

"I can't exactly say."

"Just approximately, as near as you can?"

"May be 150 to 200 yards."

Alfred estimation of the distance is grossly wrong. He had it right in the first trial when he answered 65 to 70 feet.

"Where were you going that morning?"

Jones states: "We object to the question as being irrelevant, immaterial and incompetent to the issue of this case."

Judge Mack replies: "I can't see that it makes any difference, you may ask the question." "Objection overruled."

Jones responds: "Plaintiff excepts."

Alfred's answers: "I was going to work on the mine."

"Describe the road from where it branches off the main road up to the Gap that you mentioned, as near as you can?"

"You mean the road that we went up, before branching off?"

"I want you to describe the road between the Gap and the main road." "Alfe did you state this morning that it was something like 150 to 200 yards from where you left the main road to the Gap?"

"Yes."

"Now describe the kind of road it is, what you crossed, all the surroundings for that distance."

"As you pulled off this side to go into the canyon we crossed a bridge; as Charlie crossed the bridge he stopped the team, and I was walking behind the wagon."

"What occurred after you crossed the bridge and stopped the team?"

"The boys were at the Gap and Charlie asked them if they would please open the gate and let us go through." "The boys used bad language and said, you can't go through there alive."

From what Alfred just said you would have concluded that the Litster boys were going to kill them if they tried to go through the Gap.

Dennis asks: "What next transpired?"

"Nick Rast went to open the fence and found the fence fastened and he went back to the wagon to get the axe and found he didn't need it and thrown the axe down on the ground and opened the fence with his hands."

Alfred doesn't mention the conversation Nick had with Johnny and that Johnny had consented to open the gate.

Dennis asks: "What was said and done in the mean time by you and the Litster boys?"

"All the time I was standing there at the head of the lead horses they were calling me vulgar names, cowardly sons of bitches, bastardly son of bitches." "While Nick was opening the fence Johnny jerked a gun from his coat and said, take that you son of a bitch."

I guess he means Johnny said those words as he shot point blank at him and of course Johnny's shots all missed.

Dennis asks: "Show the jury how he stood and where you stood?"

"He stood over that way and I stood over here." "I was standing up at the head of the lead horses, of course the horses were over off that way and he was standing over this way." "I was standing here and had the rifle in my hand all the time." "The rifle was pointed down toward the ground and while Nick was opening the fence, he was calling me vulgar names and said we couldn't go through there alive, and by this time he jerked his gun and said, take that, then I pointed my rifle on him and let him have it, then Willie came towards me with the axe calling me a son of a bitch and I let him have it too."

Again without the map exhibit, I have to assume the Alfred is pointing to Johnny on the left side of the road as he is in front of the lead horses. This would mean they were no more than 10 to 15 feet apart. And yet, Johnny missed as he shot at Alfred. If this position is correct, Nick and Willie may have been in the line of fire for Johnny. Remember, Jones made this point by having Nick tell where the boys were standing. Also the axe according to Nick was placed towards the rear of the wagon and on the left side far from Willie's reach. Willie was found lying on the right side near the gatepost.

Dennis asks: "Where did Willie stand with reference to Johnny, when you first discovered him with an axe?"

"He was standing a few feet from Johnny."

"What position did you have the rifle in when Johnny fired at you?" "It was point at the ground."

"Why did you have the rifle that morning?"

"I never took the rifle along for no purpose." "I never took the rifle no way." "I never knew the rifle was going to the canyon." "I never knew until Charlie came out of the house packing it, and I was on the seat ready to start off."

The more I hear Alfred's responses to Dennis's questions, the more I think Alfred's mental capacity may be lacking and that is putting it mildly.

Dennis asks: "After the shooting occurred, what transpired?"

"I told Charlie to drive through the Gap and turn around." "And we would go and inform Litster what had happened." "He drove through the Gap and as he drove through the Gap and I stepped on the brake; as the horses turned around one of the wheel horses caught his feet in the stretchers and he could not make the turn." "I got off the wagon and straightened the horses out and got back on the seat and we drove back through the Gap and went on across the bridge."

Dennis asks: "Now how did you drive the wagon down the canyon?"

"We drove pretty lively."

"Where did you go?"

"We drove on down the canyon until we came to the Litster's lower corral and he wasn't there."

The lower corral was about 400 yards below house on the south side of the canyon.

"We continued down to Mrs. Eason's and informed her." "Nick got off the wagon and went to the house and informed her, I don't know what he said."

Here again, Alfred doesn't mention seeing Jimmy or that Nick told Jimmy to go home.

Dennis asks: "When did Nick get on the wagon again?"

Dennis's question takes us back to the Gap.

"After we drove across the bridge." "Did he get on of his own volition, or did you tell him to?" "He got on of his own freewill."

Recall Nick said he was told to get on a gunpoint. Also, the Gap was just a short distance from the bridge and main road, certainly not the distance Alfred had estimated earlier.

Dennis asks: "Did Rast make any suggestion as to where you should go or what you should do, after he got upon the wagon?"

"No, Sir."

"Did he ask you about how many shots you had in your gun?"

"No, Sir."

"Nothing was said about it?"

"No, Sir."

"Now, after Mrs. Alex Eason was informed of what had occurred, what did you do?"

"We continued down the canyon to the Vaughan Ranch."

"Was there any conversation between you?"

"No, Sir, not at all."

Dennis asks Alfred how long he thought the interval might have been between passing the lower corral. Dennis asks if it was perhaps a half to three quarter's hour and Alfred said, yes. He asks Alfred what took place when they got back to the ranch.

Truman objects because this is after he shooting.

The Judge tells him that he is going to allow the question.

Dennis: "You may testify what occurred."

"Charlie drove through the gate and as he drove through the gate at the ranch, I jumped off the wagon; father and mother came out of the house, and asked what was the trouble, and I said we had trouble with the Litster boys, and she commenced crying, and asked what was the matter, and I said I killed the Litster boys in self-defense, and she said that was too bad."

Truman states: "We move Your Honor to strike out what was said by his mother."

Judge Mack agrees because Mrs. Vaughan was scheduled to testify.

Dennis asks: "What did you do then?"

"I went into the house with my mother and father."

"How long did you stay there?"

"Charlie he went down to the corral and caught two horses and come to the house." "I was coming to town to give myself up to the law."

"Did you do that?"

"Yes, I did."

"What was your mental condition during the time you were at the Gap and until you passed the house of Mrs. Alex Eason?"

Truman objects and the Judge Mack overrules.

"I was nervous and excited; my nerves were all unstrung."

Reasonable, he just had killed two people.

Dennis: "What kind of terms were you with the Litster boys, as well as the entire family, for the period of one or two years previous to the homicide?"

Jones: "Your Honor Please."

Judge Mack listens to the objection and then states: "It seems to me that he has the right to show the feelings existing between the defendant and the deceased at the time of the shooting."

Jones states: "We do not object to that."

Judge Mack adds: "Perhaps for a reasonable length of time previous to that, but I cannot see how the feelings between any other member of the family can have any bearing upon this matter."

Dennis now explains the object of the testimony would be to contradict the theory of the transaction being that this homicide was willful, and that the shooting was not done in cold blood.

"I will show that there existed between the defendant and the two deceased boys, and in fact, the entire family a feeling, inasmuch as the family or most of them have testified as witnesses, and inasmuch as the testimony already adduced before the jury shows that the father of the two boys were, within the space of an hour, on the road up the canyon to the scene of the homicide or accident." "Such feelings would tend to show to the jury that the boys were there for the purpose of having trouble that morning."

Judge Mack states: "I do not see, unless you want to contradict what Mr. Litster said or what difference the feelings between the families would make or what bearing it would have here upon it."

Dennis agrees to modify his question.

Judge Mack: "Your may ask the question."

"What kind of term were you on with the deceased boys and their father prior to the homicide?"

"We were not on good terms at all."

"You may describe what kind of terms you were on and what kind of feelings that existed between you."

"Hard feelings."

"How far back from the homicide did that feeling exist?" "From two to three years."

Nothing was said here about Mr. Litster throwing Alfred out of the Litster house for pointing a pistol at Mr. Starratt.

Dennis asks: "About how many times have you gone up and down Boone Canyon previous to the time of the homicide?"

Jones states: "We object to the question upon the grounds that it is purely incompetent, immaterial and irrelevant to any issue of this case." "We submit it cannot make any difference." "This young man may have passed up there every day for forty years."

Dennis responds: "I am asking this question your Honor, to lay a foundation for another question, to show the condition of the road and particularly of this Gap, where the homicide occurred."

Judge Mack asks: "What is the object and what is the element of the defense?"

"Your Honor please, I desire to show by this witness that for a long time previous, and in fact up pretty near to the time of the homicide that this Gap where the homicide occurred was open; that there was no wires across the road, and that there was no necessity for its being closed on that morning."

"Please make your position clearer."

"Even if it is true, in what respect does that tend to throw any light upon the homicide?"

"Your Honor please, I contend that it was a circumstance that would go to show that the deceased boys went there that morning and closed this Gap, not through any necessity, but for the sole purpose of having an encounter with the defendant."

Jones objected and after a lengthy argument the Judge sustained his the objection.

You might agree that Dennis was partially right about why the boys were at the Gap, but their father testified that he told them to close the Gap because he was going to put the cattle in the upper pasture. Even if this was not true it is still not an excuse to justify homicide, unless Johnny first shot at Alfred and then Willie came at him with an axe.

Dennis asks: "Did you ever see that Gap closed?"

"No, Sir."

Again Jones objects, by saying it make no difference whatever whether that Gap had always been open or always closed.

Judge Mack states: “The witness has already answered.”

“We move to strike it out then.”

Judge Mack agrees: “The question and answer are stricken out.”

Dennis changes his line of questions and now asks: “I want to call your attention to the testimony that you heard about this cow that got into your field, and I wish you would related all the circumstances about that without my asking any questions, and state everything that transpired.

Alfred responds: “The Litster boys were driving a cow past our ranch and Harry and I were standing up by the cabin and there was a fire above the house in the field and the cow got scared at the fire and jumped over the fence, and they went into the field and left the gate open to drive the cow out.” “I went down to the stable and got my horse and went to the field to help them drive out the cow.” “I rode down to the pasture and Jimmy was there, and I asked him what right he had to go in the field without coming to the house and asking permission to go in, or else shut the gate behind him.” “When I done that I rode to Willie and asked him what right he had to go in the field without coming to the house and asking permission to go in the field, or else shut the gate behind him.” “He said he could go in just the same and he rode up to me and called me a son of a bitch and said he would go in whenever he got ready and I told him he wouldn’t.” “He went out of the field and Harry and I drove the cow out of the field and started her up the road and they started off and Willie said, I will fix you, you son of a bitch.”

Someone is lying. You might be inclined to believe part of his story until he starts with the SOB words.

Dennis asks: “Was Willie on horseback?”

“Yes, Sir.”

“At what gate did he come along side you?”

“To our gate.”

“I mean on horseback, how did they ride with reference to speed?” “Came like a wild man.”

“State to the jury what was Willie’s treatment of you on that occasion?” “Every time I met him he always called me vulgar names.”

Judge Mack says: "That is not responsive, strike out the answer."

Dennis asks: "What was Willie Litster's treatment of you on that occasion?"

"I can't answer it."

"You don't know how he treated you...whether good or bad... did he treat you good?"

"No he didn't."

"Did he treat you badly?"

"Yes, Sir."

"In what manner did he treat you badly?" "What did his bad treatment consist of?"

Jones objects: "Your Honor please, we object to the question upon the grounds that it is leading."

Judge Mack states: "He may answer the question if he can."

Alfred answers: "Bad treatment."

"That does not answer the question, Alfe."

"I can't answer it."

"Did you or not strike Willie with a quirt that day?"

"No, Sir, I never had no quirt."

"What do you use a quirt for?"

"Riding bronco horses."

"What kind of a horse were you on that day?"

"I was on a gentle horse."

"When you went to the field, you said you were on horseback." "What about Harry?"

"He was on foot at first."

"How long did Harry remain there?"

"Until the Litster boys went out of the field, then he went to the stable and got a horse and came down here and helped me drive the cow out of the field."

Dennis asks: "Did the two of you drive the cow out alone?"

"We drove some milk cows out with it."

"Why did you do that?"

"So the heifer would go out."

"Where was the cow with reference to the gate?"

"She was down the field from the gap."

Note even here a gate opening is referred to as a "Gap".

Dennis asks: "Describe as near as you can Alfe, where she was."

"She was about three quarters of a mile down the field and I went down and drove her out."

"Why did you object to Willie and his brother going into the field?"

"I had no objection to their going in the field if they would close the gap; we had some wild horses in there, and if they get out it would be pretty hard to get them in again."

"Was Harry riding a wild horse that day or not?"

"No, Sir he was not."

"Where did the boys go after they rode out of the field?"

"They rode out of the field and went down the road."

"Were they in plain sight all the time?"

"Yes, Sir."

Dennis asks: "I will ask you again, and you need not answer until counsel has time to object; what was the uniform and general treatment of you by Willie when he met you?"

"He always wanted to bulldoze me and called me vulgar names."

"How would he act?"

"I don't understand the question."

Truman states: "I believe the question is objectionable; it is irrelevant and immaterial."

Judge Mack tells Alfred: "You may answer the question."

"I can't answer it."

Dennis is obviously disappointed that Alfred did not pickup on the point he was trying to make.

Dennis asks: "Now Alfe, going back to the scene of the homicide, and on the morning of 28th of December, where you have stated that Johnny pulled a gun and fired at you, I want you to tell this jury how you know he pulled the gun and fired at you?"

"Because, I seen it."

"From any other reason do you know it?"

"I seen him pull the gun and I fired a shot at him."

"You didn't see the shots?"

"I seen the smoke and heard the report."

"Did you hear anything else?"

"Just at the same time Willie was coming at me with an axe, and he said, I will fix you, you son of a bitch." "I didn't have time to look around, one was shooting at me, and the other coming at me with the axe; I didn't have anytime."

Judge Mack now asks Dennis: "What is the purpose of this examination by going over it a second time?"

Dennis said: "I have left out something and I am asking this to lay a foundation."

Dennis asks: "How many shots fired by Johnny?"

"He fired one shot at me."

"Was that all you heard?"

"That is all I heard, yes."

Dennis is now finished with his examination of Alfred. Remember Charlie was sitting on the bench in the wagon holding reins. If he had a pistol you would think that he just might use it to help his brother that had just been shot at. Nick Rast said he had a pistol. Both Alfe and Charlie have denied Charlie having a pistol. The one he always carried and the one that the Sheriff took from him that evening when they were arrested. Charlie is going to testify that Johnny shot three times at Alfred. You would think that these brothers would have agreed about the number shots Johnny fired. Recall Nick said Charlie told Alfred not to shot as Johnny was begging for his life.

The Cross Examination begins with Jones asking: "Alfred you testified in this case once before, did you not?"

"Yes, Sir."

Jones handed Alfred a copy and asks to look at his testimony from the first trial.

Dennis objects, but says if counsel wishes to refer to a portion of it, I will consent.

Judge Mack seems a bit disturbed as he responded: "Your objection is not well taken." "The testimony given by the witness in the former trial may be shown to him and used on this examination if desired."

Dennis responds by saying he was just referring to the volume.

"Objection overruled."

"Defendant excepts." And Dennis adds: "I object to any examination of the testimony and side talk of counsel before the Court and the witness."

Judge Mack said it is not necessary to encumber the record. "When counsel asks questions, I will have them recorded."

"I except to your rule, your Honor."

Jones repeats the question and Alfred answers:

"Yes, Sir."

Jones: "Did you tell the truth when you testified at the former trial?"

"Yes, Sir."

"Now Alfred, if you have testified differently here today to what you testified in the testimony that you have just identified, is it true or false?"

Alfred is not that dumb Counselor.

"You want to remember Mr. Jones, it was over a year ago, and I don't consider my mind is as good as it was then."

Dennis: "Your Honor please he hasn't shown the witness yet that it is a correct transcript of his testimony."

Judge Mack states: "This is a matter for cross-examination."

Jones continues his questions about him being charged with murder and what would they do to him if he were found guilty? "I suppose they will hang me." "Then would you tell a lie to save your own life?"

"No, Sir."

"You are sure of that?"

"Yes, Sir."

"If a lie hung on one hand and the gallows upon the other, and you were asked to take your choice, you would take the gallows in preference to the lie?"

"Yes, Sir."

Dennis should have objected to the hypothetical question. Instead he lets Alfred tell another lie.

"Alfred, I want you to take this gun and show the jury how you acted; I want you, if there is no objection, to show this jury how you used it when you killed Willie." "I want you to show me how you held that gun when you stood in front of Johnny and Willie, and just before you shot them?"

Alfred proceeds to show what he did.

Jones asks: "Assume I am Johnny and I jerk my pistol out here and shoot, what do you do?"

"I just let him have it."

"Now, Willie comes rushing behind Johnny with an axe raised over his head, what do you do?"

"I let him have it."

"Did Willie fall?"

"I didn't see him." "Did Johnny fall?" "I didn't see him."

"So did you go blind as you shot?"

"I was excited."

"Now Alfred, take the axe and show jury about how Willie used it when he came towards you?"

"He came at me this way."

"You mean that he had his arms just as you have it now have it?"

"I can't tell how far he had his arms." "I can't tell how far down he had his arms, or how high he had them."

"What is your judgment?"

Alfred now shows what he means and then says: "About that shape"

Jones seems to be trying to get Alfred to say the Willie's arms were above his head. I think Alfred know what he doing. Remember, Willie had a wound in his arm as the bullet entered his stomach. And if Willie was charging with an axe why are his arms down? Also, note that Jones falsely said Willie was coming from behind Johnny and Alfred did not correct him.

"What became of Johnny's pistol after he shot at you?"

"I don't know."

"You were around over the ground where he was several minutes after the shooting?"

"I wasn't looking for evidence."

"That is not what I asked you, after you shot Johnny and Willie as you described, you were around that ground for a few minutes after that were you not?"

"No Sir, I told Charlie to turn the team around." "I stepped on the brake."

Alfred is saying that he locked the wheel on one side so the wagon would make a short radius turn. Alfred did not say but he could only do this if he had gotten back on the wagon.

Jones asks: "Then you had to drive over the ground where you shot Johnny?

"Yes."

Jones asks: "Going and coming back too?" "Johnny is between you and the gate when you shot him?"

"Yes, that is where he was when I shot him."

Jones has just got Alfred to say that his body was ahead of the wagon. He was found laying nearly 30 feet back down the road as he was backing away from begging Alfred not to shoot.

"Now if Johnny was shot through the right nipple and down through the body here, he must have dropped his pistol when you struck him?"

"I didn't have time to see whether he did or not."

Jones states: "I am not asking you whether you saw or not, but suppose a man was shot through about here with a Winchester 44 caliber rifle, he would be apt to relax his fingers and drop his pistol wouldn't he?"

Dennis objects: "You're asking an opinion, he is not an expert witness."

Jones states: "I withdraw the question." Jones then asked a series of question as to how Johnny was standing when he was shot?

"He was calling me names."

Jones continues the questioning and Alfred states that Johnny was uphill from him.

"So you shot both of them and they were uphill from you?"

"Yes, Sir."

This is hardly the case when you consider the location of the bodies. Also, Alfred has both Johnny and Willie so close to him that the jury had to be thinking how could Johnny to miss his shot and how did Willie get the axe? Johnny would have been only 10 to 12 feet away according to Alfred. The brothers were found lying on the opposite side of the road near the Gap.

Jones asks: "What kind of pistol was it Alfred that Johnny shot at you with?"

"I would call it a bulldog."

"What color handle did it have?"

"I can't tell that sir." "What color was the barrel?"

"Light color."

"Do you mean a polished silver color?"

"Silver color, bright colored the same as that Mr. Easton has yesterday."

Jones continued by asking Alfred about where Johnny was when he shot him. Alfred now has Johnny downhill and laying two feet from the road.

Jones asks: "Now Alfred, I will ask you if you have read at any time since you testified here last spring the evidence you gave then?" "Have you looked over the evidence you gave at that time, at any time since?"

"Yes, Sir."

"When?"

"The other day."

"Did you read it carefully?"

"No, Sir, I just glanced over it."

Jones tries to get Alfred to say how much time he spent reviewing the trial transcript. Alfred is not about to be pinned down.

Alfred said: "Mr. Dennis brought it to him and never told him what to read."

Dennis states: "Your Honor please, I wish to state for the information of the witness that he is not compelled to state any conversation that passed between him and me."

Judge Mack responds: "Yes, he is required to state whether you required him to read that evidence over, but as to any confidential matter passing between you and the witness, he is not." "As it is now presented, the question is proper and should be answered."

Alfred: "I decline to answer."

Judge Mack asks: "Upon what grounds sir do you decline to answer; do you think if you admit the truth of it, it would be against you in this matter?"

"No, Sir, I don't think so."

"Then what reason or excuse for not answering it?"

Dennis tells Alfred to answer the question:

"If I asked you to read it, tell them so."

"No, Sir, he did not tell me to read it."

"Did he ask you to read it?"

"He left the book there and I read it."

Jones continues this line of questions and Alfred then said Dennis read part of the testimony to him.

"Was it for the purpose of giving the same testimony this time exactly as you gave it before?"

"I assume so."

"Reading it over had nothing to do with making it conform to the same as it was before is that the idea?"

Judge Mack states: "You can answer the question."

"No, Sir."

"Now Alfred were you in good humor when you got up to the Gap that day where the Litster boys were?"

"Yes, Sir."

"What time did you get mad after you got there?"

"When they was calling me names."

Alfred admits to getting mad. Yes, he was very mad, recall he had heard Johnny say this would be the last time and Willie said you don't have a mine. Yes, Alfred was very mad, mad enough to kill two brothers.

Jones asks: "Did you get pretty mad before you first shot?"

"I never fired the first shot."

"Answer, the question, did you get pretty mad before you commenced to shoot?"

"I was fixed in a position and I had to do what I done."

"Answer the question?"

"Yes, pretty mad."

"What were your mad at?"

"The language they called me."

"Were you standing there with a gun in your hand all that time?"

"Yes, Sir."

"And you didn't make a move at all until they shot at you?"

"No, Sir."

"You stood there with your gun on the ground something like this (Jones assumes the position) until after Johnny shot at you, did you?"

"Just as he made a motion to shoot and fired, I answered him."

"When you testified at this trial before that you stood perfectly motionless and did not move your gun at all until he shot at you." "Why did you say so and tell us now that as soon as he began to make a motion, you began to shoot?"

"Can you explain that?"

Dennis objects and Judge Mack says it is a proper question.

Jones states: "I will read to you Alfred, from your evidence in Book Three, page 685 commencing at line 12" (Jones reads the transcript from the first trial): "Now explain to the jury what followed." "When Nick Rast was opening the fence and the Litster boys was calling us sons of bitches and we couldn't go through there alive, Johnny Litster throwed his gun and said 'take that you son of a bitch' and commenced shooting at me. I had the muzzle of my rifle on the ground and I held it in my hand and raised it and fired and shot him; and Willie Litster at the same time was coming at me with the axe raised and said, I will fix you, you son of a bitch and throwed my gun on him and shot him.

"Now reading on further, Mr. Dennis, beginning on line 28, page 685 of the same Book." Question: When Johnny jerked his gun from his trousers and said take that you son of a bitch, what did you do? I raised my rifle to my shoulder and fired and Willie was coming after me with an axe and said I will fix you, you son of a bitch, and he was coming with the axe raised this way over his shoulder, and I throwed my rifle on him and shot him. Mr. Jones: "Now why the difference in your two statements; which one is true?" Alfred answers: "This one is true." Jones: "And the other one is false, is that right?"

"True, as far as I know."

"Which one of the statements is true?"

"Both."

"Then when you stated a year ago that you stood with your gun in your hand and shot Johnny after he shot at you, and you state today that as soon as he commenced to draw his pistol, you threw your gun on him and shot him that they are both true, is that it?"

Dennis asks: "I object to the question upon the ground that the witness has not testified to my knowledge that he drew his gun on him and shot him, as soon as he began to draw his pistol." "I insist that Johnny pulled his gun and fired and then he drew his gun and fired."

Jones states: "He said when he commenced to draw his gun, he stood perfectly still, motionless."

Judge Mack says: "That is his testimony."

Alfred again says: "Yes, they are both true."

"They are both true?"

"Yes, Sir."

"Explain to the jury how they can both be true?"

"I say they are both true, I mean they both have the same meaning that is all the way I can explain."

Jones: "Now you say that you got home, you jumped off the wagon at the gate and went toward the house, and your father and mother were standing in the yard and they asked you what was the matter and you told them you had shot the Litster boys in self-defense and they commenced to cry, is that what you said a while ago to Mr. Dennis?"

"I said after Charlie drove the wagon through the gate I jumped off the wagon and father and mother came out of the house and asked what the matter was and mother commenced to cry and asked what was the matter and I said I shot the Litster boys in self-defense."

"Did your mother commence to cry before you told that you had shot the Litster boys?"

"She asked what the trouble was?"

"I want to know whether she commenced to cry before you told her what had happened or after?"

"Afterwards."

"You testified a year ago that she commenced to cry before you told her."

"I told that today too."

Jones states: "That she commenced to cry before you told her."

"Yes, Sir."

"So when you answered the question of Mr. Dennis today, you were not correct were you?"

"I was, Yes, Sir."

Jones continues to question Alfred about the timing of when his mother started to cry. I have to assume that he trying to show that Alfred story has changed. It seems to be such a minor point here.

Finally Jones moves to another line of questions: "Now why the hurry down the canyon Alfred, when you left the boys up there where you had shot them, why did you hurry down the canyon?"

"I was coming to give myself up."

"What did you give yourself up for?"

"For killing one of the Litster boys in self-defense."

"Now if you had acted in self-defense, why were you in a hurry?"

"Did you not know that a man acts in self-defense is not committing any crime?"

"I can't answer."

"You were in a hurry were you?"

"Yes, Sir."

"You had a Winchester rifle with a number of cartridges in it?"

"After I got to the ranch, before I started for Austin, I put six more in it."

"Then you had seven when you went by the Litster?"

"I suppose so, there was thirteen when I come to Austin."

"Why did you put the extra six cartridges at home?"

"I thought I might have to use them on the road."

"And you would have used it if you had?"

"I would have used it if I had got in a pinch."

"You would have used it readily, is that right?"

"I think so."

"You are kind of a good shooter, are you not Alfred?"

"I don't know."

"You were that day were you not?"

"Yes, when a man is fixing in the same position as I was."

"You fired two shots and killed two men did you not?"

"I suppose I did."

"Is it not a fact that you did?"

"Yes, Sir."

"You killed Willie Litster there, did you not?"

"I don't know whether I killed him right there or not."

"You admit that you killed in self-defense?"

"Yes."

Jones continues to pressure Alfred: "Now can you explain or make any explanation as to why you were in a hurry going down the canyon that day?"

"I didn't want to have any more trouble."

"If you acted in self-defense, you hadn't had any trouble?"

Dennis objects: "I object to the question upon the ground that it is an untrue declaration." "A man, who takes the life of another, no matter under what circumstance, is in trouble."

Judge Mack states: "Objection overruled, you may answer the question."

Alfred states: "I can't answer the question."

"Is it not a fact that you expected to meet the father of the boys as you went down the canyon?"

"I thought I would meet him at the haystack and inform him of the trouble, yes, sir."

"Did you stop at the house and inform anyone there what had happened?"

"No, Sir."

"How far from the house were you as you passed down the road that day?"

"I suppose five or six hundred yards."

"From the Litster?"

"Yes."

Again, Alfred demonstrates his poor judgment of distances, you recall that he said the Gap was 100 to 150 yards from the main road; actually it was about 70 feet. And here the main road passes less than a 100 yards from the house.

Judge Mack now asks: "Is that the nearest point to the house as you passed going down the road?"

"I think so."

"Don't you know for a fact about what distance it is?"

"I never measured it."

While researching this story regarding roads near the house, I have concluded that some of these roads no longer exist. Still the main road is less than 100 yard from the house. The canyon is narrow, about 300 yards wide at the house location.

Jones asks: "You have been to the Litster house a good many times haven't you?"

"No, sir I have not."

"You have been there some times?"

"Yes, I have been there a long while ago."

"Do you remember having drawn a pistol on a man in the Litster house, at one time?"

"I never drew a pistol on a man in the Litster house at no time."

"You don't remember having drawn a six-shooter on H. S. Starratt in the Litster house in the presence of the Litster family?"

"I never drew in the house."

"Did you draw it out of doors?" You never went out of doors at the Litster house?"

"No, Sir."

"How did you get out of the house if you didn't go out of doors?"

"Did you go into the ground or up in the clouds, or how did you get away from there?"

Jones was trying hard to trip up Alfred. This event of the pistol being drawn at the Litster house probably occurred in 1890. Alfred would have been 18 at the time. The Starratt family ran the hardware store in Austin. H. S. Starratt is not listed in the 1880 census. The Starratt's only had two sons listed, Charles and Francis in 1880. There is no mention of him in the 1900 census and as you recall there is no 1890 census. H. S. Starratt may have been an older man and did not live in Austin in 1880. The oldest Litster daughter Mary was still living at home. She would have been 20 years old in 1890. Later in the trial Jones will ask Mary as a rebuttal witness to explain, but Judge Mack doesn't allow this testimony. So it looks like the details of this event have been lost to history. However, there is little doubt that this was the event that sparked the feud between the Litster and Vaughan families. I have speculated that Mr. Litster threw Alfred and his pistol out of the house.

Alfred states: “I will explain if that is what you want to know.”

Jones said: “I want you to answer.”

“I went out another door and got on my horse and left.”

“So that is the way you got out of the house.”

Perhaps, it was as simple as that, but still this event must have started the feud.

Jones asks: “Now you say you expected to find Mr. Litster at the corral as you went down the canyon?”

“Yes.”

“What made you believe you would find him there when you went down the canyon?”

“He was there when we went up.”

“Did you know that his wife was home?”

“No, Sir, I didn’t.”

“You naturally supposed she was there?”

“I didn’t suppose, no Sir.”

“You saw the two little children with Mr. Litster at the hay corral?”

"I saw two, yes.”

“Now, Mr. Litster and the two little children were down at the hay corral just a few hundred yards below the house and knowing the two boys were shot laying in the snow, Johnny dead and Willie wounded, didn’t you suppose Mrs. Litster was at home?”

“I didn’t know that.”

Judge Mack asks: “Did you stop at the Litster home to ascertain if anyone was at home?”

“No, sir we passed right on.”

Jones asks: “Is it not a fact Alfred, that there was a road, the road you came down the canyon on where you left the two boys, is it not a fact that it forks just above the Litster house, and you might have come by the house as conveniently as you could go around it?”

“I don’t know anything about that.”

"Is it not a fact that there are three roads and you could have taken either of them, one back of the house, one at the woodpile and the other one that you traveled that day?"

"I suppose there is."

"Don't you of your own knowledge, that you have traveled them all?"

"Yes, Sir."

"Then why did you not say you knew it instead of saying you supposed there were?"

Dennis objects to the question.

"Objection overruled and an exception taken."

"Why did you say you supposed so when you admit you knew it?"

"I supposed there were three roads."

"Have you not said you knew there were three?"

"Yes."

"Why did you say in the first place that you supposed there were three roads when as a matter of fact you know there were three?"

"I supposed one answer was as good as another."

"Now did you not know as a matter of fact that you could have taken either of those two roads with equal convenience when they were larger and would have taken you by the Litster house?"

"I don't know whether they are larger or not."

"Assuming that they circle by the Litster house, and this is water running down the canyon toward you and this is the front of the house, the house was here when this happened, it is now down here."

Jones points to a map. "Down here about two or three hundred yards below the house where the road forks that you traveled that day?"

"It turns from the house quite a way."

"I approximate it two or three hundred yards below the house?"

"Yes, Sir."

"The road you took turns off and goes back of the house doesn't it?"

"Yes, Sir."

"Then it comes right up to the house, within ten feet of the yard gate." "Does it not?" "The wood pile road, the road running through the wood pile, and into this road you traveled that day?"

"Yes."

"Doesn't the Boone Canyon road go in front of the Litster house door?"

"I can't answer."

"Don't all three of the roads come together just above the Litster house, three or four or five hundred yards?"

"The two roads come together."

"And the third one comes into the second a little below here does it not?"

Jones points again to the map.

"Yes, Sir."

"Now coming down the canyon, from where you killed those boys that day as you have described, couldn't you have taken this road that went through the woodpile back of the house, as well as to have taken that road coming down the canyon?"

"Never thought of that."

"You have done so if you had thought of it?"

"I don't know whether I could or not."

Judge Mack now instructs Alfred to answer the question:

"I could if I had wanted to."

"Then you didn't want to take either one these roads?"

"No, Sir."

"Then when you say you didn't think of it, you told an untruth, did you?"

"I suppose so, Yes."

"Then you admit in saying that you didn't think of it, that you told was not true?"

"I suppose so."

"Then you would rather be hung than to tell a little lie like that?"

"I don't know, as it would make much difference."

"You said a while ago that you would just as soon be hung as to tell a lie, what do you say now?"

"I decline to answer."

Judge Mack states: "You must answer."

"Yes, it is about the same."

Jones then walked back to his chair.

His cross-examination didn't really shake Alfred's story. He stuck to his story, however Jones did make it clear to the jury that he was prepared by his review of the first trial transcript. Jones demonstrated how unlikely Alfred's positioning of Johnny and Willie was when he shot them. He also made it clear to the jury that he had no intention of telling the Litster's about the shooting. And he had Alfred admit to a lie. Alfred said he would rather hang than tell a lie. The point that Jones didn't make was the fact the Willie's arm had a bullet wound as the ball passed through to his gut. Not likely if he was charging with an axe and his arms above his head.

Jones didn't mention either that Johnny must have been a very poor shot. I think anyone could have made the shot that Johnny missed as he supposedly shot first at Alfred. If Alfred's testimony was true then Nick Rast was a liar from the jury's perspective.

10

CHARLIE

Did He Always Do What He Was Told?

Alfred boots was the only thing to be heard as he left the stand and walked back to his chair beside Dennis. After he was seated Dennis got up and told the Court: "My next witness will be Charles Vaughan. The deputy then brought Charlie into the courtroom from the room where he was nervously waiting. Charles Henry Vaughan raised his right hand while placing his left hand on the Bible. He was duly sworn to tell the truth. Charlie knew his testimony from the first trial must be restated. Dennis asked the usual introductory questions as Charlie settled into the chair. He was now 25 years old and he said he was born in Lander County at the Vaughan Ranch.

Did Charlie need Dennis to give him a refresher course regarding his testimony from the first trial? It is hard to understand why Charlie's version of what happen was so different from Alfred's testimony. Charlie was sitting high on the bench holding the reigns of those big workhorses. He had a bird's eye view of everything. If he changes his testimony at this trial what will be the consequences of Jones's cross-examination? Charlie appeared to be relaxed at this trial. Perhaps, because all the charges against him had been dropped. Still he very much wanted to help his beloved brother?

Dennis starts by going straight to the Gap with the first question: "Now you can state to the jury what transpired at that point at the mouth of the Water Canyon, in Boone Canyon, on the 28th day of December, what transpired with reference to yourself, your brother and Nick Rast and John and Willie

Litster, now deceased?" "Beginning right at the point of the mouth of Water Canyon?"

"Well, we drove up there at the canyon to the fence and the Litster's was there and I was on the wagon driving the horses and I asked them to please open the fence."

Dennis asks: "They were there, where?"

"At the fence."

"Describe, if you saw them, where they were with reference to the fence?"

"They were on the outside of the fence, between the gate and my lead horses."

This sure sounds like they are inside the fence if they are between the gate and the lead horses. I think that is what he means?

"Were they in the road?"

"In the road."

"Show how they were standing?"

"They were standing in the road at the head of my horses."

"Can you place me and show the jury how they were standing?" "Can you represent one of them and I the other and represent to the jury how they were standing in the road?" Dennis continues to have Charlie place the boys. Charlie said they were standing close together at the gate.

Charlie said he asked them to please open the gate and one of them said:

"You sons of bitched you won't go through here alive, and if you do you won't get back alive." "They cursed each other and hard words were said before the shooting occurred."

"Now you saw the shooting did you?"

"Yes, Sir."

Dennis then asked Charlie to describe the shooting?

"I was on the wagon and my brother was on this side of the road when Johnny Litster pulled a six shooter from right here, he pulled out his gun and says"

Dennis interrupts: "Now show the jury how Johnny pulled his pistol, and what he said?"

"Well, Alfe was on this side and Johnny was standing over here, and he pulled his pistol out here and says, take that you bastardly sons of bitches and commenced shooting at him."

"What did your brother do?"

"Of course he pulled up his gun and went to shooting too, at the same time."

"After the shooting I drove through the Gap and turned around and came back."

Does Charlie's story sounds bogus? Why is he just sitting there? People are being shot at. Nick at least said he started to run for cover. Charlie was just the causal spectator and remember he had a pistol according to Nick. Also notice that Dennis doesn't ask any questions about how many shots were fired.

"I drove right through and turned around once and had to turn around the second time and come back and my brother and Nick Rast got on the wagon and we come on home down the canyon."

"What kind of a wagon did you have Charlie?"

"A four horses wagon."

Dennis asks what was loaded in the wagon and Charlie told him about the equipment they loaded that morning. Dennis now jumps ahead to the jail and asks if they ever made any threats to Nick while they were in jail. Charlie denies any threats were ever made.

Dennis then turned the witness over for cross-examination.

Truman asks: "You didn't get off the wagon at all up there, at the time of trouble?"

"No, Sir."

"You saw it all, did you?"

"I think I seen it all."

"You were paying close attention to what was going on?"

"No, sir, I had all I could do to mind the horses."

That might be a fact with Alfe shooting so close to the horses.

"Did you see Johnny pull his pistol?"

"Yes."

"Which hand did he pull it with?"

"The right hand."

"Is he not left handed?"

"I don't know."

"But he pulled it with his right?"

"Yes, Sir."

We were not told whether Johnny was really left-handed.

"Where was Willie at this time?"

Dennis states: "Objection, we submit this is not cross-examination."

"Overruled."

"He was a little out of my sight."

"You didn't see him at all?"

"I saw a part of him."

"What put him out of your sight?"

"The willows."

Charlie seems to be saying Willie must have gone some place, a moment ago he was standing in the road with Johnny.

"There were pretty big heavy willows there, that is between you?"

"Yes, Sir."

"So you couldn't see him?"

"They were rather heavy and high."

"Was there foliage on them, the leafs?"

"Yes, I believe there was not, it was the fall."

This is December 28th and there would be no foliage and Charlie should have said winter. Charlie had Willie standing behind willows in the first trial and here again he says he can only see his head and feet. Again this sounds strange, but there is a reason. He is going to say later Willie too was armed, but right now he can't see the pistol. He says he didn't see Alfred shoot at Willie. Why not if Alfred story was true about shooting Willie after he shot Johnny?

"How many shots did Johnny fire at Alfred before Alfred shoots at him?"

"I guess three."

Charlie then said he was not really sure and there could have been four or five shots. He said the horses were very excited and that he was having a hard time controlling them during the shooting.

"Did you see Alfred fire the shot that killed Johnny?"

"No, I didn't."

"Did you see the gun smoke when he fired the shot that killed Willie Litster?" "No, I didn't."

"You were paying attention to your horses?"

"Yes, I had all I could manage."

Truman asks about all the swearing when Charlie asked the boys to open the gate and where was Nick Rast standing when the shooting started:

"I forget where he was."

Truman asks how Alfred was holding the rifle?

"I believe he held it with the muzzle of it on the ground."

In the first trial he had the muzzle up.

Charlie added that he really couldn't remember.

Truman asks: "Now which boy first called you a son of a bitch?"

"Both of them."

"Both at the same time?"

"Yes, Sir."

"What was said to Alfred?" "I didn't hear it all."

"They were swearing?" "Yes."

Truman asks: Did Alfred talk back?

"Maybe he did."

Charlie uses the horse excuse again about not being sure.

Truman states: "Then don't use the word maybe, if it is not a fact that you don't know whether Alfred talked back or not?"

"They were all there at once talking and I couldn't tell who talked the most."

Then Alfred was talking?"

"I expect he was."

Truman asks a series of questions about the position of the boys and about all Charlie could say was the he wasn't sure, but he does say that Johnny is on the left and Willie is on the right road side.

Charlie seems to have forgotten about having Willie being behind the willows.

"You didn't see Willie Litster do anything to your brother that caused the shooting?"

"I say he was out of my sight."

"Answer the question."

"As I said I couldn't watch it all."

Judge Mack then told Charlie it is a yes or no and then you can explain.

Truman states: "You have already told us the bushes were there and you couldn't see anything but his head and feet. Now tell me if you saw him do anything to Alfred Vaughan that caused him to shoot him?"

"No, sir, but as I said he was out of my sight and I could not see him all the time."

Truman asks why he could see and Charlie said the willows were too high? He point out to Charlie that he was seated high on the wagon bench. Charlie continued to maintain that the willows blocked his view. But he said he could see Willie's feet and head.

Judge Mack finally out frustration asks: "Do I understand you to say that Willie was standing behind this clump of bushes when you heard the shots fired."

"He was."

Next Truman asks a long question that frustrated Judge Mack, so the Judge asks: "Where was Johnny standing when he pulled the pistol?

"He was standing up the road by the lead horses."

Charlie said that Johnny after being shot while standing by the lead horses then walked to the rear wheels of the wagon before falling down.

Not likely if you consider the fact that he was shot through the heart.

Charlie said he didn't know what kind of pistol Johnny had but he was able to demonstrate how he pulled the pistol and he repeated what Johnny said: "Take that you sons of bitches, as he commenced shooting at Alfe."

Truman asks if Nick had gone to the gate before the shooting started. Charlie said that he did know; he couldn't remember what Nick was doing.

"You were arrested, Charlie, were you not, on the charge of this killing, in the County Jail for a time?"

"Yes, I was locked up here in the jail."

"Who were you with?"

"Alfe and Nick Rast."

Truman asks a series of questions about the conversations that they may have had about the killing. Charlie can't remember and claims he forgets easily and then follows by saying that they never talked about it. "If there had been you would have been pretty likely to remember it, wouldn't you?"

"I expect so."

Charlie then told Truman he can't remember how long he was locked up and that he didn't know he was being charged with murder. Truman reminds him that he plead not guilty. Then he tells Truman he just didn't understand the questions and yes he was anxious to get out of jail.

"Now, Charlie, you are pretty anxious to see Alfe get out of here?"

"Yes, I am."

"So much so that you would sacrifice the truth in order to see him cleared?"

"I can't answer that."

Judge Mack states: "You must answer the question."

"I don't know how to answer."

Truman: "I will ask you this; would you tell a lie to help clear him?"

"No, Sir."

Truman returns to his questions about whether the three of them talked about the case. Charlie denies any talk about the shooting.

"Is it not a fact that someone said that he ought to have killed Willie dead so that he couldn't talk about it?"

"No, Sir, I never said anything of the kind."

"Your memory is good as to that?"

"Yes."

Truman: "Did you have any arms that day with you?"

"No, Sir."

Charlie continues to deny that he had his pistol. He then claimed that he gave the pistol to his brother, Harry and that Harry has since traded it to a man that was going to Mexico."

Truman asks Charlie if his father ever talked to them while in jail about their defense. Charlie said he didn't and neither did his mother.

Truman asks: "Did Harry ever come into the jail during any of the time you were incarcerated and say you ought to have killed Willie so he couldn't talk?"

"No, sir he never did."

Truman asks him if he remembers seeing his mother and father come out of the house when they got back to the ranch. Charlie couldn't remember anything other than he went to get two horses, because Alfred wanted to go to Austin.

Truman asks: "You were a witness, Charlie in this case at the last trial?"

"Yes, Sir."

"You know the evidence was taken down in shorthand and written up the same as now?"

"I guess it was."

"Have you ever read that, your testimony?"

"Part of it, I believe." He said he read some and that Dennis didn't read it to him. He then told Truman it was just a matter of curiosity.

Truman asks another question: "Charlie, about how far were your horses from the gap when you stopped them?"

"Maybe eight to ten feet somewhere along there."

When asked he says the boys were standing four or five feet in front of the lead horses. And they had their backs turned and they turned when Charlie said, "Please open the Gap." Charlie said he asked them in a pleasant way.

"You were not accustomed to use the kind of language to them that they used to you?" "You testified that they were quarrelsome and used vile, bad language to you."

"Not that I know of."

"If you had been accustomed to talk that way, you would have known it?"

"Yes, Sir."

"You had a pistol, Charlie, hadn't you, when you came into town?"

"Yes, Sir."

"Was it yours?"

" It was."

"Where did you get it?"

"I had it."

"All the time?"

"Yes, Sir."

Dennis quickly interjects because what Charlie has just admitted would make him a liar.

Dennis states: "Do you mean you had that pistol all the time from the scene of the shooting, until you came to town?"

Charlie answers: "From the time I went to the ranch and got in town."

"You got it at the ranch?"

"Yes, I got it at the ranch, and I had it with me when I came to town."

Dennis asks Charlie why they took the rifle? He said just to shoot any game that they might see alone the road.

Charlie admitted that he normally carried his pistol, but does not admit that he had it at the Gap. You have to wonder why it was important for him to say this? It would have been reasonable for Charlie to use his pistol when Johnny shot first at Alfred.

Judge Mack calls a recess till 10 o'clock Saturday morning. Charlie will again be back on the stand. I'm sure Dennis did not feel good about Friday's testimony from either of the Vaughan brothers.

This trial was a hardship for the people living out of town. No doubt this was the reason why the Judge was having a Saturday session. Dennis would have time to talk to Charlie about the way he was answering the questions.

Jones would continue the cross-examination of Charlie and he would soon find Jones's questions more difficult.

"Mr. Vaughan, I will ask you during the time you were in jail with Alfred Vaughan and Nick Rast, did you have any weapons in your possession?"

"No, Sir."

"At no time during the time you were in jail in the custody of the Sheriff, you had no kind of weapons with you?"

"No."

Is this the trap for Charlie? We know from the Nick's

testimony they were allow to have pocketknives to make quirts to help pass the time. So we can expect Jones to come back to this subject.

"Now, I want you to tell about those shots that Johnny fired again." "How many shots were fired and how he acted when he fired them, and who he fired at, and all about it?"

Charlie has this act well rehearsed and Jones tries to get him to act out the scene. He asks him to demonstrate how fast Johnny shot. Charlie doesn't want to do this. "Did you not demonstrate to the jury in the former trial that they went bang, bang, bang, like that in the quick succession?"

"I don't know."

Judge Mack asks: "Did you testify at the former trial that way?"

"Not that I know of."

Charlie continues by saying he doesn't remember.

"I am not asking if you remember, I will give you another chance that you may have time to recollect if you can." "If you testified at the former trial that the shots were not over a second apart or were as quick as a man could fire then, and it was bang, bang, bang…one two three, if you did so testify at the other trial, was it true or false?"

"I can't answer the question."

Judge Mack tells Charlie that he must answer.

Jones asks: "Did you testify so, is it true or false?"

The Judge then explains to Charlie that he is not saying you did so testify, but only if you did.

Dennis objects and he states that if the witness is to be confronted with testimony he gave at the former trial it is to be read to him so he can state whether it is true or false. The purpose should only be for testing the memory of the witness. The Judge reminds Charlie that he must answer.

"If I did so, I expect it was true."

Judge Mack says: "In justice to the witness, Mr. Jones, you must show whether he did or not."

Jones proceeds to ask Charlie about the shots and he now answers that four or five shots were all fired at once.

Recall, Alfred had reduced Johnny shots to only one.

Jones tries to get him to tell how fast the shots were fired. Charlie final says that it was over in about two or three seconds. As Jones tries to pin Charlie with a fixed time, but Charlie won't pin himself down.

"Now, Charlie, tell the jury why you and your brother and Nick drove away from the place where your brother had shot these two boys down and left them there without attempting to assist them in any manner?"

"We drove on toward home, we thought we would find Mr. Litster at the haystack and inform him, but when we got there he wasn't there."

"Would it not have been easier to have taken the boy home than to have gone to the haystack to tell Mr. Litster?

"I don't know."

Jones asks the question again. This time Charlie says he forgot the question. Jones repeats it.

"We just got on the wagon and drove off, we fully intending to inform him."

"You fully intended to do that?"

"I guess we did."

"How did you feel about it personally?"

"I can't say how I felt."

Jones was zeroing in on Charlie. His lies are become obvious.

"Did you think about it at all?" "Is it not a fact that you did not think about it?"

"Well, I was excited."

"That is not the question."

"Is it not a fact that you did not think anything about it?"

"I can't answer that."

"Then you don't know whether you thought about it at all?"

"I can't tell whether I did or not."

"Now think about it and tell the jury whether you thought anything at all about Willie Litster, after you left him there in the snow?"

"I can't tell whether I did or not."

Charlie goes on to say that they were in a hurry to get back to the ranch. When asked, why the hurry, he again says he can't answer that question.

Jones asks him what place they passed first going back and of course it is the Litster house. When asked how far the house was from the road Charley can't answer. Jones asked him if it was a quarter of a mile and Charlie says he doesn't know how far a quarter of a mile is. Then he said they passed the hay corral that was about seventeen feet away and then they passed the Eason's house. He said she lived right along the road. Jones asked why they didn't stop at the corral. Charlie said, because Mr. Litster wasn't there. He added that they did slow down as the passed the corral.

Jones continued his questions and Charlie went more to his now stock answer. "I can't answer that." You might be right if you assumed Dennis told him to respond accordingly if he doesn't recall exactly how to the question.

About all Charlie has proved was that he does not know why anything was being done, he cannot judge distance, he could not see all of Willie because the willows were in the way from where he sat high on that wagon. Yes, he had his hands full holding the reins of those big horses.

Jones asks Charlie a new series of questions regarding the positioning of the bodies after they were shot. Charlie has Johnny lying on one side of the fence and Willie on the other side. He said he didn't know how he got on the other side of the fence, but that was where he was lying.

Jones asks if the testimony in the former trial was true or not.

"True."

"Every word of it?"

"I suppose it is."

"Now if your testimony given in the former trial differs from this which of the two statements shall we take as being the true one?"

"What I said before is just the same as that."

"Say that we find they differ, which one is correct?"

"I can't answer that."

Judge Mack states: "Yes, you can, it is very simple, and you must."

"Well it is the same."

"It might be different in a sentence or two, that is all I can say."

"Then the statement you made this morning is a correct one isn't it?"

"I can't say whether it is correct or not."

Jones will now read a portion of Charlie's testimony from the first trial. It didn't seem to phase him as he continued by saying he couldn't answer.

Jones continues to read: "Do you know who fire them?" "I know Johnny Litster fired three shots at my brother while he was standing with the rifle in his hand with the muzzle down, and then my brother fired two shots, and there was four or five shots fired in all." "What length of time did it take?" "From the time the shooting commenced until was over, it was in a second or two; you might say it was all at once." "From where you stood, you could not tell whether Willie Litster fired any shots or not?" "He was standing behind a small bunch of willows almost out of my sight, and I could not state what he done because all the time I had to spare I was with my horses." "You stated that Johnny after the firing was over walked ten or twelve feet?" Jones finishes reading the testimony from the first trial.

Jones asks: "I want to repeat to you Charlie, not withstanding that you and your Counsel have both stated that that is a true statement, which of the two statements shall we take, the one you made here a while ago in explanation of the time that elapsed from the first to the last shot, or this statement, which shall we take as the true one?"

"I can't say, it was a long time ago, I couldn't remember how many feet it was."

"Then most likely the statement that you made at the other trial is more correct than the one you made here today, that is because it was nearer the time when it happened."

Dennis adds: "Do you assume there is a difference, Mr. Jones?"

You might be thinking about that too. What is the difference?

Jones continues: "I say not withstanding you made the admission and the witness himself made it, I will read the question." "You stated that Johnny Litster after the firing walked over ten or twelve feet." "Is that right?"

"I don't know how to answer it."

"Then you don't know whether you can make a statement, or a statement you recollect better shortly after a thing happens than you can a long time after if happened?"

"There might be some difference in it." "Then the longer it has been since you witnessed a thing the more unreliable your memory?"

"I don't know."

Jones now brings two pocketknives for Charlie to look at. "I will ask you Charlie, if either one of those knives belong to you?" "Please take them and examine them and tell the jury whether or not either of those knives belong to you?"

It appears that the missing knives that were evidence from the first trial have now been found. Recall the question Jones started with about having a weapon in jail and Charlie said no. "At no time during the time you were in jail in the custody of the Sheriff, you had no kind of weapons with you?" "No." How is Charlie going to handle this?

"I don't know whether they are or not."

"Did you ever see either knife before?"

Dennis knows what was about to happen and states: "I object to the question upon the ground that it is not cross-examination; and on the further ground that it is immaterial and irrelevant and is introduce for the purpose of corroborating a witness for the State; and that it is collateral and therefore is clearly and wholly inadmissible."

Lawyers must be taught this language in law school.

Jones fires back: "I will submit it is offered for the purpose of testing the credibility first, and second as to his memory." "The witness testified some time ago that he had no weapons of any kind in his possession at any time during the time he was in County Jail with Nick Rast and his brother.

Yes, Charlie took the bait, but can he get off the hook?

Objection overruled. Defendant excepts.

"Have you examined the knives?"

"Yes, sir I have."

"Is either one of them your knife?"

"This one I had when I was arrested."

"When did you last see that knife before I showed it to you now?"

"I don't remember."

"You have no idea when you last saw it?"

Jones must have enjoyed trapping Charlie.

"I don't remember."

"Did you have that knife Charlie, in you possession, in your pocket and carry it during all the time you were in the County Jail with Nick Rast."

"No, Sir, I never had a knife in there."

Has Jones been given some bad information? If not Charlie has just totally discredited himself.

"You didn't have this one at all?

"No, Sir."

"It was taken from you when?"

"When I was arrested."

"You are sure of that?"

"Yes, of course."

Jones now offers the knife evidence as the knife belonging to the witness and kept and carried by him in the County Jail, of this County, and marked Plaintiff Exhibit No. 5.

Judge Mack states: "He denies that he carried the knife in the jail."

Is this going just the way Jones planned?

Jones states: "We would like to introduce this testimony that we may introduce this Exhibit."

Judge Mack responds: "Just lay the knives aside for the present and proceed with your examination of the witness."

Jones: "All right." "You can't be mistaken about Willie being on the upper side of the fence?"

"He was on the upper side of the fence."

"On the opposite side of the fence from Johnny?"

"Yes."

"How was he acting when you saw him there and when you left?"

"I can't say."

"You can't say whether he was standing up or lying down."

"No Sir."

"You can't say whether he was hollering, crying or lying perfectly quiet?"

"No, Sir."

Judge Mack asks if he heard him say anything after he was shot and Charley said he didn't.

Jones asks: "Did you see any weapon laying by Willie"

"I never seen nothing."

"Did you see any in his hand or about his hand?"

"I don't remember; as I said I had about all I could handling my horses."

"Was he lying on the snow when you saw him?"

"I don't know that even."

Charlie's selective memory is now worse than ever and he says he cannot remember Nick getting on the wagon either. But he knows that he did not have his pistol. Jones is going to stop at this point, but the jury can bet they will hear more about those pocketknives.

Dennis needs to do a little damage control so he will ask a few questions on re-direct examination. He wanted Charlie to state that during all his travels to the Water Canyon the Gap was always opens. He erred by asking Charlie to explain why he wanted his brother out of this trouble. Charlie couldn't explain, and he only would say that he just want it so. Dennis had him repeat that there were four or five shots fired and that was what he had said in the former trial. Dennis points out to the jury that Charlie was not able to remember exactly so he could not answer some of the questions. And what Charlie had said at the former trial was true. "Your witness."

Charlie is not through as Jones returns with his re-cross examination. As for the pocketknife, you'd be right if you had guessed that we would hear more about them when the Sheriff returns to the stand. But for now Jones asks Charlie how many times he has passed through the Gap and he says he doesn't know but many times. "It was always open?"

"Every time I went through there, the gate was always open?"

"I passed there going to our mine, we were building a house at the mine and hunting cattle and we often went that way." "It was always open."

Perhaps, we are hearing a good reason why Charlie should have kept his mouth shut. Perhaps, this mining claim was really going to be base for a little cattle rustling. As I said earlier, I never found anything about a worthwhile mineral discovery at this site. So I have my doubts about the Vaughan's real plan at the Water Canyon.

Jones: "Did you ever see a gate here in your life time?"

"Only at the upper end."

"I am talking about this particular place, between these two posts."

"No, Sir."

"Never in your life."

"No, Sir."

Jones asks Charlie a few questions about what type of gate was there. He explained that it just was a wire gate that had wires from the two posts. Jones asked if it was like fence panel, Charlie could not answer because he didn't know what a fence panel means. To Charlie it was just a hole in the fence.

Judge Mack was now curious and he asks: "When was the last time you went through there previous to the homicide?"

"We was going up there on Saturday or Sunday morning, I think somewhere along there."

Jones tells him that would have been either the 23rd or the 24th. Charley cannot figure how many days that would have been. It was probably a few days before because there was a snowstorm on the 21st.

A Juror was allowed to ask a question:

"Mr. Vaughan, did you say there was a wire gate there?" "You know what a wire gate is?"

"I do, it is two posts with wire stretched between, and you can throw it back to open."

"You said there was a wire gate there; that you would open or close if you wanted to."

"There was on that morning."

Jones asks: "I say previous to that was there a wire gate?"

"I don't understand."

Judge Mack must be getting a little incensed too as he now asks: "Do you know what a wire gate is?"

"Yes Sir."

"Is it just as the Juror says?"

"Yes Sir, it is just as the Juror says."

"Was there wire there, a wire gate at that place any time previous to the morning of the homicide?"

"Not that I know of there wasn't; it was always open."

The Juror is allowed to asks another question: "I understand you to say that it was always open; that the gate was there, and you can carry the wires around in the fence; was there such a gate there?"

"No, there was not."

The type of gate the Juror may have had in mind is the common ranch gate. This was not the case here at the Gap. You had to splice or tie the wires to close the opening.

Judge Mack asks: You have no recollection of seeing a gate as described by the juror, at that time?"

"No. Sir."

The Juror is not through. "You mean by the wire gate, that you could lay the wire from one post to another and go through?"

"Yes, Sir."

"You could undo it from this post and lay it aside and go through there?"

"Yes, Sir."

Judge Mack now asks the Juror: "Does each wire have to be separated, undone, or unfastened?"

"That is the way I have it."

Jones should have thanked the Juror for finally getting Charlie to describe the gate at the Gap. The juror must have been a rancher and was familiar with that set up. So while Charlie contends he never saw it closed doesn't mean it could not have been closed. The Litster would have had a lot of stray cows if that gate was always open.

Charlie was finally excused

Both Jones and Truman pushed for answers to questions they knew Charlie wasn't going to answer. Charlie certainly did not appear to be very bright, perhaps his dumb act was just his way of not answering those questions.

Dennis has to know that Jones was going to recall the Sheriff about those pocketknives. If Alfred and Charlie did have those knives, then Nick was right about being afraid while he was in jail.

The veracity of Charlie's testimony must have been in question by the jurors. It would be surprising if even one juror would accepted his story about Johnny pulling a pistol and shooting at Alfred. The part where Willie was partially hidden behind the willows was first told at the Coroner's Inquest and again at the Preliminary Examination. He said he thought Willie had a gun but could not see it. During that testimony Charlie said Willie was shooting at Alfred. He could not admit that he had his pistol for an obvious reason.

Recall the question: "Did you ever see a gate here in your life time?" Charlie's answer: "Only at the upper end." He wasn't talking about the Gap when he answered this question. Here, he was referring to the gate that crosses the main road as you leave the ranch traveling east in Boone Canyon. This gate would have been farther up Boone Canyon.

I was at the ranch in May 2001 and I found a gate across the main road below the road to the Water Canyon. When I returned to the ranch in October 2002, I concluded the gate crossing the main road had been moved to a new location below the road to the Water Canyon. As for the fence across the mouth of the Water Canyon, well it does not exist.

Charlie's statements as well as Alfred's did indicate that there were other roads existed 109 years ago in the vicinity of the Boone Creek Ranch house. It seems that there was a road that forked from the main road below the old ranch house and that was a road to Silver Creek.

11

OTHERS

Can This Testimony Help?

Dennis was glad to call his next witness? Charlie did not come across as a creditable witness. Harry Vaughan, the younger brother of Alfred will take the stand. Harry was 20 years old. Dennis may have had a few second thoughts regarding his other witnesses and certainly about Frank Vaughan. He knew Frank would have to explain his reported comment about why they left Willie alive to testify and the same for Mrs. Vaughan. She would have to face cross examination regarding what she said about telling her boys to lie. Harry could refute what Jimmy said about Alfred when Willie was retrieving the heifer from the Vaughan's pasture.

Dennis asks: "Did you see the deceased, Willie Litster enter your pasture on the Reese River in 1893?"

"Yes, Sir."

"You may state what transpired relative to a cow going into the field."

Recall, this was about ten days before the shooting on December 28, 1893. Willie and Jimmy went in search of the heifer that came up missing. Harry said the Litster boys were herding the calf on the road by his parents ranch. He said the calf jumped through the fence and into the pasture. He said the Litster's opened a gate and went into the field and they left the gate open. Alfe and Harry went to see what they were doing and why they left the gate open. Harry said: "Alfe told Jimmy he wished they would ask before going into the field and that they should have shut the gate."

"When Willie rode back Jimmy told him what Alfe said and Willie called Alfe a son of a bitch."

Harry said the Litster brother then went out of the field and we found the cow in the field and took it to them.

Dennis asks: "Was anything said between the defendant and Willie?"

"Yes, Willie said to Alfe that he would fix him."

"How long was this before the homicide?"

"About twelve or fifteen days?"

"I don't remember just how long for sure."

Using Harry's approximate timing that would be on about December 16th. Jimmy's estimate was the 18th.

Harry said Alfe was riding the Chestnut sorrel he had just saddled and there was a riata (lariat; a lasso) on the horn. He said Alfred did not have a quirt. He also stated that Alfred did not try to lasso Willie.

Dennis asks: "How long have you known the Litster boys?"

"Every since I have been big enough to remember."

Without being asked, Harry added: "The last three year every time Willie would see us he would call us damned sons of bitches and swear at us."

Jones started the cross-examination by asking Harry if he understands the charge that has been brought against his brother. "Do you know what the penalty is for murder?"

"Yes, Sir."

"What is it?"

"Hanging."

If people today had a clear understand of what the penalty was for a crime, there would be less crime.

Jones reminds Harry that he has testified before. He asks Harry a series of question about how they got the cow out of the field. Harry said he was on foot until they went for the cow. Then he said he rode a horse bare back and the calf was found near the railroad tracks not far from Willie and Jimmy.

Jones asks: "What is the difference in the size, if you can say between Alfred and Willie?"

"I don't know, but Alfred is bigger".

Jones states Alfred age was twenty-one and Willie was

sixteen years and four months. Harry said Willie may have been a little taller than Alfred, but Jimmy was smaller.

Jones asks: "You are anxious to see him get out of this case?"

"Yes, Sir."

"Would you stretch the truth?"

"I wouldn't tell anything unreasonable." "Mr. Dennis didn't tell me to tell anything but the truth."

Harry continues to say that he would just tell the truth as Jones continued the pressure.

Jones asks: "In other words you would let him be convicted before you would tell a lie?" "Do you mean to convey the idea before this jury that Willie Litster was quarrelsome and abusive when your brother would meet him, and this was for about year three years before Willie was killed?"

"Yes Sir."

Harry admits he had been a good friend with Willie at one time and that they went to school together. He said he didn't know how the hard feelings started. When asked about visiting Alfred in jail, Harry said just a few times because he was very busy and didn't have time to come to Austin. He admitted reading over his prior testimony and because he said he forgot some things. He claimed he had never talked about his testimony with his brothers.

Re-direct by Dennis: "Harry you stated to Mr. Jones that you would do almost anything in reason to get your brother out of this trouble?"

"Yes, Sir."

"Why do you wish to see him out of this trouble?"

"I think he is innocent and what he did was in self-defense."

"What makes you think he is innocent?"

"The Litster's are always quarreling and wanting to fight."

Dennis asks several questions to support the idea of self-defense. Again Harry said every time Willie saw them he would curse at them.

Dennis asks: "Did Alfred always go armed?"

"No Sir, not very often."

Harry said his first visit to see Alfred and Charlie was

about six week after the shooting when

Dennis asks: "Did you ever tell your brother that he ought to have killed Willie outright?"

"No, Sir."

"Did you ever make threats toward Nick Rast?"

"No, Sir."

Dennis concludes by asking Harry several questions so that Harry could say he never said anything or heard anything about killing Willie outright would have been better.

Judge Mack calls for the noon recess until two o'clock that Saturday afternoon.

Harry had been on the stand all morning. Since he was not at the Gap on the day of the shooting there really wasn't much he could add, except to show that Willie and Alfred didn't like each other and his story surely conflicts with Jimmy's version of the cow in the pasture event. He made Willie out to be very quarrelsome. Harry did loose credibility when he denied every discussing his testimony with anyone. This would be humanly impossible and nothing would have been wrong by just saying that he had and that he was telling the truth. Also, Harry said he was not at the Vaughan corral when the wagon came home. He arrived shortly after they came back. You may recall Nick said Harry also said they should not have left Willie alive to testify.

After the Lunch Recess, Dennis called Indian Munsey to the stand. Munsey did not testify at the first trial.

Judge Mack wants to know if this Indian knows the nature of an oath?

Munsey said: "It means to tell the truth."

"What will happen if you don't tell the truth?"

"The law will punish me for it."

Munsey said he was 26 years old and he was living in Austin. There was a sizable Indian population living below Austin in the Reese River Valley. When asked where he worked during the summer of 1893, he said the he work for Duffy's in June and then for the Litster's till sometime in August.

Dennis asks: "Did you know Johnny and Willie Litster?"

"Yes, very well."

He went on to say that he worked with the brothers and that Johnny, Willie, Jimmy and he slept in the granary.

"You may state whether Johnny or Willie Litster had any pistols or fire arms at that time?"

Jones responds: "We object on the grounds that it is immaterial to this case to show whether or not Johnny or Willie carried pistols unless it can be shown that they had pistols when they were shot, but that they might have had them in June or August, can make no difference in this case." "As suggested by my associate, Mr. Truman, it would make no difference if they had pistols when killed unless they tried to use them."

Dennis states: "Mr. Litster testified that his boy had no fire arms, and I offer this testimony for the purpose of showing that they had constantly had fire arms and I want to show by this witness that they had fire arms and kept them in the room where they slept under their pillow and took them out into the field with them." "I intend to show that subsequent to this time, but during the time the witness was in the employ of Mr. Litster this defendant went down the road and passed through the field and that Johnny Litster said there goes that son of a gun that leaves gates open and if I saw him do it I'd kill him."

Judge Mack wants to know if this witness testified about this at the former trial?

"No, Sir, this witness was found after the former trial."

"I shall allow this question, but again I want to ask a question first."

Judge Mack states: "You took an oath here a moment ago?"

"Yes, Sir."

"Do you believe in God?"

"Yes, Sir"

"What is He?"

"He is the good man up there." (As he point to the sky.)

Objection overruled.

Jones asks: "Will you permit me to question this witness as to his capability?"

"You may do so."

"Munsey, suppose you tell a lie, how would you be punished?"

"Sent to prison, I guess."

"Who told you that?"

"I read a little, not much, some boys told me."

What boys told you?

"Steiner boys, Litster boys and Vaughan boys, I am acquainted with them all."

"They all told you, that you would be send to prison if you told a lie?"

"Yes, Sir."

"What were they talking about when they told you that?"

"I couldn't remember."

"You think you are a pretty smart Indian, don't you?"

"No, I don't think so."

"You are not very smart?"

"No."

"Where were you raised?"

"In Austin, here."

Jones continues to ask simple questions. Jones wants to know who ask him about this case. He said Justice Weller did and he told him what he knew. Jones asks if he talked to anyone else about the case. He said only Charley Steiner and Justice Weller. He later admits that he talked to Mr. Dennis. Jones tells Munsey he didn't tell the truth when he said only Steiner and Justice Weller. Munsey said he forgets.

Jones asks: "Did you talk to the old man, Mr. Vaughan about it too?"

"Yes."

"You talked to Charley Vaughan about it?"

"No, just Frank Vaughan."

"You talked to Mrs. Vaughan?"

"Yes."

Jones tells him that he has talked to five people about the case.

Jones adds: "Say Munsey, don't you know all Indians lie when they want to?"

"Yes."

It sounds like Jones was being unfair to Munsey, but Jones is familiar with his background. Munsey liked being a witness for the U. S. Marshal. Munsey could speak fairly good English and he liked to make money or profit from other Indians when they came to court. Jones knew Munsey had quit a job three days ago just to be here for this trial. Jones tries to get him to say who is paying or feeding him while he isn't working. Munsey steadfastly maintained no one promised anything to him. Jones either gives up or feels he had duly impressed the jury.

Dennis resumes his questions about the revelation of pistols the Litster boys had when Munsey worked at the ranch.

"You may state whether the Litster boys had any guns in the room with them and where they kept them and if they took them out?"

"They had pistol under their pillow, I see them take them out of there."

"What kind of pistol?"

"Bull Dog, they call them."

"Now state what you heard Johnny say about the Alfred when he rode down through the field when you was with Johnny?"

Truman objects.

Dennis says that he wants to show malice and ill feelings towards the defendant.

Judge Mack allows the question.

"Alfred rode past them and Johnny said, I bet five dollars he will leave the gate open when he goes through and if I was down there I would take a shot at him."

If you thought Jones was rough before, well now he is going to apply some heavy pressure to Munsey. He asks a series of question to show that Munsey was far from an educated man.

"Everything you know a white man told you, make you 'sabe'?"

"Yes, Sir."

"Everything you know white man makes you 'sabe'?"

"No."

I'm not familiar with the word "sabe"; by the way it is used here it must mean, " savvy" for these Lander County Indians.

Munsey admits to Jones he had been taught by Charley to say the year was 93 when he saw the Litster's pistols. But he really didn't know the year that was two years ago because he said he didn't know figures.

"You might be mistaken?"

"Yes, I guess."

At this point Indian Munsey was excused.

There is no question about the fact that Indians were not citizen and they were not treated with much respect. I noticed that Jones did not once address Munsey as Mr. Munsey. People today are very judgmental about those that came before us. We've all heard some self-righteous person say how wrong or terrible those people were for the way they treated Indians. These people do not understand history and what it took to develop a civilized nation. When you study history you should set aside our modern politically correct thinking.

Dennis calls his fifth witness, Mr. Vaughan to the stand. This is Alfred's 71 year old father. He was born in Clinton County, New York. He came to Lander County in the fall of 1867 and has resided here ever since. His ranch is about 25 miles north of Austin along the Reese River at the mouth of Boone Canyon. He said he and his wife with their four sons, Frank, Charles, Alfred and Harry were living there.

Dennis asks: "You may state, if you know, how many guns, pistols or fire arms you sons Charles and Alfred took with them when they started to go to the mine?"

"Nothing but a rifle"

Judge Mack asks: "A rifle, so far as you know?"

"Yes, I saw the rifle."

"Are you sure they didn't take a pistol with them?"

"There was no pistol taken from the ranch." "The pistols were at the ranch."

This is important. Dennis needs to discredit Nick Rast's testimony and to avoid the obvious questions about Charlie not defending Alfred when Johnny shot at least three times at his brother. If this were true then you would think that Charlie would have used his pistol. He did not.

Jones began the cross-examination: "You don't know whether Charlie had a pistol on that day or not?"

"He didn't have to my knowledge."

"You don't know to your own personal knowledge?"

"I didn't see that he did and I didn't see that he didn't have."

Jones asked him how many guns they have at the ranch and Lee Vaughan tells that they have two shotguns, one rifle and three pistols. He admits as he is being questioned about Charley having a pistol that he just did not see it on his person, however he could have had it under his coat.

Jones asks: "Is it not a fact that he could have one in his pocket and you not know it?"

"He might have one, but I didn't see it."

"Did you examine their room for one?"

"Mrs. Vaughan went to make up the bed and she found Alfred's pistol under the pillow"

"I walked out into the dinning room and she was making the bed and took it out of the bed and laid it on the stand."

"Did she show it to you?"

"She didn't show it to me, she just laid it on the stand."

Mr. Vaughan said nothing about the location of the other two pistols. The fact that Alfred's pistol is mentioned and Charlie's pistol is not sure sounds like he could have had it, just like Nick Rast said.

Dennis states:

Your Honor the Defense Rests.

Jones will now call his rebuttal witnesses. The first is James Ryan. Mr. Ryan was called to testify about the creditability of the local Indians living in Lander Counties.

"Do you know the reputation of the Indian Munsey, in this community for truth and veracity?"

"Well, I don't know much about that Indian." "I can't say that I have heard them say anything good or bad about him."

"Then you do not know anything about his reputation for truth and veracity?"

"No."

Jones calls Sheriff Easton. "I will ask you to look at these two knives; do you know this one?"

"Yes, Sir."

"Where did you get that knife?"

"I got it from Charley Vaughan."

"Now going back to the time when he was in jail, in your custody as Sheriff of this County, I will ask you to tell us whether or not you took knifes away from Charley, and if so, about when?"

Dennis sees the trap Jones has set for Charlie and he states: "I would like to interpose an objection to this; that the proof of that knife is a collateral matter in this proceeding, and that the matter was brought out upon cross-examination."

"The objection is overruled." "It is proper cross-examination."

Dennis responds: "I will offer authorities on that."

"I will listen to your authorities, but I think most of it is admissible that tends to impeach a witness on the stand."

Dennis reads from a book entitled: "Rice on Evidence."

Afterwards, Judge Mack responds: "Rast made three different statements that he was in fear. Charles Vaughan when he was on the stand denied he had a knife." "I think it is material and relevant to show whether he made that statement, and whether Charles Vaughan told the truth." "The objection is overruled."

"Defendant excepts."

Jones: "We reserved the right to put the knives in the original evidence because we could not find the knives."

"Mr. Miller had the knives locked up and we now can offer them."

Jones asks: "Mr. Easton have you see these knives before?"

"Yes, I believe that is the knife."

"About what time before the former trial did you take the knife from Charles Vaughan?"

Dennis objects to the leading question and he was overruled.

Jones asks: "Take that knife and look at it." "Did you at the former trial identify two knives, and how many days before the trial that you took them?"

"I don't know if that was asked at the former trial."

"If you testified at the former trial that it was three days, is that correct?"

"Yes."

"Then if you took the knife away from him about three days before the former trial, he either procured it while he was in jail or had it in his pocket in jail."

"Yes, he had it in his pocket all the time."

"So then, during all the time you had him in your custody, in jail, which covered several weeks up to and within a few days before the former trial of this case, he had that knife in his pocket?"

"Yes, Sir."

Jones then asks the Sheriff to read this examination beginning at page 607, book 3 of the former trial in this case, beginning at line 5 and ending on line 23.

"Examine that please and see if it is correct."

Sheriff Easton said it says here that it was two day instead of three.

Jones now shows the Sheriff the other knife and ask who does this knife belongs to?

"It was Alfred's knife and I took it at the same time as I took Charlie's knife."

Jones again asks: When did you take the knives?

Dennis now states that it was two days before the former trial. Jones then offers the knives that Alfred and Charley had as evidence.

Dennis asks: "What is the purpose?"

Bad question Mr. Dennis.

"For the purpose of showing that Alfred and Charley had dangerous weapons upon their person at the time Nick Rast was incarcerated with them, in county jail."

Dennis states: "Defendant objects on the grounds that it is irrelevant, immaterial, and only tends to corroborate one of the State's witnesses in rebuttal, and that being rebuttal that the State seeks to corroborate one of its own witnesses, rather than to show any material facts in the case."

Judge Mack states: "It is rather introduced to impeach Charley Vaughan."

"Counsel doesn't say so."

"Objection overruled." "Defendant excepts."

This went very bad for Dennis. Jones had set the trap as I suggested for Charlie at the beginning of his testimony. And now Charlie's lie has been confirmed.

Can Dennis salvage some of the damage?

He asks: "Mr. Easton did you ever know of the defendant or Charlie Vaughan trying to use those knives?"

Jones objects and Dennis withdraws the question.

Dennis asks: "Mr. Easton, how long did you have Charlie and Nicolas Rast under your charge, in jail?"

"From the time they were arrested until they were released during the first trial".

Dennis asks the Sheriff about the work details that they would be asked to perform and were they under close supervision? He also wants to know about the times that Nick was out of the cell alone and away from Alfred and Charlie.

Dennis asks: "Did Nick ever talk to you about his condition in the jail with the Vaughan's? "Did he ever tell you that he was afraid of the defendant and his brother?"

"No."

"Did he ever intimate that they had made threats against him?"

"No."

"Or that they attempted to use any knives or anything of that kind?"

"No, Sir."

"Did he ever make any such intimation?"

"No, Sir."

"He had plenty of opportunities to do it without their hearing him?"

"Yes."

He reminds the Sheriff that he took him alone to the Coroner's Jury and the Grand Jury. The Sheriff said he complained only once but he was not separated from them.

Jones asks:: "Wasn't it something like this Mr. Easton, that a complaint reached your ears that he wanted to be separated from them, and you heard that?"

"Yes."

"And you asked if that was so, and he said he did want to be separated?"

The Sheriff said he brought Nick into his office and Nick told him that he was afraid and wanted to be separated. The Sheriff said he told him that he could only put him in the Assessor's Office. We have to assume that all the jail facilities were full. The Sheriff said Nick got angry and he said he didn't want to be put in that office so the matter was dropped. The Sheriff said he didn't remember all the details and couldn't recall what he had said during the first trial.

Judge Mack asks: "Did you know those boys had those knives on their person all the time?"

"Yes, they were making bridles and quirts in there and used the knives."

"You were frequently away from town for days at a time during the time you had them in there?"

"Yes, I think so."

The Sheriff explains that they were only together during the day, but at nights they were in separate cells.

Jones concludes by asking one more time: "And you knew that the Vaughan boys had those knives all the time?"

"Yes, Sir." The Sheriff was then excused.

I mentioned earlier, they were together during the day in the outer cell room where they made quirts and ate meals. It was difficult for Nick's brother to talk without the Vaughan's overhearing.

Jones calls George W. Steiner to testify regarding Indian Munsey's character. George said that his father had employed him several time to work in the hay field with other Indian's. He said he was a good worker but the other Indian's did not like him because he was a liar.

Jones asks: "You say that his reputation among the Indians for truth and veracity is bad?"

"Yes, Sir.

"They say he won't tell the truth?"

"Yes; they don't like him and they won't have anything to do with him." " "Yes, they say he is no good and they won't have anything to do with him at all."

Another rebuttal witness is called, Frank J. Whaley, however he was absent. Counsel for the plaintiff asks to have his testimony from the former trial as to the identity of the bunch of willows reads to the jury. Dennis consents to the reading subject to the same objections.

"State what you did on the tenth of April 1894, in relation to the examining the place where you went out on the Litster Ranch?"

MacMillan responds: "I would like to have it understood that this all goes under the objections that we have made." MacMillan has been very quiet while assisting Dennis during this second trial.

"It will be so understood."

"Please point out the place that you examined and what you did?" "Mr. Litster, Mr. Dunsdon, Mr. Egan and myself went to the place where the boys were killed" "Do you know the boys were killed there?

"No, Sir; they told me that was the place."

MacMillan states: "We object upon the grounds that is hearsay."

Judge Mack responds: "Of course the hearsay testimony will be ruled out."

"Describe the place you went to and examined."

"We crossed a bridge and passed through a bunch of willows; there was willows on both sides of the road, and we came to a Gap in a fence."

"On the left hand side, seven feet back from the gate post we took up a bunch of willows, and fifteen feet and six inches from the same point we took up another bunch and brought them town."

"From the same gate post we measured down forty- five feet in the road, and opposite that point on the left hand side from the bridge towards the gate, we found where there had been a willow cut, and we found a willow that had been cut, and we took the willow and place it on the stump to see if it would fit, and we found it corresponded exactly with the stub, and so also brought that willow into town, and we have them all here."

Jones said: "We will strike out the testimony relating to the willow cut from the stump."

"I am willing to have all stricken out except as to the bunch of willows which has been identified as the bunch of willows behind which Charlie Vaughan says Willie stood."

The Judge then instructed the jury to disregard the testimony except for the purpose of identifying the bunch of willow Charlie said Willie was behind.

"Do you have the willows here?"

"Yes, Sir."

"Will you produce them?"

"Yes, Sir."

MacMillan objects and says the jury should have been taken to the ranch to judge for themselves.

The objection was overruled.

The willows were then brought into the courtroom.

"You may arrange those willows from the post about as you found them." "We will say that the bridge is back here and that it is the post of the gap; this willow was seven feet from the post on the right side." "How far was it from the road?"

"I should judge about three feet from the track and seven feet from the post." "Now, as near as I can get at it, that is about the position these willows occupied with reference to the Gap and the road." "From the gate post on the Litster house side (the right side), seven feet from the post and three feet from the track was this first bunch of willows?"

"Yes, Sir."

"You dug up those willows from those places?"

"Yes, Sir."

"After you dug up those two bunches of willows what remained for seventeen feet back from the post?"

"Nothing; no willows at all."

"No sprigs of willows or anything?"

"There were a few little sprigs left, about as large as a foot."

"Were they scattered around?"

"There might be two or three little sprigs in some places only one and they were very small."

The reason for this rebuttal is to refute Charlie and his tale about Willie standing behind the distance willows. Charlie had to place Willie away from the gate to fit the story about Alfred first shooting Johnny.

James Egan was the next to be called and as mentioned by the prior witness he was on the same trip when the willows were cut.

Jones asks: "Tell the jury where you got that bunch of willows as near as you can without looking at the map?"

"I got them about seventy feet above the bridge and about seven feet from the Gap near the fence on the Litster Ranch."

Egan places the location of the willows with respect to the gatepost as he said: "Seven feet from this post and about one yard from in from the road track is where this bunch of willows stood."

Judge Mack asks if it was on the upper side, as you would go up Water Canyon.

"Yes, Sir."

"On the right side or the left?"

"On the right side as you go up the canyon."

Going up the canyon toward the Gap?"

"Yes, Sir."

Egan describes two clumps of willows; the first clump was seven feet back from the post and the second clump was another eight feet behind the first. Both were at the edge of the road.

Dennis begins his cross-examination of Egan by asking what month did he go there and he reply that is was during the first trial.

Jones under re-direct returns with a series of question about Egan's ability to recognize which of these two clumps was the first from the post.

"Save except for the grass that was there, there was nothing back of those willows for a considerably distance?"

"Nothing."

Egan said he judges that it was clear for 50 yards before some more willows were growing along with a few small trees that were about the same size as the willows near the Gap.

Dennis asks: "When you speak of open space back, do you

mean as to the lower side of the road, to the right going up?"

"Yes, Sir."

"You don't mean to be understood as going back down the road?"

"No."

Jones asks: "How was it looking back from this post and still on toward the bridge?"

"Clear ground."

This line of questioning is hard to follow without a map. The significance of these willows seems to be that they are obviously not where Charlie placed them with reference to Willie.

George Watt, Jr. follows as the next rebuttal witness. He was still living at Silver Creek with his parents. He was being called to testify about Willie's reputation.

"Was it good or bad?"

"Good."

And he said the same about Johnny. He knew Willie all his life and went to the same school, but he said didn't play with him because of the age difference. He had ridden horseback many times with Willie.

Jones asks: "Did you ever, at any time, during the life of either Johnny or Willie Litster, know them or either of them to carry a deadly weapon of any kind?"

"No Sir, I did not, I never saw a weapon on either of them."

"If they had carried one you would have been mostly likely, that is, if they had carried it to considerable extent you would have most likely seen it from your intimate association with them?" "Yes, Sir."

"Do you know the reputation of Charlie Vaughan in the community in which he has lived, for truth and veracity?"

"I do, and it is very bad."

Dennis then asks the obvious: "George what relation are you to John and Willie?"

"I am a cousin."

"Their father and your mother are brother and sister?"

"Yes, Sir."

Miss Stina Wagner was the schoolteacher at Silver Creek

and she was the next to take the stand. The Litster boys had been her pupils.

"Do you know the reputation of Willie Litster in the community in which he lived for peace and quiet?" "Yes, sir, it was decidedly good for both boys." And she said the same when Jones asks his question about honesty. When the teacher was asked about Charlie, she said she could help knowing about his bad reputation. Dennis knows better and he doesn't ask any question of Miss Wagner.

Another rebuttal witness, John Mullen was called to the stand. He has worked for the Litster Ranch for several years and was well acquainted with the boys. Jones asks: "In your work there on the ranch were you constantly associated with those boys?" "Yes, Sir."

Jones asks: "I will ask you Mr. Mullen, if you know the reputation of Willie Litster during his life time, or during the time you knew him for peace and quiet?"

"What I knew was good."

Mullen said he had work with Johnny and Willie for four and a half months in 1893.

Dennis declines to cross-examine.

Jones calls Thomas Dunsdon. Tom was William Litster's closest friend. Tom's sons John and Nate were the young men that rode to Austin to get a doctor for Willie. Tom said that he has known the boys all of their life.

"I will ask you if you knew the reputation of Willie Litster in the community in which he lived for truth and veracity?"

"I never knew the boy to tell anything…"

Jones has to clarify his question.

"The question is do you know it; answer yes or no?"

"Yes, Sir."

"Was it good or bad?" "It was good."

How was it as to Johnny? "It was good."

Dennis objects, "I object your Honor. On the ground that the reputation of Johnny Litster is not material, it has not be attack in the least and cannot be pertinent to the case. Also, we are not attacking Willie's reputation for truth and veracity."

"Objection overruled."

"I will ask you Mr. Dunsdon, as a neighbor of the Litster family for a number of years before the two boy died, and being frequently in the company of the boys, did you ever at any time see either of those two boys with a deadly weapon of any kind?"

"No, Sir."

Dennis again declines to cross-examine.

Johnny and Willie did not carry firearms. We have six more rebuttal witnesses to be called to the stand. It certainly appears that neither Willie nor Johnny were wild or disrespectful teenagers.

George Watt, Sr. was the next to be called. Mr. Watt was the Willie's Uncle George. As I have said he was patriarch of these Scottish people living in the Silver Creek and Boone Canyon area. He will testify to the good character of both Willie and Johnny.

Jones asked: "Do you know the reputation of Charlie Vaughan in the community in which he lived for truth and veracity?"

"I never had much dealing with Mr. Vaughan."

"I mean Charlie, his son."

"I never had no transaction with him."

Next Mr. Jones calls Mary Christian. "I will ask you if you at any time you witnessed Alfred Vaughan draw a pistol on a person?

Dennis knew Jones had called her for that purpose and he quickly said:

"Your Honor please, I object to that upon the ground that it will be a collateral matter, one brought out on cross-examination."

Judge Mack now asks: "State your position Mr. Jones." "We offer it for the purpose of impeaching Alfred Vaughan; he said on examination the other day that he had never drawn a pistol on any one in the Litster house."

Dennis states: "You fixed the time indefinitely."

Jones responds: "I don't know the time myself, I asked him if he didn't at any time and he said he did not.and I asked him if he didn't draw a pistol on Mr. Starratt when they were preparing to eat a meal while Mrs. Christian and the children were at the table, and he said, No."

Objection sustained. State excepts.

I wonder why the Judge did not allow this question. This was obviously the incident that started the feud between the Litster and the Vaughan's. It would have been interesting to hear what Mary could have said about that occasion.

Jones now recalls John Mullen to the stand. He forgot to ask John if he ever saw the boys with a deadly weapon and he said he did not. He also asked: "During all the time you were associated with them on the ranch working with them and sleeping in the same room where they slept, and possibly in the same bed, you never knew them to have a deadly weapon of any kind, did you?" "No, Sir."

The next rebuttal witness was Dougal McGregor: He testified that he had known the boys ever since they moved to Boone Canyon, about thirteen years before the shooting. He was well acquainted with the boys. He was not related to the boys and he said he often slept at their ranch. He too stated that they were peaceable boys. And said they had a good reputation.

Dennis declines to cross-examination.

Jones now calls Matt Edwards and asks: "Are you acquainted with Charlie Vaughan, Mr. Edwards?"

"Yes, Sir."

"I will ask you if you came over from Kennedy to Austin during last summer at any time?"

"I came over in the fall, September, I think."

"I will ask you whether or not he had anything to say to you, when you were traveling with Charlie as to a pistol?" "I am not asking you what he said, but I am asking you whether he said anything to you about a pistol?"

"Yes, Sir."

"Tell the Jury what he said about the pistol."

Dennis states: "I object to the question upon the ground that it is irrelevant and immaterial and the proper foundation has not been laid for its introduction, it is not shown that it had any connection, remote or otherwise, to the purposes of this case."

Jones responds: "We offer it for the purpose of impeaching Charlie Vaughan." "I asked Charlie if he ever showed the pistol to any one and I named Matt Edwards and asked him if he told him that this is the pistol I had when my brother killed the Litster boys and he denied it."

Judge Mack: "That would be admissible on another ground." "That would tend beyond the question to show that he did have a pistol on the day of the shooting." "You may proceed if that is the object."

"That is the object, to show that Charlie had a pistol on that day, and tends to corroborate the evidence of Nick Rast that he and his brother may have changed weapons."

Mr. Edwards explains: "Charlie had a pistol with him and I was examining the pistol." "I asked Charlie if this is the pistol he had when they had trouble with Litster boys?"

"And he said, yes."

Dennis asks: "He didn't refer to any particular time?"

"No, Sir."

"He did say that he had it with him when he was up the canyon on the day of the homicide?"

"No, I asked him if it was the pistol he had when they had trouble with the Litster boys and he said yes."

Jones asks: "He didn't say he didn't have it with him?"

"No, Sir."

Looks like Charlie's big mouth did too much talking as he is caught in another lie.

Judge Mack now tells Dennis that he is going to permit him to ask two questions that he had not permit before. You may ask whether that Gap was open before or whether he passed through there?"

Dennis states: "Your Honor, I think I proved the same thing by another witness and I would not desire to put the defendant on now, at least not until the State closes."

"You asked the question in direct examination and he has the right of rebuttal; if you put him on; you must put him on before they rest; they might want to controvert the fact."

Jones calls James Litster to the stand. "Jimmy, I will ask you if you know if you know how long the Gap or fence where your brothers were killed, had been up before the day they were killed?"

"About a month, I guess or a month and a half."

"How do you know it had been up for that length of time?"

"We put it there."

"For what purpose?"

"To keep the cattle in the field."

Describe to the jury why you know it, why you put it up; give your explanation?" "I don't understand it?" "You say it was to keep the cattle in; in where?"

"In he field."

"In which field?"

"In the big pasture."

"In the field where you raised hay, barley and such like?"

"Yes Sir."

"Was this fence where your brothers were killed; a cross fence in the middle of you ranch?" "Yes, Sir."

Jones asks: "Do I understand you to mean after the harvest was over and the hay stacked and the grain harvested, that you put up that fence gate when ever it was down, to keep the cattle on the pasture side, is that the idea?" "Yes, Sir."

"And you used the back pasture, the one on the other side of the fence for your horses, did you?"

"Yes, Sir."

"And you have farmed and harvested on the ranch and watched for these things, and know that that fence had been up where your brothers were killed, for all the time you stated?"

"Yes, Sir."

"Anyway until shortly after harvest time of that year?"

Yes, Sir.

This is interesting as Jones leads the witness to testify, without objections. Jimmy describes the purpose of the interior fence that had the Gap. He said the fence was used to separate the horses from the cattle. The current USGS Quad Map shows another fence line outside the boundary of the ranch. The interior fence with the Gap is not shown on the Quad map.

The last rebuttal witness to be called was Doctor Huntsman. He was asked if he examined the wounds in

Johnny's body.

Dennis objects and states that it is irrelevant.

Judge Mack allows the question.

Dennis reminds the Judge that his testimony is under objection as the doctor proceeds to describe to the jury nature of the bullet wound. Dennis continues to object; by saying a proper foundation has not been laid. Judge Mack says he see no defect in the foundation for the introduction and the testimony.

Doctor Huntsman states: "We will suppose this is the outside of the body, and I will begin the description from the positive point of the body and take the right nipple as such point." "I would locate the nipple about here." (The doctor makes a mark on a body chart). "I found a gunshot wound in the right breast two inches above the nipple and two inches to the left of the nipple, and it ranged inward and downward to a point on the left side in a line with the axilla." (the armpit) "The axilla is a point under the arm near the ninth or tenth rib." "You cannot always be positive as to the rib." "You understand from the description I am giving of this wound that the ball must have entered in this direction and passed inward and downward to a point in a medial line between the axilla and the center of the body on the left side at the point of exit."

Jones asks: "Take myself and show the jury where the ball entered the body and came out."

You would be right if you recognize that his testimony is contrary to Johnny being uphill from Alfred when he was shot and that was why Dennis objected.

MacMillan begins the cross-examination of the doctor. He is going to challenge his qualifications, as he did during the first trial. "You are a graduate of a medical college?" "Also a graduate in surgery?" "Is there anything said about surgery in your diploma?" "Your diploma is on record?"

"The answers to these questions are yes"

He states has practice medicine going on twenty years. He admits that he has not done a great amount of surgery. MacMillan asks him if he has ever since college dissected a human body. "Not what we would term dissection, but I have held many post mortem examinations, and have opened bodies."

MacMillan continues to demean the doctor's experience. "Your surgery practice has been confined to you country practice here?"

"I don't know how to answer that." "If you will ask my any question in surgery, I will endeavor to answer you." "I have practiced here twenty odd years, and have had more or less surgery practice, and have had experience with gunshot wounds and amputations and general surgery practice."

Dennis adds a statement to the cross-examination: "I wish to have it admitted that he did not probe the wound."

"It is so admitted?"

"Yes."

Jones states:

"If your Honor please, we now Rest."

Dennis states:

"The Defendant Rests, your Honor."

Judge Mack now tells both attorneys that must submit immediately all instructions they wish to have given to the jury. Judge Mack then declared a recess until 8 o'clock that evening. Perhaps you were wondering what they did in Austin on Saturday night. Again, I feel this is because the Court was aware of hardship attending this trial had caused. Some have had to travel more than a days ride to be here. All that remains for the trial is the closing arguments by the attorney's and Judge Mack instructions to the jury before they would wait for the jury's verdict. The courtroom was full that evening, many citizen wanted to hear the closing arguments. Jones was ready. He obviously was a very good orator judging from the newspaper reports. He spoke for two hours before the Judge interrupted by calling a recess till Monday morning.

Twenty days have now lapse since the court had convened to select a jury. It was 9 a.m. Monday, June 10, 1895 and Judge Mack orders Jones to resume his closing argument. He picked up from the place where he stopped on Saturday night and continued his summation until eleven o'clock that morning. The words for the closing arguments were not recorded. So no one will ever be able to study the style or what was actually said by these attorneys. Dennis took the floor and spoke till noon at which time the Judge called a recess. Dennis resumed his summation at 1:30 p.m. He turned the floor back to the State and Truman used two hours and ten minutes during which Judge Mack overruled several times Dennis's objection to Truman reading the State's desired instructions that were given to the Judge.

Judge Mack had done his homework on Sunday too and he was prepared to read his instruction to the jury. He had received two instructions Jones wanted and no less than thirty by Dennis. The Judge's instructions were long and read like a textbook. It took the Judge forty minutes to read these instructions to the jury and it was 5:15 p.m. when the Judge excused the jurors for their deliberation.

The instructions were well prepared. The Judge knew that the first trial decision was overturned because the instructions were found to be in error. This would not be the case this time. The following instructions are an exact copy from the trial transcript by Judge Mack. They are vastly superior to instruction given at the first trial.

Judge Mack's Instructions:

Gentlemen of the Jury: The Defendant, Alfred Vaughan, is accused of the murder of William Litster, Jr.

The Defendant, Alfred Vaughan, admits that he shot the deceased with a gun. The deceased died a few hours after the wound was inflected.

It is for you to determine from the evidence whether by shooting the deceased, the defendant, Alfred Vaughan, is guilty of any offense.

In the commission of every crime, or public offense, there must be a union, or joint operation of the act and intention. The intention is manifest by the circumstances connected with the perpetration of the offense and the sound mind and discretion of the accused.

It devolves upon the prosecution to establish by competent proof beyond a reasonable doubt all the material facts constituting the crime of which the defendant is accused. The burden of proof is on the prosecution. All the presumptions of law independent of evidence are in favor of innocence, and every person is presumed to be innocent until he is proven guilty.

Murder is the unlawful killing of a human being with malice aforethought, either expressed or implied, and may be affected by any of the various means by which death may be occasioned.

Express malice is that deliberate intention to take away the life of a fellow creature, which is manifested by external circumstances capable of proof.

Malice shall be implied when no considerable provocation appears or where the circumstances of killing show an abandoned and malignant heart.

Malice aforethought, as used in the definition of murder, means the intentional doing of a wrongful act without legal cause or excuse. It is not confined to homicide committed in cold blood with settled design and premeditation but extends to all cases of homicide, however sudden the occasion, when the act is done under such cruel circumstances, as are the ordinary symptoms of a wicked, depraved and malignant spirit. It includes, anger, hatred and revenge, but also every other unlawful and unjustifiable motive. It does not imply deliberation or the lapse of considerable time between the malicious intent to take the life and the actual execution of that intent, but rather denotes purpose and design in contradistinction to accident and mischance.

Murder in the first degree consists of a willful, deliberate, premeditated killing. The intention to kill must exist. The intention may be ascertained from the acts and circumstances such as the use of a deadly weapon calculated to produce death, the manner of its use and attendant circumstances characterizing the act.

The intention to kill need not have existed for any given length of time before the act of killing. They may be as instantaneous as successive thoughts of the mind. It is sufficient, the killing being unjustified or unexcused by the circumstances, if it were formed even at the moment of inflicting the mortal wound. When the killing is ascertained to be intentional, the next inquiry will be whether it was willful, deliberate and premeditated. Every intentional act is necessarily a willful one; the one implies the other.

Deliberation and premeditation signify that the act was done with reflection and was conceived beforehand. If a person has time to deliberate or reflect for a moment as well as an hour or day before committing the act, it is sufficient to constitute deliberation.

If you believe, from the testimony, that at Lander County, Nevada, on or about the 28th day of December, 1893, the defendant with his malice aforethought, either expressed or implied, with premeditation and deliberation, willfully and unlawfully shot William Litster, Jr. with a gun with the intent to kill him and did so kill him, you should convict the defendant of murder in the first degree.

Murder in the second degree is the unlawful killing of a human being with malice either expressed or implied, but without the admixture of deliberation.

If you believe for the evidence, that at Lander County, Nevada, on or about the 28th day of December, 1893 the defendant with malice aforethought either expressed or implied, but without the mixture of deliberation or premeditation, willfully and unlawfully shot William Litster, Jr. with a gun with the intent to kill him and did so kill him, you should convict the defendant of murder in the second degree.

Manslaughter is the unlawful killing of a human being without malice aforethought expressed or implied and without any mixture of deliberation. It must be voluntary upon the sudden heat of passion caused by a provocation apparently sufficient to make the passion irresistible.

In cases of voluntary manslaughter there must be a serious and highly provoking injury inflicted upon the person killing sufficient to excite an irresistible passion in a is reasonable person or an attempt by the person killed to commit a serious personal injury on the person killing. The killing must be the result of that sudden, violent impulse of passion supposed to be irresistible. For if there should appear to have been an interval between the assault or provocation given and the killing, sufficient for the voice of reason and humanity to be heard, the killing shall be attributed to deliberate revenge, and punished as murder

If you believe, from the testimony, that at Lander County Nevada, about the 28th day of December, 1893, the defendant unlawfully without malice either expressed or implied, and without, any mixture of deliberation, upon a sudden heat of passion caused by a provocation apparently sufficient to make the passion irresistible, killed the deceased, William Litster Jr., you should convict defendant of manslaughter

When it legally appears that a defendant has committed a public offense, and there is a reasonable doubt in which of two or more degrees he is guilty, he can be convicted of the lowest of such degrees only.

The killing being proved, the burden of proving circumstances of mitigation to justify or excuse the homicide will devolve on the accused unless the proof on the part of tile prosecution sufficiently manifests that the crime committed only amounts to manslaughter, or that the act was justified or excused in committing the homicide.

Justifiable homicide is the killing link of a human being in necessary self-defense, or in the defense of habitation, etc.

If a person kill another in self-defense, it must, appear that the danger was apparently so urgent and pressing, that in order to save his own life or to prevent his receiving great bodily harm the killing of the other was absolutely necessary; and it must appear also that the person killed was the assailant, or that the slayer had really and in good faith endeavored to decline any further struggle, before the mortal wound was given.

One who is without fault himself, when attacked by another, may kill his assailant if the circumstances be such as to furnish reasonable ground for apprehending a design to take away his life or to do him great bodily harm, and there was also reasonable ground for believing the danger imminent, and that such design will be accomplished, although it may afterwards turn out that the appearances were false and there was in fact no such design, nor any danger that it would be accomplished.

The killing of one who is an assailant is excusable if there be reasonable apprehension of loss of life or of receiving great bodily harm: and if the danger is so imminent at the time or moment of assault, as to present no alternative of escaping consequences but by resistance, thought it afterwards appear that there was no actual danger.

If you believe, from the evidence, and from all the acts and circumstances in the case, that the defendant, had reasonable ground for apprehending a design to do him great bodily harm by the deceased, and that there was reasonable ground for believing the danger imminent that such design would be accomplished, and he acted upon such appearances and killed William Litster Jr. to save his own life or to save himself from receiving great bodily harm, the killing would be in self-defense.

If the homicide appears, from the evidence, to have been justified or excusable, the defendant should be acquitted.

You are made the sole judges of the testimony and the weight to be given to the same, and you must there from determine all questions of fact involved. It is your province to award such credence and. weight to the statements of the various witnesses, as in your judgment they may be entitled to.

In determining the credibility of the witnesses examined it is your right to take into consideration their interest or feeling in the result of the subject matter, their appearance or deportment while being examined, the possibility or probability of the truth of their statements as compared with other testimony given, or facts established; their opportunity for observation, or knowledge of the matters to which they testify; their friendly or unfriendly feelings toward either side; how far they may have been contradicted, etc. It is a general principle of law, that if a witness has willfully sworn falsely with respect to a material ma matter, you are at liberty to disregard the testimony of such witness.

I state this rule of law that you may be assisted in

reconciling any differences or conflict in the evidence, and arrive at the truth and clearly determine all questions of fact.

The defendant has offered himself as a witness in his own behalf in this trial, and in considering the weight and effect to be given to his evidence, and in addition to noticing his manner and the probability of his statements taken in connection with the evidence in the case, you should consider his relation and situation under which he gives his testimony the consequences relating to him from the result of this trial, and all the inducements and temptations which would ordinarily influence a person in his situation. You should carefully determine the amount of credibility to which his evidence is entitled. If convincing and carrying with it a belief in. its truth, act upon it; if not, you have a right to reject it.

If, upon a review of the testimony, there is a reasonable doubt remaining as to the guilt of the defendant, he is entitled to the benefit of such a doubt by an acquittal.

What is meant by reasonable doubt is one based on reason. It is not mere possible doubt, but is such a doubt as would govern or control a person in the more weighty affairs of life. If the minds of the jurors, after an entire comparison and consideration of all the evidence, are in such a condition that they can salt they feel an abiding conviction of the truth of the charge, there is not a reasonable doubt. Doubt to be reasonable, must be actual and. substantial, not mere possibility or speculation.

You are instructed that you are to judge of the weight and credit to be given to dying declarations, as in the cafe of other testimony by all of the circumstances. And in dealing, with this kind of evidence, you should consider the following matters: First: The trustworthiness of the relater, or those who repeat the same. Second, the capacity of the declarant at the time of making the same to remember accurate the past, and third, his disposition truly to tell what he remembers.

After thus carefully considering such declarations as above mentioned, and weighing them in connection with the other evidence, and circumstances in tree case, the law is that on account of the improbability that one who realizes he is about to die, will willfully and intentionally tell an untruth, such declarations are then admitted as though there had been an opportunity to cross examine the declarant, and when so admitted in evidence you are the sole judges of their weight and credibility, keeping in mind the liability of a misunderstanding of those who relate the declarations and. the liability to perversion of the same, and that it is proper that it should be carefully considered as above mentioned, and then after subjecting such declarations to those considerations, you believe the same to be true, you should act on the same, but if you do not believe the same to be true, you will have the right to reject the same just as you would in the case of any witness who comes upon the stand and testified before you in person.

The defendant has interposed the additional plea of former jeopardy; and you are instructed that there is no evidence to sustain a verdict in favor of defendant, upon his plea of former jeopardy.

You entered upon your duties as jurors in this case by taking a solemn oath that you would a true verdict render, according to the evidence. That duty and obligation are performed only when a verdict is rendered which is in accordance with the evidence. While you have a right, to use your knowledge and experience as men, in arriving at a decision as to weight and credibility of witnesses, yet your finding and decision must rest alone upon the evidence admitted in this trial. You cannot act upon the opinions and statements of counsel as to the truth of any evidence given, or as to the guilt or innocence of the defendant. The argument of counsel often is a. most valuable assistance in enabling jurors to sift, consider and collect the testimony to the end that you may determine its re liability or we fight, and f or this purpose a you should give the arguments of the respective attorneys fair and candid consideration.

You must consider all the evidence in connection with the law as given you, and there from reach a decision. In doing so you must consider, without fear, favor or affection, bias or prejudice or sympathy; compare, weigh and consider all the facts and circumstances shown by the evidence, with the sole, fixed and steadfast purpose of doing, equal and exact justice between the State of Nevada and the defendant at the bar.

In criminal cases it requires the unanimous concurrence of the jury to render a verdict.

Signed: C. E. Mack, District Judge, June 10, 1895

What were the two instructions that Jones wanted?

No. 1: You are instructed that the words or actions or gestures, however grievous or provoking unaccompanied by an assault will not justify or excuse murder.

No. 2: If you believe, from the evidence in this case, that at the times Nicholas Rast testified before the coroner's jury, at the preliminary examination of the a defendant, Charles Vaughan and said Nicholas Rast, and before the Grand Jury that indicted the defendant, Charles Vaughan and. Nicholas Rast for the killing of William Litster Jr., that said Rast was in fear of his life from said defendant and his relatives if he did not testify on said occasions as he had been directed to testify by the defendant or his relatives; and that during the time he so testified and before he so testified, he was confined in the County Jail of this County with said defendant and said Charles Vaughan, and by reason of the threats of the defendant or his relatives made to him, said Rast was put in fear of his life, and bar reason thereof said Rast gave a statement of the facts of the killing of William Litster Jr., tending to exculpate the defendant thereby, but has testified on this trial to a different state of facts, yet you are still the sole judges of the weight and credibility of said Rast's testimony; and if you believe the testimony as given by him here on this trial is true, you have the right to rely upon it to the a extent you believe it to be true.

I would say the Judge covered the first, but not the second. Recall Truman in his summation did covered the second requested instruction. So the jury heard and also heard Dennis objections to what Truman was saying.

Dennis requested instruction are numerous, and they seem to follow a pattern, but here are a few of his requested instructions for the jury:

No. 1: The jury are instructed, that justifiable homicide is the killing of a human being in self defense or in defense of habitation, property or person, against one who manifestly intends or endeavors by violence or surprise to commit a felony on earlier.

No. 2: A bare fear of any of these offenses is not sufficient to justify the killing. It must appear that the circumstances were, sufficient to excite the fear of a reasonable man and that the party killing acted under the influence of those fears.

No. 3: The jury are instructed, as a matter of law, that, if a person believes, and has reasonable cause to believe that another has sought him out for the purpose of killing him or of doing him great bodily harm and that he is prepared therefore with deadly weapons and the latter makes demonstrations manifesting an intention to commence an attack, then the person so threatened is not, required to retreat, but he has a right to stand, and defend himself and. pursue his adversary until he has secured himself from danger; and if, in so doing, it is necessary, or upon reasonable grounds it appears to be necessary, to kill his antagonist, the killing is excusable upon the grounds of self defense.

All of Dennis's requested instructions followed the theme of these first three with different wording.

No. 17: If the jury believe from the evidence that the witness Nick Rast, has willfully sworn falsely at any time in this case, whether before the a coroner's jury, committing magistrate, the Grand. Jury, or on the present trial, as to any matter or thing material to the issues in the case, then the jury are at liberty to disregard his entire testimony.

No. 18: The jury are instructed: that the policy of our law deems it better that many guilty persons should escape rather than one innocent, person should be convicted and punished; so that, unless you can say, after a careful consideration of all the evidence in the case, that every material allegation of the indictment is proved beyond all reasonable doubt, you should find the defendant not guilty.

These requested instructions, especially by the defense are naturally self-serving. The remaining points that Dennis want covered had to do with a lesser sentence than murder in the first degree. The Judge did an outstanding job to clarify this for the jury. But as you will soon see the jury didn't have a problem with all these legal ramifications.

The Jury reached their verdict within ninety minutes, barely enough time for the Judge to have his evening meal. I'm assuming that the jurors did discuss the case perhaps as their evening meal was served. It simply boils down to Nick Rast testimony. He might lie to save himself, but it would be hard not to believe his testimony. And his fear of the Vaughan's is easy to understand.

Court was reconvened at seven o'clock. The verdict had been passed to Judge Mack. After reading it he handed it back to the Clerk to be read aloud by Mr. Christian: "State of Nevada vs. Alfred Vaughan: We the jury in the above entitled cause do find the defendant guilty of murder in the first degree. Dated June 10, 1895, John B. Paul, Forman."

Alfred sat still in his chair and seemed to strain as he held back any show of emotion. Charlie and Harry were the only members of his family present as the verdict was read. They left the courtroom immediately. Do you suppose that there could have been any other verdict? As stated throughout this book Alfred and Charlie both lied. How can you sympathize with them?

Nick Rast testimony must have been overpowering in the minds of the jurors. The lack of agreement between Charlie and Alfred's testimony certainly made the verdict easier. The physical evidence did not support either of their stories. How could the jurors have not been impressed by the testimony about Willie's dying declaration? Yes, that young boy knew he was dying because of Alfred's painful gut shot wound. He was bleeding internally for nearly six-hour before death came.

Dennis did ask that the jury be polled and each answers that it was his verdict. Dennis made a motion for a new trial and that was overruled. Judge Mack then granted Dennis forty days to file his motion for a new trial. That would be July 20, 1895. Dennis waives the time of the sentence:

Judge Mack thanked the jury for there service before

dismissing them.

As soon as the last member was out of the room the Judge asked: "Will the Defendant please rise." "Alfred, I want you to know that Mr. Dennis has fought very heroically for you and he has done all in his power for your defense."

"Alfred Vaughan do you have any cause or reason to show why sentence should not now be passed upon you?"

Alfred said: "I am not guilty and I did not have a fair trial and could not as the people are prejudiced against me and I could not get justice."

Judge Mack states: "It is ordered and decreed that you Alfred Vaughan, be hanged by the neck until you are dead." "The day upon which you are to be executed will be set by the Court at some future time." "May our Father and dear Savior have mercy on your soul."

"Sheriff Easton, please remove your prisoner to his jail cell."

This was just down the stairs, only a few feet from the courtroom. This cell has been Alfred's home for the last 18 months.

After the sentence was given Dennis thanked the Court and the attorneys for the State for the kindness and many courtesies shown him during the trial. Messrs Jones and Truman both shook Dennis hand, but their words were restrained and they knew that this matter had not come to an end.

The observers during this trial noted that Alfred seemed withdrawn. At times paid little attention to the trial. Hope that came following the State's Supreme Court was now gone. Dennis went to Alfred's cell before leaving the Courthouse. He told him his plan for an appeal and he want Alfred to know that it was not over. He was a young man and he was suffering the loss of freedom of being a buckaroo out on the ranch.

Alfred was never the same after this second trial. Hope seemed to be gone.

12

APPEAL NO. 2

Is Justice Really Blind?

After Messrs Dennis and MacMillan had time to reflect on the trial. They filed the Notice of Appeal, August 5, 1895. There was never any doubt that they would appeal to the State's Supreme Court. They used all the time granted by Judge Mack to make the following appeal:

To William Christian, Clerk of said Court, and W. D. Jones District Attorney of Lander County.

You will please notice that the defendant, Alfred Vaughan hereby appeals to the Supreme Court of the State of Nevada, from the judgment and orders of the Court herein and every part thereof.

From its order overruling defendants motion for a new trial and from its order overruling his motion for as arrest of judgment. Said Defendant appeals, from each and every part of the judgment orders and rulings herein.

Both attorneys signed the Notice of Appeal as well as W. W. Christian.

Alfred's attitude changed following the second trial. He knew the chance of ever getting out jail was fading and he may have been thinking that he would most likely swing from a rope. If any hope was left for him it may have been to try a jailbreak. Yes, a plot was discovered for an attempted escape. Nearly two month has passed from his last day in court. Alfred just sat solemnly in his jail cell. He was extremely bored and the heat had been miserable during these summer months. Mr. Dennis made it a point to see him at least once a week. His mother and father had only been to visit once since the verdict on June 10, 1895.

However, his favorite brother Charlie came every Sunday. Charlie could remember those Saturday nights when Alfred and he came to town and went to the saloons. Now Charlie would just sit at the jail and visit with his brother. Charlie's didn't carry a pistol anymore either. Although, it would be a safe bet claiming he still had that pistol. Do you really think he gave it to Harry and he traded it to a guy going to Mexico?

After the Sheriff return his pistol last year following the first trial he started to carry it again until he was on the short end of some smart remarks. "Hey, Charlie, you're not going to shoot me with that pistol, are you, or is it just Alfe that does the shooting?" He decided to leave the pistol home. When he testified about the gun being traded probably caught him by surprise. I really don't think he was prepared for the question and the trade story just popped out. I really doubt the story about the trade.

When Charlie came to see Alfred, he found his brother's mood changed. Charlie sensed Alfred's state of depression and he felt sorry for his brother. He was trying to encourage Alfe. Charlie probably had a conversation one day that was something like the following.

"Alfe, if you can get out of here would you go to Mexico with me?"

"What in the hell you talk-un-bout Charlie?" "I'm behind these bars and I'm gonna hang."

"All you have to do is remove one of them bars at that back window."

"How in hell am I gonna do that?"

"With what I brung ya."

Charlie was a regular visitor and Sheriff Easton's jail wasn't a place of high security. Charlie had a hacksaw blade and file tucked in his right boot.

"With what I have in my boot, Alfe." "The deputy, he ain't watchin and ya gotta hide it quick when I give it to you."

The following story was taken from the Reese River Reveille, dated September 14, 1895.

The Sheriff's office has discovery and obtained additional implements used by the murderer, Alfred Vaughan, in his attempted escape from the Austin jail two weeks ago. It will be remembered that two saw blades and two pieces of lead were recovered from his cell, as reported heretofore. The Sheriff and Deputy Smith moved Vaughan from his old cell to another at that time, and they then believed that all the tools had not been recovered. A few days ago a closer search was made of the old cell, and in the hollow of the iron bedstead they found a new nine-inch saw blade and a six-inch saw file.

Someone from the outside furnished him the new saw blade and file. Vaughan is kept closely watched in his cell and continues sullen and defiant and is liable to do violence if he gets any kind of a chance. He is closely watched and is considered more dangerous now than at any time since he was locked up on the 28th of December 1893. His case is now in the Supreme Court and his keepers are anxious for a decision that they may be relieved of their desperate charge as soon as possible.

It sounds like more than just one trip was used to bring these items to Alfred. The Sheriff had to have known where these items came from. Why didn't the Sheriff pursue this with an investigation? I think he exercised some judgment. The Vaughan family was hurting with one son about to die if the high court denies the appeal. Alfred did not escape and no damage came from this attempt to escape. The Sheriff may have felt a little responsible for not having better security.

Just imagine how big this story would have been if Alfred had escaped. Could he and Charlie have gotten very far before being recaptured? We'll never know. Austin is a long way from Mexico. They no doubt would have headed south towards Ione. Could they have lived off the land without resorting to robbery? When you are out in the middle of Nevada you really get a feeling of the meaning of big country. Hiding from the law would have meant that they would have to avoid most of the small western towns showing wanted posters. It would have been an adventure for sure just trying to make that ride to

Mexico. Anyhow, it is safe to say the Sheriff Easton had a long talk with Charlie about this. I'm sure he impressed Charlie that he was very lucky that his plan failed, because that would have meant prison time for Charlie.

Alfred was not allowed in the outer cell room without being watched by the deputy. Charlie's next visit to see Alfred had Deputy Smith do everything but a strip search. Charlie too must wait for the Supreme Court's ruling.

As it was done for the first appeal, the following text in this chapter was taken from the book at the Supreme Court Library: Report of Cases, January Term, 1896, No. 1447. I've added both rulings by the high court to show how this legally entangled case evolved. Again, several legal references were deleted from the copied text. The Supreme Court focused on the dismissed juror. This is not a surprise. Throughout this book no effort has been made to conceal the fact that high court ruled both times for a new trial. The first trail concluded in April 1894 and the second trial in June 1895.

As you followed the second trial, you probably guessed that Judge Mack made a critical error when he removed the Juror A. A. Flint. I was surprised at the time it took to select the twelfth juror. The remaining eleven were qualified and to remove them all from Lander County's limited jury pool seemed a waste of time. Now day's jury alternates would have filled Flint's place. Judge Mack should have allowed Dennis the opportunity to reexamine the eleven jurors, but if the Judge did, then he would have had to grant Dennis the additional peremptory challenges. Flint's removal added several days and cost for this trial.

If you can look past the legal references in the arguments by the appellant and the respondent to the written opinions by the Justice's you will see that these Justice's were very concerned about the rule of law. They were not saying one way or the other about the guilty or innocence of Alfred Vaughan. Their duty was to determine whether or not he had a fair trial as prescribe by law. It was clear that Judge Mack rightfully found A. A. Flint to be an unfit juror. You'll see that the Justices felt the manner in which the removal occurred could not help but to produce prejudice for the eleven remaining jurors.

State of Nevada Respondent, v. Alfred Vaughan, Appellant

Criminal Law - Juror Excused After Admission of Evidence - After a Jury has been sworn, and evidence admitted in a capital case, the court may, in its discretion, excuse a juror against defendant's objection, on proof that he is disqualified, the fact of his disqualification having come to the knowledge of the prosecution during the trial.

Idem-Jury-Juror Discharged After Evidence Introduced - Error to Retain Balance without Allowing Defendant to Examine - When in a capital case a juror, because disqualified, is excused by the court against defendant's objection, after evidence has been admitted, it is error to accept the other jurors without first discharging them and giving the defendant the privilege asked for of re-examining them as to their then state of mind before being re-sworn to try the case with the new juror.

APPEAL from the District Court of the State of Nevada, Lander County; Charles E. Mack, District Judge:

Alfred Vaughan was convicted of murder, and appeals. Reversed.

The facts sufficiently appear in the opinion.

Argument for Appellant: James F. Dennis and J. H. MacMillan, for Appellant:

I. The statement of the district attorney, in reference to the juror Flint, was contrary to law, as there was an assumption of the guilt of the prisoner while stating a public offense against a juror duly qualified and sworn to try the issues between the state and prisoner, which should not have been permitted at that time in the trial of so important a case.

II. No challenge of the juror was made, and there was nothing before the court; no issue of law or fact when witnesses were put upon the stand, and the testimony of the witnesses was prejudicial and irrelevant to the issues between the state and appellant.

III. Could the court look into the juror's mind and say that it had not changed since the declaration sworn to by witnesses Kassell and Moss? Was there anything to justify the court, in the presence of a jury it had then decided to retain for the future trial of the accused, in saying that the juror had perjured himself in order, if possible, to acquit the defendant?

IV. Take the entire proceedings against the juror Flint, his examination, the statement of counsel in reference to him, the testimony of the witnesses against him, and it fails to show any necessity for his discharge from the jury. He, speaks of having had a different state of mind when on his voir dire, but says he had got rid of it. The testimony and proceedings as to his past declaration do not prove or tend to prove that his mind was not, at that time, equally balanced between the state and defendant. There was not that imperative necessity for his discharge that the law contemplates in such cases.

V. The discharge of juror Flint, against the objection of the defendant, terminated the legal existence of the jury sworn to try the issues between the state and accused, a jury that had heard the opening statement of counsel for the state and the testimony of all the witnesses against the prisoner.

VI. What becomes of the constitutional guarantee of the right of trial by jury? Can it be for a moment supposed that eleven men, who heard all the state's testimony, were indifferent or impartial at the beginning of the trial which resulted in the conviction of appellant, or will it be assumed that the instruction of the trial judge purged and rendered the minds of the eleven jurors a blank as to what had transpired on the previous presentation of the state's case. If these eleven jurors attended to their duty on the first presentation of the case, they could not have been impartial at the beginning of the trial.

VII. The trial court refused to allow defendant to examine the eleven old jurors as to their state of mind after the discharge of the juror Flint, or the right to exercise any peremptory challenges to the reconstructed jury or the new part of it.

VIII. The only safe way to prevent an injustice and to secure an impartial jury, such as is guaranteed to us by the constitution of our country, is to discharge the entire twelve men, under the circumstances of this case, and empanel a new jury, allowing to the defendant his statutory right of challenge, peremptory and for cause.

Argument for Respondent: Robert M. Beatty, Attorney General, W. D. Jones, District Attorney, and D. S. Truman, for Respondent:

I. The court was fully authorized to draw another juror to take Flint's place. (Gen. State. 4262; State v. Pritchard, 16 Nev. 101; State v. Vaughan, 22 Nev. 285.)

II. The eleven jurors had been passed by both the state and the defendant, and had been sworn. No attempt was made to show that any one of them had been disqualified; the fact that Flint had been shown then to be disqualified raised no presumption that any of the other eleven jurors were disqualified. No one had a right to examine any of those eleven jurors at that stage of the trial without showing good cause, and no cause being shown, it was not error to refuse the request.

III. The eleven jurors had been sworn, and this court long ago, decided in State v. Anderson, 4 Nev. 65, that: "The allowance of a peremptory challenge to a juror who has been accepted and sworn is not a matter of right and a refusal on the part of the court to allow it is not error."

IV. No cause was shown, or attempted to be shown, why any one or all of the eleven jurors should be peremptorily challenged, and unless good cause be shown, according to the statute it is not error to refuse it

V. It was unavoidable for the proof as to Flint's disqualification to be made to' the court in Flint's presence and in the presence of the other eleven jurors. At that time Flint was as much a part of the jury as any of the other eleven, and there was no jury without him and each and all of the other eleven jurors; they could not legally separate (Sec. 340, Crim. Prac. Act), until the "urgent necessity" arose, was proven, and found by the court.

BY THE COURT: JUSTICE, BELKNAP, J.

Respondent was convicted of murder of the first degree. At the trial, after a jury had been empanelled and sworn and the witnesses examined, the district attorney called the attention of the court to the fact that one of the jurors was disqualified and asked leave to present testimony in support of the charge. Upon permission given, witnesses were examined whose testimony tended to show that A. A. Flint, the juror against whom the investigation was directed, had said several months prior that the defendant was guilty; that he had conscientious scruples against capital punishment and would never vote for a conviction of murder of the first degree were he one of the jury. The court, excused him, another was substituted, the witnesses were re-examined, a verdict of murder of the first degree returned, and judgment entered thereon. Various exceptions were taken in behalf of the appellant to the rulings of the court in this particular.

First, as to the discharge of juror Flint:

Lord Coke lays down the rule that a jury sworn and charged in case of life or member cannot be discharged by the court or any other, but they ought to give a verdict. Following Coke, Hawkins, in his Pleas of the Crown says: that no juror can be challenged either by the king or prisoner without consent after he hath been sworn, unless it be for some cause which happened since he was sworn.

In Wharton's Case, one of the jurors that had been accepted and sworn was challenged for a cause when he was sworn, but unknown at the time to the Queen's Counsel. The challenge was denied.

But in the case of the two Kinlocks the power of the court to discharge jurors underwent careful examination, and it was decided that the general rule as laid down by Lord Coke had no authority to warrant it and could not be universally binding. In that case it was determined that the court had power to withdraw a juror at the request of the prisoners for the purpose of imparting to them a defense which they could not otherwise have taken.

The decisions in this country sustain the position that a juror may be excused when his detention upon the jury would defeat the ends of public justice.

In U. S. v. Morris, it was decided that after witnesses had been examined the prosecuting officer could, in the discretion of the court, examine witnesses upon the question of the bias of a juror.

In discussing the subject, after stating the common -law rule, Judge Curtis said: But it by no means follows that it is not in. the power of the court, at the suggestion of one of the parties, or upon its own motion, to interpose and withdraw from the panel a juror utterly unfit, in the apprehension of every honest man, to remain there. Suppose a prisoner on trial for his life should inform the court that a juror had been bribed to convict him-that the fact was unknown to him when the juror was sworn and that he had just obtained plenary evidence of it, which he was ready to lay before the court, is the court compelled to go on with the trial? Suppose the judge, during the trial, obtains, by accident, personal knowledge that one of the jurors is determined to acquit or convict without any regard to the law or the evidence, is he bound to hold his peace? In my judgment such a doctrine would be as wide of the common law as it would be of common sense and common honesty. The truth is that this rule, like a great many other rules, is for the orderly conduct of business. There must be some prescribed order for the parties to make their challenges, as well as to do almost everything else in the course of a trial. As matter of right, neither party can deviate from this order. And it is the duty of the court to enforce these rules, which are for the general good, even if they occasion inconvenience and loss in particular cases. But there goes along with all of them the great principle that, being, designated to promote the ends of justice, they shall not be used utterly to subvert and defeat it; being intended as a fence against disorder, they shall not be turned into a snare; they do not tie the hands of the court, so that when, in the sound discretion of the court, the public justice plainly requires its interposition, it may not interpose; and it would be as inconsistent with authority as with the great interests of the community to hold the court restrained.

A very eminent English judge has treated this rule concerning challenges just as I believe it should be treated. Chief Justice Abbot says: I have no doubt that if, from inadvertence, or any other cause, the prisoner or his counsel should have omitted to make the challenge at the proper moment, the strictness of the rule which confines him to make the challenge before the officer begins to administer the oath, would not be insisted on by the attorney-general, or, if insisted on by him, would not be allowed by the court. That is, like other rules of procedure in trials, it is in the power of the court to dispense with it when justice requires.

In U. S. v. Coolidge, Lee an indispensable witness to the government, refused to be sworn. Judge Story said: The question is simply this. A party is on trial before a jury, and a circumstance occurs, which will occasion a total failure of justice if the trial proceeds; have the court, in such an emergency, power to withdraw a juror? It has been stated from the bar that, in capital cases, the court has not this power; but in a case in Foster's Crown Law, and in several other cases, it has been held that they have. In misdemeanors, there is certainly a larger discretion, and until the cases just mentioned, capital trials were generally supposed to be accepted. It is now held; that the discretion exists in all cases, but is to be exercised only in very extraordinary and striking circumstances. Were it otherwise the most unreasonable consequences would follow. Suppose, that in the course of the trial the accused should be reduced to such a situation as to be totally incapable of vindicating himself-shall the trial proceed, and he be condemned? Suppose a juryman taken suddenly ill, and incapable of attending to the cause; shall the prisoner be acquitted? Suppose that this were a capital case, and that, in the course of the investigation, it had clearly appeared, that on Lee's testimony depended a conviction or an acquittal; would it be reasonable that the cause should proceed? Lee may, perhaps, during the term, be willing to testify. Under these circumstances, I am of opinion that the government is not bound to proceed, but that the case be suspended until the close of the term, that we may see whether the witness will not consent to an examination.

In State v. Allen, upon the trial, after witnesses had been examined, the court heard evidence touching the disqualification of a juror, who had before being sworn expressed the opinion that defendant was guilty. The disqualification was proven, the juror excused, and the jury discharged.

In State v. Bell, it was held that the duty of courts to guard the administration of justice against fraudulent practices was an exception to the rule that a jury sworn in a capital case cannot be discharged without the prisoner's consent until they have given a verdict. So when a juror had fraudulently procured himself to be selected for the purpose of acquitting the prisoner the juror was properly excused.

In People v. Ollcott, Justice Kent stated his conclusions as follows: I conclude, then, that as no general rule or decision that I have met with exists to the contrary in a case of misdemeanor, and as the rule, even in capital cases, abounds with exceptions, and is even questioned, if not denied, by the most respectable authority, that nine of the judges of England, it must from the reason and necessity of the thing belong to the court, on trials for misdemeanors, to discharge the jury whenever the circumstances of the case render such interference essential to the furtherance of justice. It is not for, me here to say whether the same power exists in the same degree (for to a certain degree it must inevitably exist) on trials for capital crimes, because such a case is not the one before the court; and I choose to confine my opinion strictly to the facts before me. With respect to misdemeanors, we may, with perfect safety and propriety, adopt the language of Sir M. Foster, which he, however, applies even to capital crimes, that it is impossible to fix upon any single rule which can be made to govern the infinite variety of cases that may come under the general question touching the power of the court to discharge juries sworn and charged in criminal cases. If the court is satisfied that the jury has made long and unavailing efforts to agree that they are so far exhausted as to be incapable of further discussion and deliberation, this becomes a case of necessity, and requires interference. All the authorities admit that when any juror becomes mentally disabled by sickness or intoxication, it is proper to discharge the jury, and whether the mental inability be produced by sickness, fatigue or incurable prejudice, the application of the principle must be the same. So it is admitted to be proper to discharge the jury when there is good reason to conclude the witnesses are kept away, or the jury tampered with, by means of the parties. Every question of this kind must rest with the court, under all the particular or peculiar circumstances of the case. There is no alternative; either the court must determine when it is requisite to discharge, or the rule must be inflexible that, after the jury are once sworn and charged, no other jury can, in any event, be sworn and charged in the same cause. The moment cases of necessity are admitted to form exceptions, that moment a door is opened to the discretion of the court to judge of that necessity, and to determine what combination of circumstances will create one.

In the inquiry touching the disqualification of the juror three witnesses were examined. Two of them, Kessell and Moss, swore, among other things, that Flint had said some months previous, in their presence, that he was opposed to capital punishment; and Dunham, the third witness, said that he had often heard Flint say that the defendant was guilty.

The court excuse the juror for two reasons: First, that he had formed and expressed an opinion that the defendant was guilty, and, second, that he was opposed to capital punishment.

For either of these reasons the juror may have been excused. The subject was within the sound discretion of the district court, and we cannot interfere with its exercise except in cases of its abuse.

Second-Whether it was correct to empanel another juror in the place of Flint, or to discharge the jury:

In People v. Damon, after a juror had been sworn in chief and taken his seat, it was discovered that he was incompetent to serve. He was excused and another juror substituted. In the opinion of the court, Chief Justice Savage said: "I apprehend no authority can be necessary to sustain the proposition that the court may and should in its discretion set aside all the persons who are incompetent jurors at any time before evidence is given." The inference to be drawn from this language is that, after evidence is given, no substitution should be made. At the common law, if, during the trial, an incompetent juror was discovered, the whole jury was discharged.

The rule has not been changed by the legislation of this state. It is as binding upon courts as statutes adopted by the legislature.

Adhering to it, I conclude that a mistrial took place when Flint was excused. The substitution of another juror in his stead was contrary to all precedent. The case illustrates the evil of the course pursued. The jury had been occupied for upwards of three days in hearing the testimony on the part of the prosecution when Flint was excused. Under these circumstances it is not presumable that the jury was indifferent.

Defendant was entitled to a legal and impartial jury, and all the substantial requirements of law should have been observed in its empanelment.

The judgment should be reversed and a new trial granted, and it is so ordered.

JUSTICE, BONNIFIELD, J., Concurring:

In view of the character of the charges preferred against juror Flint, and of the examination and proceedings had thereon and in connection therewith, all being made and had in the presence of the jury and against the objection of the defendant, the vital question, in my opinion, in this case is: Was the court vested with legal discretion to retain the eleven jurors on the panel against defendant's objection? Or, in other words, was not a fatal error committed in empanelling juror Savage in place of juror Flint, who had been discharged, instead of discharging the eleven jurors and empanelling a new jury?

In the first place, it was not necessary to have preferred said charges, or to have held said examination or proceedings in the presence of said eleven jurors, but I am of the opinion that it was improper to have done so. It appears to me that it would have been proper and the right course to have pursued for the court to have put said jurors in charge of the sheriff to be retired from the court room, and the juror Flint retained during the examination of the charges made against him; then it might have reasonably been said that the remaining jurors could not have been prejudiced by anything which had occurred in the matter of the impeachment of Flint; that, therefore, no error was committed to defendant's prejudice thereby, and, upon the authority of the Pritchard case, the action of the court might be sustained, if, at all.

It is provided by statute, and binding on the courts as any other statutory provision, that: The common law of England, so far as it is not repugnant to, or in conflict with the constitution and laws of the United States, or the constitution and laws of this state, shall be the rule of decision in all courts of this state. And it seems to be settled by the common law writers and by nearly, if not quite, all of the decided cases on the subject, that under the common law, in all cases where a juror is discharged during the progress of the trial from any cause of necessity, the balance of the jurors must be discharged, or rather the discharge of the one by the court operates to the discharge of all the balance, but the balance may be immediately recalled into the jury-bog and their examination be entered into as originally upon their voir dire, if either party so desires, and the respective parties may have their challenges over. By our statute the common law rule is abrogated to this extent and no further, that is: If before the conclusion of the trial a juror becomes sick, so as to be unable to perform his duty, the court may order him to be discharged. In that case a new juror may be sworn and the trial begun anew, or the jury may be discharged and a new jury then or afterwards empanelled.

Only in the class of cases above named does our statute give the court discretion to either empanel a new juror or to discharge the whole, jury and empanel a new one at its option. In the case at bar the juror was not discharged on account of sickness, and hence the above statute is not applicable to it, and we have no other statute on the subject, but we have the common law, with its mandate that in such cases the jury shall be discharged. At this point in the procedure we come to the parting of the ways between the common law and the statute. The statute plainly points out the course to be pursued in empanelling a new jury, which, of course, must be followed, unless the parties consent to proceed under the common law rule of immediately calling the remaining jurors back to the box for re-examination and challenges; so, if there be any, authority for retaining the eleven jurors, as was done in this case, we must look elsewhere for it besides the statute or the common law.

No judicial authority has been cited in point, and in my

opinion none can be found to sustain the respondent's contention on the question under consideration, except in those states where the statute authorizes such practice as was adopted by the trial court in this case. Cases have been cited and seem to be relied on as to such, authority. But I am of the opinion that they cannot be properly so considered. In the Pritchard case, upon the question whether the court below erred in empanelling another juror in the place of the juror who had been discharged, instead of discharging the remaining eleven jurors and empanelling a new jury, the supreme court said: In considering the facts of this case, in connection with the authorities to which our attention has been called, we have arrived at the conclusion that this action of the court was correct. The remaining eleven jurors were competent. No objection was urged against them. They had been selected, agreed upon and accepted in the mode provided by law. No testimony had been offered. It seems to us that the discharge of an incompetent juror creates no necessity for the discharge of the eleven remaining competent jurors.

Now, the facts in that case were these: The jury was empanelled and sworn to try the case; thereupon the court took a recess till next morning. Upon the reconvening of the court counsel for the defendant was permitted by the court to ask the jurors the following questions, to wit: Since you were examined by me before, touching your qualifications to serve as jurors, has anything happened or occurred to your recollections to render you improper jurors to your knowledge? Thereupon one of the jurors informed the court and counsel, in substance, that there had been some misapprehension or some mistake made in his examination as to his qualifications as a juror, and stated that he could not find a verdict of guilty on a charge of murder upon circumstantial evidence. Upon this statement and ground he was discharged. It is apparent that in that preceding nothing occurred so that it could reasonably be said that it might have prejudiced the balance of the jurors against the defendant. Indeed, it was admitted on the record by stipulation of the parties and confirmed by the court: That neither the plaintiff, the defendant nor said juror had been guilty of any intentional fraud or deception in procuring the swearing of said juror to try the case, except in so far as the answers made by said juror on his voir dire may operate as such fraud.

But in the present case the record shows a materially different state of facts. Here the juror was charged, in effect, with deception, fraud and the crime of perjury, with the view, on his part, of getting on the jury to favor and acquit the defendant, and the court found, in effect, that the charge was true. Here, also, by the strongest implication, the defendant and his family were charged with being accomplices in the crime of said juror, and this imputation was left resting on them by the district attorney and the court, instead of exonerating them there from.

During the progress of the examination of witnesses in support of these charges, the district attorney put defendant's attorney on the stand as a witness, evidently for no other purpose than to connect the defense with the alleged fraud and perfidy of said juror. He was subjected to quite a lengthy examination, and all the questions put to him by the district attorney appear to have been put with said view. The witness having stated that he had received an intimation the evening before that there was one juror on the panel favorable to the defendant, juror Flint asked him from whom he had received this intimation; the witness declined to answer, on the ground that it was privileged. The district attorney then said to, and asked, the witness as follows: Let us find out whether it is so or not: Was it from your client, his father, or brother, or mother? The witness declined his answer. The court, in passing upon the question of discharging Flint, expressed the opinion that the juror had deceived both of the counsel and the court. This relieved defendant's attorney from all blame in the matter, so far as the opinion of the court was concerned, but it did not remove the imputation cast upon the defendant and his family of complicity.

After Flint had been discharged, and in explanation of the grounds of his discharge, the court remarked in the presence of the eleven jurors, to wit: I became convinced that he came upon the jury to aid and assist the defendant in this case, for what inducement I do not know. The remaining jurors might reasonably have inferred from that remark that, in the opinion of the court, the juror had inducement, and that such inducement moved from the defendant or from some one in his behalf.

Counsel for defendant asked that the remaining eleven jurors be discharged on the ground, among others, of the evidence adduced before them, tending to disqualify them, and tending to bias and prejudice them against the defendant, and he asked to be allowed to examine them on their voir dire as to their qualifications, and asked to be allowed a peremptory challenge to the new juror Savage. The court replied: If I thought your challenge was taken in good faith I should be induced to set aside them all.

By counsel: "I assure your honor it is in good faith."

By the court: "I will pass upon that; the law gives you eight; I am impressed with the fact that you simply desire to obtain from the court that (which) is erroneous. The challenge is not taken in good faith, and it will be denied. You may have the benefit of an exception." By counsel: "I will take it."

It seems, to me that the above remarks impeaching the sincerity of counsel cast discredit on the whole defense of the defendant, and would have a tendency to create fatal prejudice in the minds of said jurors against the defendant.

The charges having been made and the examination thereof had before the jury against the defendant's objection, and the above remarks made in their presence, can it be reasonably said that the eleven jurors were not thereby prejudiced against the defendant and the theory of the defense, and hence remained competent jurors? Under these facts and circumstances was the court clothed with discretion to retain said eleven jurors on the panel against the objection of the defendant, and without giving him the privilege asked for of examining them as to the state of their minds? Certainly the ruling in the Pritchard case does not go so far as to sanction such practice or authorize such discretion as were adopted and exercised in this case under the state of facts existing here, nor was it intended by the court that the rule adopted in that case should have such effect as is clearly manifested by the language used in the above quotation from the opinion of the court. It is equally clear to my mind that the case of People v. Stone, supra, does not support the action of the court in the present case. In that case a juror was discharged on the ground of alienage, and a new juror empanelled, and like the Pritchard case there was nothing occurring in the proceedings relative to the juror discharged that could reasonably have tended to prejudice the remaining jurors against the defendant or his defense, so far as we can learn from the opinion there rendered. The court held in that case, as in the Pritchard case, that the discharge of the one juror did not necessitate the discharge of the eleven, for the reason that no injustice had been done, that the rights of the prisoner had not been infringed, and no law violated. The court then says: If a doubt could, however, remain on this point, that is, on the point of empanelling a new juror, instead of a new jury, it is definitely and conclusively settled by the statute relative to jurors. So it seems that the decision was finally based on the statutes of Illinois, which give the courts discretion to fill one or more vacancies on the jury, where one or more jurors are discharged from necessity, and to retain the other jurors on the panel. But we have no such statute.

It seems to me further, that if, from what the court said in that case can be construed as basing the decision on general principles, and not solely on the statute, it was done so on the ground of the peculiar facts of that case, and is not authority in any other case containing materially different facts. The court said: The case is sui generic. We have been referred to authorities, which are admitted to be the rule in the British courts, and if the facts in this case were of the nature, which marked the cases that have been decided there, and in like cases in our own courts, we should have no difficulty in coming to the same results on the present occasion.

Can it be said no injustice was done in the present case, no law violated, no rights infringed, and that the eleven jurors were not prejudiced on account of these proceedings had in their presence on matters outside of the proper investigation of the charges contained in the indictment? I am of opinion that we are not warranted in entertaining such presumption.

Can it be held with any reasonable plausibility that the

action of the court, in the matters under consideration, should be sustained because it is not shown here that these proceedings prejudiced the eleven jurors against the defense when the only means by which defendant might or could have shown it was denied him in the court below? This question is susceptible of but one answer, and that in the negative. It is clear to my mind that to so hold would be denying the accused in such cases the right to protect himself against such prejudice, however great in degree it might be, created by such procedure.

It seems to me that it cannot reasonably be presumed that these charges against the defendant, and the proceedings had, and imputations made of complicity of the defendant and his family in procuring Flint to be placed on the jury through his alleged deception, fraud and perjury, did not prejudice the eleven jurors against the defendant and the theory of his defense, so as to render them incompetent.

I am of the opinion that nothing scarcely is more potent to create such prejudice against a party than arousing suspicion that such party has packed, or attempted to pack, a jury by which he is to be tried, and that but few men are capable of resisting such prejudice and to rise above its influence, in their deliberations as jurors.

Further, it is evident, to my mind, that to affirm the judgment of the trial court, in consideration of the facts developed in this case, would be establishing a rule in this state without law and without precedent, and which would operate, in many cases, in the practical denial of the right of trial by jury-such trial as is contemplated by the statute, the common law and the constitution. It seems to me that such rule would be unwarrantable judicial legislation, instead of proper adjudication.

In what has been said above, it is not intended as a criticism of any matters occurring on the impeachment of said juror Flint, or on the trial thereof, or of any remarks made by the court in connection therewith, except in so far as the same occurred in the presence of the eleven jurors.

In consideration of the facts above given, I am of opinion that the court was not clothed with legal discretion to retain said eleven jurors on the panel without the consent of the defendant, and against his objection, and without giving him the privilege asked for of examining the said jurors as to the state of their minds before being sworn to try the case with the new juror. Upon this ground, and for the reasons here in above given, I concur in reversing the judgment and granting a new trial.

JUSTICE, BIGELOW, C. J., Concurring:

I am of the opinion that the discharge of the juror Flint was a matter in the discretion of the court. He had sworn, upon voir dire, that he had not formed or expressed any opinion as to the defendant's guilt or innocence, and that he had no conscientious scruples against the infliction of capital punishment. But upon the examination held after the district attorney moved to dismiss him from the panel it appeared quite clearly that he had several times expressed the opinion that defendant was guilty, but that, if he were on the jury, he would not vote to hang him, and when pressed for a reason why he would not had said that he was opposed to capital punishment. It may be that these remarks were simply idle talk, and had been forgotten by the juror, but if such were not the case, and especially if he did have such conscientious scruples, then certainly he was not a fit juror.

The trial judge was in a better position to determine this fact than we are, and his conclusion thereon is not unsupported by the evidence. It follows, the same as in any other case where a point has to be determined upon conflicting evidence, that the discretion of the trial court cannot be overruled upon appeal. As the juror was properly discharged, the evidence was insufficient to support the plea of former jeopardy thereafter entered by defendant.

I am also of the opinion that while perhaps the court did not commit reversible error in refusing to discharge the entire jury, it should either have done so or have given the defendant his challenges over again, as demanded by him. This would have been, substantially in accordance with the rule at common law, which, in the absence of a statute, must be our guide.

State v. Pritchard, relied upon as justifying the action taken below, does not cover these questions, because there no testimony had been taken, which is particularly referred to as one of the grounds upon which the decision is placed, and because no question was raised concerning the defendant's renewed right to his challenges, which were always given him at common law. If that rule is unsatisfactory, and doubtless it can be improved upon, it should be changed by statute, as has been done in many states.

I also agree with much that is said by Justice Bonnifield concerning the proceedings taken against juror Flint, and which could not well have failed to have a prejudicial effect upon the minds of the jurors retained in the case.

For these reasons I concur in the judgment.

Author's Summary:

A layperson cannot say much about the application of the law regarding the decision by these Justices. However, this case was a good example for needing juror alternates. Perhaps, this was one of the cases used to bring about that needed legislation.

The real problem for the second trial was that the case had been very graphically presented to Lander County residents by the Reese River Reveille. Many understood what happened and to them it was a clear-cut case of cold-blooded murder. The emotions within the community continued to run high. Yes, the second trial should have had a change of venue.

The courts of the past were not entirely blameless for the many lynching that took place in our nation. There is an excellent book, "Contempt of Court" by Mark Curriden and Leroy Phillips, Jr. This book provides some history of lynching in the U. S. They have in their appendix a listing by Year, White or Negroes, Type of Crime and the States where lynching were recorded from 1882 to 1944. It might surprise you to learn there were 4708 lynching recorded during this period. They've occurred in all but six States and the District of Columbia. Most of these lynching took place between 1882 and 1900.

Nevada was one of the least States for lynchings where only six lynching were recorded. It is hard to think of anything worse than a mob bent on hanging or doing worse as often was the case. I am sure many and may be most of these victims deserved to die, but not in this way. I think the citizen of Austin should be commended for not taking justice into their hands. In an earlier time Flint might have been strung up along with Alfred. Perhaps that would have been Hollywood's version of an Old West murder such as this. Recall, Austin did have one lynching in 1881. This was not included with the records shown in the above book, so you know that Nevada actually had more than six lynchings. I am guessing that the Old West ended somewhere between 1881 and 1895.

13

TRIAL NO. 3

Is This Going To Be In Reno?

The State Supreme Court action did produce an unexpected hardship on Lander County. As you know, they had a very difficult time seating the jury for the second trial. Now there is going to be a third trial. It should not be surprising to find Jones petitioning the Court for a Change of Venue. His request provides a great deal of first hand history about Austin and Lander County in the affidavit he presented to the Court. Here you have a good word picture of the entire community as he reviews the eligible and ineligible jurors. Remember women were not part of the jury pool.

He has a list of citizens with occupations that placed them in the ineligible category. His affidavit also gives the date, March 20, 1895, when the Supreme Court ruled for the first retrial. Nearly a year had lapsed since the first trial held in April 1894. The Supreme Court ruled again on January 20, 1896 for the second trial that concluded June 10, 1895.

There must have been considerable anxiety by the families as they waited for these rulings. The last ruling was not without pain to the Litster's and it certainly gave hope for the Vaughan's. Jones' affidavit documented the fact that the community as a whole was upset with the time spent and the cost of these two trials.

Did the legal system fail when the juror, A. A. Flint perjured himself? The trial was interrupted and he was arrested for his perjury. His bail was set a $750 and that was a lot of money in those days. His sentence was not reported so it is not known whether there was any jail time associated with his perjury. Whatever, it could never balance with the prolonged suffering caused to the Litster family.

Perhaps Judge Mack as well as Jones shares the blame by trying to speed up the second trial. Dennis capitalizes on the idea that trial should not have been restarted with the former eleven jurors. I think he knew this was going to provide him with a good argument if he had to appeal the decision. Therefore, he made the most of the dismissal of Flint as he even refused to examine any of those called to be his replacement.

If not before, but now for sure all the citizens in Austin were familiar with the details of this case. They had been described many times in the local newspaper and many had taken off work to come to the courtroom. Dennis had asked to enter a motion for a change of venue at the start of the second trial, but he shortly withdrew the motion. I think Judge Mack would have overruled his motion in any case. The County Commissioners knew that the jury pool for a second trial for Alfred had in fact exhausted the jury pool. Jones was asked by the Commissioners to prepare an affidavit for the Court. The order to move the trial must come from the judge.

The following is the text from W. D. Jones's Affidavit for the Change of Venue:

Jones: "I now desire, if Your Honor Please, to ask up the motion for a change of venue in this case."

The affidavit and notice of motion were filed on 12th day of February 1896, and both have been served on counsel for the defendant.

The Court: "You may read the affidavit."

Jones: The affidavit reads as follows:

In District Court of the 3rd Judicial District of the State of Nevada, in and for Lander County. The State of Nevada, Plaintiff vs. Alfred Vaughan, Defendant

W. D. Jones being duly sworn says that he is the duly elected, qualified and acting District Attorney of said County, and attorney for said plaintiff.

That he has resided in said County for over twenty-seven years next preceding the making of this affidavit, and has been District Attorney thereof for more than nine years of said time, and by reason thereof is very thoroughly and intimately acquainted with the people of said County.

That said defendant shot and killed William Litster, Jr., in said County on the 28th day of December 1893, and that the Grand Jury of said County duly indicted said defendant for the crime of murder therefore, on March 1, 1894.

That the defendant was tried on said indictment in said court, at Austin in said County, for April 3rd to 22nd, 1894 inclusive, and that upon said last named date said defendant was convicted of the crime of murder in the first degree.

That thereafter the Judge of said court duly pronounced judgment against said defendant, upon said conviction, and sentenced him to be hanged by the neck until he should be dead for said murder of said William Litster, Jr.

That on the 20th day of March 1895, the Supreme Court of said State duly reversed said judgment and ordered a new trial of said action.

That on May 21st to June 10th 1895 inclusive, a second trial of said defendant on said indictment took place in said District Court at said Austin, and on said last named date, said defendant was again convicted of the crime of murder in the first degree.

That thereafter the Judge presiding in said court duly pronounced judgment against said defendant, upon said conviction, and sentenced him to be hanged by the neck until he should be dead, for the said murder of said William Litster, Jr.

That on the 20th day of January 1896, the Supreme Court of said State duly reversed said judgment and ordered a new trial of said action.

That on said two trials about 383 of the eligible jurors of said County were summoned to appear and did appear in said District Court, to answer as to their qualifications to serve as jurors in said action, and in order to obtain twelve qualified jurors at each of said trials, about 244 jurors were examined on their voir dire, and the remaining 139 jurors summoned heard so much of the proceedings of said trials that they thereby became disqualified to serve as jurors in this action.

That there were 17 Grand Jurors who found said indictment, about 25 witnesses in said action, six jurors who served at the Coroners Inquest, upon the body of said William Litster, Jr., some 20 relatives of said defendant and said deceased, all of whom are disqualified to serve as jurors in said action.

That there are, of the eligible jurors of said County, three Justices of the Peace, one County Clerk, one Sheriff, three Constables, one Recorder, three Attorneys-at-law, three Physicians, two Ministers of the Gospel, three Telegraph Operators, about twelve Locomotive or Stationery Engineers, about ten Mail Carriers, engaged in the actual carrying of the United States Mail, on a regular mail route; about twenty-five members and officers of regular enrolled fire companies, and in all about sixty-seven jurors, who, by virtue of law of this State, are exempt from jury duty.

That since the last general election in said County; fifty-nine of the eligible jurors of said County have left said County, fourteen have died, and nine are either deaf, blind or too feeble to perform jury duty.

That at the last general election in said County there were about 485 votes cast in said County, and at this time there is not to exceed 412 of said votes in said county.

That since the 28th day of December 1893, affiant has heard more than 400 of the eligible jurors of said County express the unqualified opinion that said defendant is guilty of the murder of said William Litster, Jr.; and very many of the residents of said County, who are eligible jurors have also expressed said opinion in the hearing of said affiant, during said time.

That very many, to wit: at least 1000 of the residents and more than 300 of the eligible jurors of said County heard some material portion, or all, of the evidence offered against said defendant, at one or both of the said trials.

That affiant has been in every township in said County, since said 28th day of December 1893, and has heard very much comment by the residents thereof against said defendant, for the killing of said William Litster, Jr.; and was also engaged in both said trials for said plaintiff, as counsel thereof, and therefore alleges the fact to be, that it is now impossible to obtain a qualified jury in said County to try said charge against said defendant.

That it would be impossible to obtain a fair and impartial jury in said County to try said charge against said defendant, and that such a state of public excitement exists in said County against the defendant as would likely overawe and intimidate even a fair jury, even if it were possible to obtain one.

That said Indictment is now pending in said County.

WHEREFORE, as District Attorney of said County, and attorney for said plaintiff, and for and on behalf of the State of Nevada, I hereby apply to this Honorable Court to make and enter its order changing the venue of the action of the State of Nevada, Plaintiff, vs. Alfred Vaughan, Defendant, indicted for the killing of William Litster, Jr., in said County on or about the 28th day of December 1893, now pending in the District Court of said County, from said Court to the Honorable District Court of some County in this State where a fair and impartial trial of said action can be had.

W. D. Jones: Subscribed and sworn to before me, this 12th day of February 1896.

W. W. Christian, Clerk of said County,

The Judge ordered the third trial to be moved to Reno. This was an added expense for Lander County. Now they must pay for the transportation for the witnesses that would be required to attend the trial in Reno. After contacting officials in Reno, a trial date was set for April 6, 1896. It has been almost two years to the day following the beginning of the first trial.

The parties for the Plaintiff and the Defendant were served with subpoenas. They were told that travel expenses would be paid. Four of the people on the witness list had since moved to Reno. These were Mrs. H. H. Clark; J. B. Jones; Nathan Dunsdon, this is Tom's son, he made that ride to get the doctor for Willie; and Robert Eason. Jones was notified that the trial would be in Judge Cheney's Court. Jones ask Judge Cheney to provide another nine subpoenas to: Dr. Huntsman; Wm. Litster;

Thomas Dunsdon; Mrs. Alex Eason; James Litster; Nicholas Rast; Mrs. Wm. Litster; James B. Egan; and Wm. Easton. Dennis also requested subpoenas for: Charlie Vaughan; L. S. Vaughan; Frank Vaughan; Harry Vaughan and William Brey.

The people traveling from Austin at County expense had to ride on the same train, first to Battle Mountain on the Nevada Central and then transfer to the Union Pacific for the ride into Reno. It wasn't said but I assume Alfred was taken separately to Reno a few days earlier. Still there must have been considerable tension during that train ride for the Litster's and Vaughan's.

You can imagine the stress these folks were now experiencing for this agonizing legal mess. It is common in our modern world. But did it start here in Austin? The process was taking a toll on both families as well as the attorney's. At least the witnesses would have a chance to see Reno, the Biggest Little City in the World or did that come later? Jones made arrangements with the Nevada Central to schedule a special train leaving Austin in time to connect with the mainline traveling through Battle Mountain to Reno. They left Austin in the morning and didn't get into Reno until 9 p.m. They were told; if they traveled any other way it would be at their own expense.

Jones and Dennis were told to have their witnesses in the courthouse on Monday at 10 o'clock in the morning on April 6, 1896. The Judge knew it would be easy to empanel a jury because no one from Reno was familiar with the case.

The Reno Gazette-Journal reported on April 6, 1896:

The courtroom was crowded and much interest manifested in the trial. Vaughan is an innocent looking young man and one whose conversation would not indicate that he was a "bad man." At 3 o'clock there had been eleven jurors selected and the State had one preemptory challenge and the defense had exhausted their challenges.

While researching the Reno trial, I had hoped to find another transcript. It was shortly discovered that there was no transcript. The reason became obvious, as there was no need. So the only written record of this trial comes from the Reno

Gazette-Journal and the Reese River Reveille.

The Austin newspaper reported that the Gazette-Journal said: *A venire for 60 tales men was issued, 49 of whom were examined as to their qualifications, and the following persons were selected and sworn as a jury to try the case: E. A. Morril; E. E. Warden; G. H. Fogg; W. L. Middour; D. W. O'Connell; I. N. Bakeless; Frank King; S. J. Bryant; James Sullivan, Jr.; James Shepley; M. Hawcroft and W. J. Luke.*

The trial here was moving much faster than it did in Austin. The attorney's did not waste a lot of the Court time. Jones made his opening statement and Dennis followed him. This time Dennis would make an opening statement at the beginning, something he did not do in the first two trials. Court was adjourned following his statement.

A good crowd was again on hand for the Tuesday morning for this now well-publicized trial. Jones called his first witness, Dr. Huntsman. His testimony was mainly about the location of the wound on the body and the course of the bullets. William Litster; Mrs. Litster; Thomas Dunsdon; Mrs. Alex Eason; William Easton and James Litster followed him.

The local newspaper said:

Their evidence covered statement made of the young boy that was shot just before he died. The evidence is very strong and, notwithstanding the frequent objections by the defense, was admitted in most every instance. The testimony of Mrs. Litster, the mother of the poor dead boys caused many a tear to fall, even among strong men, and Judge Cheney seemed affected by as the mother told the story of what occurred soon after the shooting and gave the last words of her dying boy.

Dennis objected many times, perhaps this was his all or nothing defense. It must have seemed like an uphill battle for Dennis even when the Judge did sustain some of his many objections. After the noon recess Jones called Nick Rast to the stand. Jones has changed the sequence of his witnesses.

The trial here in Reno may have been more interesting to the jury, because it was all new to those hearing the testimony. Again, Nick Rast proved to be the State star witness.

The local newspaper reported:

Nick Rast was with the Vaughan boys at the time of the shooting and witnessed the killing, gave evidence that would seem to be almost convincing. He is a foreigner and owing to this fact appeared easily confused, but stuck to his statements and insisted that he was telling nothing but the truth. His evidence is very important, as he saw the trouble from first to last and it is probable that the jury will note every word spoken by him on the stand.

The State rested after the evening session on Tuesday. Wednesday morning was Dennis's turn. He calls Charlie to be the first witness in defense of Alfred. The newspaper reported that he told substantially the same story as in the former trials. There was no mention of Jones's cross-examination. It would have been interesting to see how Charlie explained the pocketknives at this trial. Alfred was put on the stand after Charlie. This time Alfred had the benefit of hearing what Charlie said before coming to the stand. Still their testimony from the former trials had to govern and they really could not change their story at this time.

The local newspaper reported the following for Alfred:

He related the circumstances of the killing of the Litster boys with apparently no remorse of conscience.

Jones must have come down on Alfred very hard. He had heard Alfred's unbelievable story perhaps one to many times.

The local newspaper reported:

The attorney's for the defense frequently objecting to cross-examination. Judge Cheney overruled the main objections and noted the exceptions by the defense.

The testimony continued into the evening session and the testimony of all the rebuttal witnesses was completed on Thursday morning. The closing arguments followed. The prosecution opened with Truman. He spoke for nearly two hours following the noon recess. Dennis was up next and he made according the Reno Gazette-Journal, "the effort of his life." J. H. MacMillan followed and he spoke until 4 o'clock. Judge Cheney called a recess until 7 o'clock. At which time Jones would address the jury.

I wish the transcripts included summation by Jones. He

seems to have been a excellent public speaker. The jury would hear his description of the evidence. Jones knew as did Alfred that the case would end here in Reno.

He reviewed the testimony and he made a strong plea for justice. He painted a word picture over the next ninety minutes as he spoke about the scene where Alfred first shot Willie and then killed his brother, Johnny. Jones has lived with this matter nearly day and night for the last two years. He knew all the details of the case and he explained to the jury that Alfred suddenly lifted the rifle and shot Willie. The bullet grazed Willie's arm before entering his stomach. This was at point blank range. Willie could not have had an axe raised above his head for this wound to his arm. Alfred shot Willie as Johnny was helping Nick Rast open the fence gate at the Gap. He graphically told the jury how Johnny was backing down the road begging Alfred for his life and when Johnny turned to run away Alfred shot and killed him. This was happening while Willie was down on the snow cover ground crying in great pain. Willie would soon vomit his morning breakfast mixed with blood. He told how Willie continued to cry in agony as the Charlie and Nick listened to Alfred's orders to open the Gap and turn the wagon. Jones asks the jury to visualize the scene as the big wagon drove off. They could have easily helped Willie, but instead left him to die an agonizing death.

The Reno Gazette-Journal reported:

It was quiet pathetic for everyone listening in the courtroom and you could see how solemn the jury had become.

Jones made it very clear that it was Alfred's unjustified rage, filled with hate did cause him to commit two murders. Yes, two senseless murders because of his temper. Alfred would soon learn that just as the other two juries had found a verdict for the ultimate consequence for that act. He would hear it again.

Judge Cheney then gave his instructions to the Jury. He didn't ask the attorneys for any instructions or perhaps it just wasn't noted in the newspaper. I'm sure the Judge had reviewed the transcripts from the first and second trials.

The Local newspaper reported:

His charge was concise and clear, and not one of the jurors could fail to understand.

The jury was allowed to retire to deliberate at nine o'clock that evening. About an hour later they did ask the judge for one clarification.

Friday morning the judge was notified that the jury had a verdict. A little after 9 a.m. on April 10, 1896 the jurors were brought back into the courtroom. Judge Cheney asked if they had a verdict and the Foreman, G. H. Fogg responded that they did and it was passed to the Judge. He returned it and asked that it be read. Here again Alfred was found guilty of murder in the first degree. The Reno jury had reached the same conclusion as the Coroner's Inquest, Preliminary Examination and the two former trials. Judge Cheney thanked the jury for their service and discharged them.

Alfred was standing when the verdict was read and he again showed no emotion whatsoever. He obviously knew that his chances were slim and at best may be something less than first degree. The Judge calls a recess till 1:30 p.m. and stated that he would pass sentence at that time. As Alfred was led away he was heard telling the deputy:

"Well they gave it to me hard and it didn't surprise me, but I want to die today." "Well it can't be helped."

What did Alfred mean by this statement remains a question? The deputy told him that he must be strong and take this like a man.

Just before 1:30 p.m. Deputy Caughlin went to Alfred's cell. It was the appointed time to get his prisoner. Here he found him suffering and he appeared to have been crying. Alfred did not respond to the deputy's order to get up. He just sat there on the bed with his back to the wall. The deputy quickly passed the word that the prisoner could not or would not move. And that he appears to be in pain. The word was rushed to the Judge Cheney and he told the deputy to call a doctor to examine the prisoner's condition. The doctor arrived at Alfred's cell about 2:15 p.m. The doctor told the deputy to summon more help. Soon two more doctors came to assist with the examination of the prisoner.

The doctors agreed that Alfred had taken poison. Someone

somehow was able to give Alfred the poison that was now slowly taking life from his body. The doctors were sure that he had taken an overdose of morphine. He must have taken the poison during the lunch recess. The hours passed and the doctors Thoma, Lewis and Phillips did all in their power to keep him alive, but as the hours slipped away so too did the life of Alfred. They tried to pump his stomach to no avail and they tried walking him. They called for his two brothers, Frank and Charlie to help. During all this time Alfred never spoke one word to anyone, even at times when he stared directly at them. As the hour of 10 o'clock approached that night they had to pronounce Alfred dead. His heart had stopped. The doctors each agreed that he died from morphine poisoning.

The next day the Reno Gazette-Journal reported:

No one knows how Vaughan got the death-dealing drug, but that he was determined to die if convicted goes without saying. The Gazette continues by saying, "*...that a higher court will pass judgment more than any tribunal in this world. His family will be saved many heart aches, and while it is true that they have suffered much in the past, and have been almost ruined financially in trying to save the of their boy from a ignominious death, the trouble is over now.*"

I know very little about morphine other than it is used as a painkiller. I've heard that many people around the world are addicted to this drug. The question still has to be asked. How did Alfred get this poison?

They were a number of suggestions as to how he might have got the drug. Some thought it might have been in his clothing. It was reported that Alfred had said he would never be sentenced a third time and that he had made arrangements for the worst. A brief inquest was held Saturday and nothing of substance was presented and the matter was closed.

The State of Nevada did not pursue an investigation. Why? They must have known the identity of the likely person that gave him the drug. They apparently were happy to see this case finally come a conclusion. Logic rules out his defense attorneys as the source. They had worked diligently for two years to save his life. The deputies at the jail would not likely be the source of morphine. There was a lot of speculation about how did he obtained the drug.

Twelve day later the Reese River Reveille dated April 22, 1896 reported:

Charlie bought him a bunch of flowers, some oranges and strawberries, which were examined before given to Vaughan

This also was the story that has been passed down through the Litster family. Recall, Charlie was the brother that would do everything Alfred asked? There is really little doubt that it was Charlie.

All hope by Alfred was gone and there was no doubt regarding sentence for his third conviction. It would be the same as the first two trials. Alfred knew that time had run out and he did not want to hear his sentence read again for murder in the first degree. He knew the penalty would be hanging. His parents also knew what the sentence would be. There should be no question about whether Alfred knew what he was doing when he took the overdose of morphine. According to those that watched throughout these trials, they said he appeared tired and that his demeanor had changed.

It was time to end it all. Did he as the newspaper declared cheat the gallows? He took the drug during the lunch recess, perhaps around 12:30 p.m. He was officially declared dead at 10 o'clock that night. Three doctors work hard to revive him. The gallows would have been swifter. The real punishment in a formal execution is waiting for that final moment to come. Therefore, I agree Alfred did cheat the hangman. Make no mistake; he did not cheat that higher court where we all will give an account for our lives. We can be saved and forgiven because of His grace or we can take our chances and stand before Him as an unsaved person to hear judgment at the Great White Throne. Perhaps, Alfred did believe that he could be forgiven by calling on the Lord's name.

"Everyone who calls on that name of the Lord will be saved, how, then, can they call on the one they have not believed in? And how can they believe in the one of whom they have not heard? And how can they hear without someone preaching to them?" Rom 10:13-14.

The following words that seem appropriate:

> *Death is so limited*
> *It cannot cripple love, It cannot shatter hope,*
> *It cannot corrode faith, It cannot destroy peace,*
> *It cannot kill friendship, It cannot suppress memories,*
> *It cannot silence courage, It cannot invade the soul,*
> *It cannot steal eternal life, It cannot conquer the spirit,*
> *Author Unknown*

While these words may be sweet to the ear there is a problem, because they are not true for everyone. The Vaughan family had a funeral for Alfred on the following Sunday. Do you think that brought closure? Whatever, "closure" is supposed to mean? Closure is an over used word today. The true and simple answer is a fact, the hurt and pain never goes away. Life is a collection of memories, good and bad.

The Vaughan family placed an ad in the Reno Gazette-Journal that thanked the Sheriffs of Lander and Washoe Counties and all the other persons for kindness shown to Alfred Vaughan while in his confinement. Even here you can see that Vaughan's cannot express any regrets for what their son had done to the Litster's. I've placed biography in the appendix for W. D. Jones stating that during Alfred's trials, his brothers and mother frequently threatened him and others associated with the trials. What kind of people were these Vaughan's? Soon they would all leave their ranch in Lander County, but still as you drive State Highway 305, you will find a sign that reads: "Boone Canyon Vaughan Ranch". The old ranch house can be seen at the mouth of Boone Canyon. If only this house could talk.

The Reese River Reveille reported it is has been rumored:

Mr. and Mrs. Vaughan had decided to permanently reside in Reno.

It was also reported:

Alfred was buried with Episcopal rites, although it was stated on good authority that before his second trial he had embraced the Catholic faith.

The Reno Gazette-Journal published the following:

"The Vaughan murder trial just completed in the District Court is not without its' lessen. The awful crime of killing the young boys, the pride of the Litster household was the result of the unbridled temper of young Vaughan. He was just ready step into the busy life of the world, now he languishes in jail almost at the shadow of the gallows. Aside from the sorrow the two families have been crippled and financially one of the fairest counties of Nevada almost bankrupt in handling the trials. The example of the ungovernable temper that was aroused over a land dispute with its after results renders words unnecessary.

Since this was a famous murder case in Lander County, it is appropriate that the memory of the three trials live on as part of Nevada's recorded history. I have stated my bias on behalf of the Litster family and for that reason I've included text copied from the two Supreme Court rulings, as well as the quotations taken directly from the trial transcripts of the first and second trials. There was no transcript made for this third trial because there was no need for any appeal to State's Supreme Court. Thus the shorthand notes were destroyed. The act of murder certainly cost Lander County more than the lives of Johnny Litster and Willie Litster. Alfred Vaughan did pay with his life. but this did not relief the taxpayers as they had to restore the financial health of Lander County.

14

CLOSURE

Is That Really Possible?

Yes, life goes on as some may say, but in what way? Does anyone really believe that life could ever be as it was for individuals that have experienced the ordeal of murder? No one needs to ask because you know that neither Litster's nor Vaughan's could ever resume the life they once had here in Lander County. The killing at the Gap occurred twenty-seven months before the third and final trial of Alfred Vaughan. His act of murder changed the lives for more than just two families. It was easy to see that these families tried hard to avoid each other during the time of the trials.

The Vaughan's seemed to have hope for their son right up to the end. Did the Vaughan's ever express regrets to the Litster's? Not according to any record that I have seen. Considering the reaction of the Vaughan's on that December morning in 1893 as the wagon returned to the ranch it is not surprising that they never apologized to the Litster's. After the Reno trial, it was time for Mr. and Mrs. Vaughan to leave Lander County. As I said earlier, the Vaughan's worst day would come and it did on April 10, 1896. Alfred's parents must have been shattered. They were old, nearing the end of life and their son's uncontrolled hatred hurt them deeply. They had used most of their resources to pay for his legal expenses and they had become outcasts in the community. Yes, it was time to leave their ranch home where they had lived for 29 years. They moved to Reno.

The 1900 Census only listed Charlie Vaughan's name in

Lander County. The County tax records does not have the Vaughan's paying any property tax for the year 1896. The Vaughan's apparently sold the ranch. Mr. and Mrs. Levi Vaughan had their personal items moved from the ranch to Reno where they remained following the third trial. Also, Frank and his stepbrother Harry relocated. Using the 1880 as a base the ages of the Vaughan family in 1896 would have been: Levi, 72; Elizabeth, 61; Frank, 31; Charlie, 26; Alfred, 24; and Harry, 22. There is little doubt about the fact that the family would have remained on the ranch had Alfred been acquitted. I have made no effort to find the actual dates when the Frank, Charlie and Harry may have left Lander County.

The name of the old Vaughan Ranch and the ranch house remains to this very day. As mentioned in a prior chapter, there is a road sign along the side of Highway 305 that reads "Boone Canyon Vaughan Ranch." You can find State maps of the Nevada today still showing the location of the Vaughan Ranch. It seems that no Vaughan has lived here for more that a century yet the name remains. Is this sign like some of the old ghost towns in Nevada? Is it truly a forgotten monument in memory of Alfred Vaughan's murder of the Johnny and Willie Litster?

I am assuming the name of Vaughan actually continued because the Nevada Central Railroad had a siding here that was identified as the Vaughan Station. Recall, James Litster referred to this station as "the Switch".

The real historic site of the murder does not have a monument or a sign. It was at a place they called "The Gap" and it is about five miles up Boone Canyon near the mouth of the Water Canyon. Perhaps, "The Gap" should have a monument considering the impact the three trials had on Lander County's economy 109 years ago. The exact location seems to be buried with the memories of the characters that lived this tragic story. There is no fence here today. I believe William Litster could not stand to look at this short section of fence with a gate that was called "The Gap". So he removed the part of the fence crossing the mouth of the Water Canyon.

The Litster's ranch house has survived and it can be reach from the Silver Creek Ranch Road by traveling the fork that passes the abandoned site of the Silver Creek School. The road up Boone Canyon from SR305 is closed now. The road remains but it has locked gate. In a spiritual sense the Vaughan's or no one else should trespass on this private ranch property.

The Vaughan Ranch was much too close following the third trial for the Vaughan's to continue to be neighbors with the Litster's. I think it is safe to assume that had Alfred been set free it would have been the Litster's moving out of the County. The newspaper reported that it was hard for these people to be together in the same courtroom. Think about the train ride to Reno when they had to travel on the same train. Surely, W. D. Jones insisted that Sheriff Easton had to do a better job than he did when he first put Nick Rast in the same cell with Alfred and Charlie.

The Sheriff must have made every effort to see that these families would not confront each other. He didn't want another situation like that mentioned during the second trial when William Litster had an exchange or some type of incident with Alfred in the Austin Courthouse hallway. The details were not clear, but Dennis said William tried to shoot Alfred. This happened on a day when the deputy was bringing Alfred down the hallway and as they passed William words were exchanged. I doubt the charge about William trying to shoot Alfred, but I think it would be a good guess that William did respond to Alfred remarks by taking a swing at him.

Whatever happened to Nick Rast? He died June 7, 1922 at the age of 70? It appears he continued to live the rest of his life after the three trials with his brother's family in Lander County. This is where he was living when the 1900 Census was taken. Nick was a good man. He just had the misfortune of taking a job with the Vaughan's on the day of the tragedy. According to his testimony he was living in fear of his own life while he was locked up in jail with Alfred and Charlie. Remember, Alfred asked Nick: "Do you want to be in a dead man's coffin too?" Also, Alfred was pointing his Winchester at Nick when he told him to get on the wagon and shortly after he made the above threat

The Reese River Reveille reported that Vaughan's were

brazen enough to even threaten the Judge and the District Attorney. That would not happen today. I think the Vaughan brothers could easily have scared Nick with those pocketknives. It is hard to believe Sheriff Easton allowed them to keep those pocketknives when they were being charge with murder. That too would not happen today. Nick owes a lot to his brother for telling him that he had to find the courage to tell the truth. He didn't do that until his brother arranged a meeting with W. D. Jones. Yes, Willie Litster's dying declaration was compelling, but without Nick's testimony I doubt whether justice would have prevailed.

Sadness came again to the Litster family when Lizzie died in 1901, just five years later at the age of nineteen. The cause of Lizzie's untimely death is unknown. However, diphtheria was taking a toll in this part of Nevada during the winter of 1901-02, according to a letter written by Tasker Oddie to his mother. Now three of the Litster children have died without reaching the adult age of twenty-one. Still the worst was to come for Elizabeth, as her husband too would soon die in 1903. William was two months short of his 58th birthday. William had suffered greatly following the loss of Johnny and Willie and then again when Lizzie died.

Elizabeth was fortunate to have her other children. Her three remaining sons continued to work the ranch. In 1903 the ages of her sons were: James 24, George 18 and Louis 15. Life on the ranch was not easy and they were not making a lot of money working this ranch. They didn't have welfare or any of the government's subsidies for farming or ranching that exist today. Yet, Elizabeth did survive William by 23 years and she continued to live at the ranch until her death in 1926. She was buried next to her husband and daughter at the Austin Cemetery. Johnny and Willie's common gravesite as well as the grandparents James and Christina are just a few feet away.

The 1910 Census shows that James had married and his family was living at the ranch. By the time of the 1920 Census, James 39 and wife, Rosalia 40 were found to be still living in Lander County with their two daughters Ethel 12 and Caroline 3, but they were not living at the Litster Ranch. James' family eventually would leave Lander County for the San Francisco East Bay Area. His youngest daughter Caroline died in 1996 where she had continued to live here in the East Bay Area.

Louis was very close to his mother. He didn't get married until he was 31 years old. The 1920 Census shows that Louis 31, his wife, Ida 20, and their son Louis Jack, 5 months were also living at the ranch. Louis and his wife may have remained a while at the ranch after Elizabeth died, but they too would leave. Louis was an excellent horseman and he was on the rodeo circuit for a while before he married. He lived the latter part of his days in Reno with his sister, Mary (Litster) Christian. Louis died August 10, 1956, while being treated for an illness in San Francisco. He too is buried adjacent to his parents at the Austin Cemetery.

Marilou said, George Watt Litster was not fond of the lonely ranch life and Boone Canyon had too many bad memories. George moved to Austin and took a job in town shortly after his father died. Here he lived with his sister, Mary and his brother-in-law, William Christian. George married William Easton's daughter Della Louise Easton on August 15, 1910. He was 25 and Della was 19 years old. Their only son, William Glenn Litster was born July 29, 1911. Della (Easton) Litster died July 18, 1915, at the age of 24. The cause of death was not stated on the certificate.

George asked Mary and William if they would care for his son, William Glenn Litster, while he went to Reno in search a new life away from Austin. He then proceeded to go to California in search of work. Glenn's aunt and uncle continued to raise him as their own child and he only saw his real father on rare visits when George came from California to visit in Reno. George married twice more during his life. He became a rice farmer near Willows till the Great Depression caused his bank note to be foreclosed. George died on June 14, 1953. He has lived in the following places after leaving Austin: Reno; Willows; Sacramento; Vallejo; Whispering Pines; Ukiah and Paradise.

William and Mary Christian also left Austin and moved to Reno and continued to raise George and Della's son, but they never adopted the boy. William Glenn Litster is Marilou

(Litster) Colson's biological father. Mary (Aunt Maine) survived her husband by many years here in Reno where she died at the age of 93 years. She did have many more News Years to celebrate as her brother, Johnny Litster, wished in his letter dated December 26, 1893.

Marilou Litster was four years old when her real mother, Gladys (Bailey) Litster died. Two years later she was adopted by her grandparent, George and Ida Litster. Marilou has a half brother and half sister. The half brother was the last of the Litster's to carry the surname for her family's branch. He died in March 2002. This is what I meant when I said the murder of Johnny and Willie changed many lives and even lives of those yet to be born. It cannot be said for a fact, but it would not be surprising had Johnny and Willie lived to find other relatives still living in Lander County and just maybe on the ranch in Boone Canyon.

There is a lot of history from the old west here in Lander County. Ranching continues throughout the County and for sure this too has changed a great deal with the advent of modern equipment. However for Austin, mining is the town's true foundation. That is how the town started and the town has strained without that activity. Is the Toiyabe Mountain Range still hiding the gold and silver that could start another rush for those that would claim her treasure?

The old Litster Ranch is now called the Boone Creek Ranch. Mary Jeanne Ansolabehere is the present ranch owner. She currently lives on the ranch and she said the old ranch house has been remodeled for twentieth century. Mary Jeanne has lived here for the last forty-two years. When asked, she was not aware of the double killing or where it took place. The fence with the Gap no longer exists at the mouth of the Water Canyon. She did know that one Litster boy had been killed at the ranch. This little canyon valley as I have said several times is very pleasant and certainly nicer than the neighboring terrain. This is high desert plateau country, the air is very dry and the winters are very cold. The more familiar I became with the history for the story and those that lived here, well the more impressed I became by how hardy were these western ancestors.

If this Litster Ranch could talk, I would like to hear the true answer for several questions that were never described during the three trials of Alfred Vaughan and by this I mean:

1. What was the true timeline for December 28, 1893?
2. Did the Litster brother's plan a confrontation at the Gap?
3. Why didn't William Litster hear those two shots that were fired? However, Mary Jeanne says sound does not carry in this canyon.
4. Why did the Vaughan's leave Willie alive there in the snow?
5. Why did Alfred draw his pistol on Mr. Starratt that evening at the Litster ranch house?
6. Why didn't William stop the Vaughan wagon as it came through the ranch and explain that the gate was closed at the Gap?
7. Why didn't William ride a horse to check on his sons?
8. Why did William walk up on the ridge instead of the road when he went to check on his sons that morning?
9. Why did Elizabeth wait for William to come to the house before insisting that he must check on the boys?

The records that remain for Lander County's most famous murder trial did not answer these questions. And like the ghost towns of Nevada, the history of the three-murder trials has nearly passed leaving only a few memories from that time now long gone. Ordinary people are very poor about passing a family history to the next generation. They do not have time nor do they think anyone would be interested in their life.

When the details of history are lost, we are left to speculate and most likely we'll be wrong when we do. We may be close to the truth, but that is not really good enough. We can see in our modern society that there are many similarities from one generation to the next. The way people think is truly the glue that binds a culture together. America will not have a culture to pass on without preserving the history of those that settled and built this nation we call America.

The culture of our nation seems to be second to the media's

desire for politically correct thinking. I have titled the next and last chapter of the book "Epilogue". Here I've listed a few comments that I think modern Americans should consider about Alfred Vaughan's trials with respect to where we are heading and by how much we have changed from that time a century ago.

I'm reminded of a comment from my daughter. She is married to Marine Major, Mathew K. Hays. They are now stationed in Okinawa with our three granddaughters. She said, she remembers the pastor at their church when they were stationed at Cherry Point, NC. He asked for a show of hands from the people attending a morning service of those that knew the names of their Great Grandparents. About half of the audience raised their hands. Does this really mean anything? I think it means a lot.

15

EPILOGUE

Author's Comments

Alfred Vaughan's senseless killing of Johnny and Willie Litster was not new to the commonwealth of man; it has been replayed throughout history. Those that yield their emotions with anger, rage, revenge, and jealous continue these senseless murders. They fail to understand the consequences. Not only for the victims but also for themselves. Is murder a continuing reflection of Cain's hatred for his brother Abel? I'm sure that everyone could offer comments regarding the current criminal justice system. Your's are probably different from mine.

I have made the following observation as result of looking back at the history of the murder of the two Litster brothers. A century ago Lander County's criminal justice system bought Alfred to trial within four months of his double murder. You have to give the County high marks for the speedy pursuit of justice in contrast to what we have today and the difference is unrecognizable. Modern defense attorneys are experts at stalling. Clever lawyers for both the defense and the prosecution share the responsibility for entangling the criminal justice system. Why does it now take years to bring a person to trial when they are charged with murder?

Did you notice there was no testimony about Alfred's childhood or any thing from his past that may have caused his violence? There was none of that nonsense. As a matter of fact, testimony regarding events that may have had a relationship to the feud between these neighbors was ruled immaterial to the case. Now the system listens to all of the immaterial and irrelevant excuses? This is nothing more than the defense attorney trying to confuse the jury by encumbering the case with a multitude of details? Excuses do not alter the malice of a criminal act. Why should personal problems be an excuse for murder?

Today the media is concerned about "WHY" someone would commit a crime such as murder. Is it really possible or necessary that we know "WHY"? The guilty person and their attorney will say whatever is needed to get a lesser sentence or an acquittal. The "WHY" has been emphasized to such a degree and many people today seem confused about punishing the evil people who commit homicide. You hear daily where some defense attorney is blaming society or a corporation by saying they are responsible for the crime their client committed.

Of course, you have noticed the accused most always seems to enter a plea of "Not Guilty". They may have been caught red handed. Still the defense attorney will have the client enter that plea. What are the ethics of these modern defense attorneys? I see the conduct by some of these attorney's that makes me think of them as accomplices to the crime that has been charged. Is this really what an adversarial trial system is supposed to be or has it just evolved to this over the years?

The prosecution is not without blame. They often appear more interested in another conviction and their only concern is following the rule of law, which they often fail to follow. An example would be by misrepresenting evidence or not disclosing the same when it would aid the accused. The prosecution often makes a deal with those that have committed a crime. For example, I've read about a woman agreeing to plea guilty to avoid the death penalty for the slaying of her pregnant niece and the unborn child. Is this right? We have really deviated from the true goal for justice.

One thing about the three trials for Alfred that stood out; there was no sanity phase or penalty phase for his trials. I seriously question this concept, or that it makes the rule of law more just. Today, not only are the trial dates prolonged, but it also takes years for the judgment for a capitol sentence to carry out the execution. In the mean time, there is the never-ending pursuit of appeals to be heard. As long as we the taxpayers withhold our voice we must continue to pay for this evolved criminal "nonsense" system.

It galls me when I hear a bleeding heart expressing opposition to capitol punishment. They are largely responsible, though not legally, for the continuing acts of murder. They say capitol punishment is not a deterrent. First off, that is a big lie. I know of no one executed who ever committed another murder and if there is deterrence, it can only be a pleasant by-product. But deterrence is not the true reason for a capitol punishment; it is just and a fitting punishment for the crime of murder and it pays honor to the victim.

Most of the people now that have committed murder are not even given a capitol sentence. If the criminal justice system were less inclined to lock people behind bars and instead practice absolute justice for the victim's of these acts of murder, you would see a great decline in murder. Would you like to bet? But, I suppose it is foolish on my part to suggest such a practice that will never be on this side of the second coming of Christ.

Assuming that I could ask Alfred one question, it would be: Did you really want to kill the Litster brothers? Truthfully speaking, he must answer affirmatively. The ultimate expression of what is meant when anyone says "I hate you" is the act of killing. Alfred's state of mind from the testimony shows the act was premeditated, willful and with malice. It is a simple answer and you don't need a psychiatrist to explain Alfred's childhood or other personal problems that have nothing to do with his evil act of cold-blooded murder. Wishing someone dead is not a crime. Yet, Alfred apparently was guilty of mental murder for nearly three years before he carried out the physical act. He finally committed the ultimate and complete act of hatred. Without hatred there would not have been anyone "Killed At The Gap".

Let me comment about on our modern society and hate-crimes. The point I want to make is that our government has demonstrated the stupidity that apparently comes from being a multi-cultural society. Being charged with a criminal act isn't enough anymore. The government must have "thought control" for what they now define as hate-crimes. You see people of a different races or religions can commit crimes against the other. Alfred would not have been charged today with such a crime. Accordingly, I would not be surprised if Alfred today would only have been charged with voluntary manslaughter following many months or years of investigation. Yet, had these boys today came from a different race or religion it may well have been a hate-crime. Why do we let our modern politicians get away with playing the "race card" as they try to appeal to various ethnic voting blocks? The only thing they have produced is a nation divided against itself. If you think I'm wrong, well we can respectfully disagree.

The consequences of Alfred's murder did more than changing lives of two families. It brought fame to: W. D. Jones; he became a renowned judge in Nevada; and to William Easton, he became a State Senator. It also brought shame to the perjured juror, Mr. Flint, not to mentions the Vaughan family.

Most of us know little about criminal procedure and few outside the legal profession have any understanding of the criminal justice system. Simply stated it is the process of investigating a crime, adjudicating the guilty or innocence of a criminal charge and imposing punishment. If you are interested in law, you should go to your local bookstore and ask where they keep the legal books.

After reading about the three trials for Alfred Vaughan you have probably noticed places where procedures have changed from that time. The most notable was the problem with juror, Mr. Flint. Also, there was no penalty phase for these verdicts. Murder in the first degree didn't have a variety of sentences. It was death by hanging, no ifs' ands' or buts'. Still a defendant found guilty had the right to appeal to the State's Supreme Court. The high court would review and rule on the appealed verdict before the sentence could be carried out.

Most of us do not see a need to concern ourselves with criminal procedure because we respect the rights of others and do not feel that we will be caught up in the system. Yet, there are occasions when the ordinary citizen is called for jury duty.

These days, the less you know about anything the better the attorney's will like you as a juror. At least it seems that way. Also, it appears that most judges want you to believe that you are bound absolutely by their instructions. You've probably heard about cases where a judge overturned the jury's verdict. It is not wise for a layperson to discuss what they know about the law to any trial attorney or a Judge.

Most citizens support those that fight crime. Our interest can be seen by the television shows we watch. You can go all the way back to the days of Perry Mason and Dragnet or to the current shows like Law & Order, The Practice and Crime Wave plus many more that could be listed. Why are these shows so popular? Is it the human drama? Is it our interest in seeing justice done? Are we so concerned that an innocent person might wrongly be conflicted of a crime? Are we frustrated when a likely guilty person is released due to some technicality or plea bargain?

Fortunately, criminal procedure has to deal with the U.S. Constitution, without it we would not be living in a Country with the freedoms that we take for granted. Consider the Fourth Amendment (1791):

The right of the people to be secure in their persons, houses, papers, and effects, against unreasonable searches and seizures, shall not be violated, and no Warrants shall issue, but upon probable cause, supported by Oath or affirmation, and particularly describing the place to be searched, and the persons or things to be seized.

We should all remember the Fourth Amendment. The founding fathers greatest concern was freedom for the citizens. Yes, this Amendment has aided criminals, but that is better than the alternative of not being a free person. Privacy is the basis of all our freedoms. I once heard a pastor address this truth from the Scriptures many years ago. We need to realize privacy is paramount if we are to remain a free people. No one should have to live in a police state. Freedom is more important than safety. Many have given up safety and died for freedom, but never for safety. We should be careful not to let our fear of the modern terrorist strip our freedoms. Homeland Security could be the instrument used to strip our remaining freedoms. Now consider the Fifth Amendment (1791):

No person shall be held to answer for a capital, or otherwise infamous crime, unless on a presentment or indictment of a Grand Jury, except in cases a raising in the land or naval forces, or in the Militia, when in actual service in time of War or public danger; nor shall any person be subject for the same offence to be twice put in jeopardy of life or limb; nor shall be compelled in any criminal case to be a witness against himself, nor be deprived of life; liberty, or property, without due process of law; nor shall private property be taken for public use, without just compensation.

We all heard about people taking the “Fifth”. You may even think this is wrong. No, it is wrong for people enforcing the laws of the land to attempt to abridge our Constitution in the name of expediency. Our nation has found many ways to abridge the Constitutional protections and the Supreme Court has ignored many unconstitutional laws and regulations imposed on modern citizens. This too is wrong. Also take a look at the Six Amendment (1791):

In all criminal prosecutions, the accused shall enjoy the right to a speedy and public trial, by an impartial jury of the State and district wherein the crime shall have been committed, which district shall have been previously ascertained by law, and to be informed of the nature and cause of the accusation; to be confronted with the witnesses against him; to have compulsory process for obtaining witnesses in his favor; and to have the Assistance of Counsel for the defense.

After you stop laughing about the part for about speedy trial you should think about the following: The Bill of Rights (first ten Amendments) came with the Constitution all in the year 1791. Our new nation was operating under the Articles of Confederation following the War of Independence. In 1787 the Constitution was drafted to replaces the Articles, but there were many that were afraid of an all powerful federal government, so Congress added the first ten amendments, calling them the Bill of Rights. This was done to ensure the Constitution's passage four years later in 1791. It took awhile for this great document to be settled upon.

What should happen when a citizen's rights are violated? It would be even longer before the U.S. Supreme Court answered this question. The Court's ruling for the case: Weeks v. United States in 1914 became the basis of the exclusionary rule.

Evidence obtained by the government in violation of the Constitution may not be used against the defendant whose rights have been violated.

Law enforcement officials should follow the rule of law. Therefore, Criminal Procedure for our Criminal Justice System is a must and it assures freedom. I have a good friend that has a standard speech where he describes what it means to be a Sovereign Citizen. He argues that the ultimate power, the power to forbid or to allow is truly vested with the people because we are meant to be Sovereign Citizens. Government does not grant us freedoms. Our Constitution simply recognizes that freedoms precede government. It is therefore government's primary responsibility to protect this fundamental truth. He warns us about a government that gives permission for something that it has no right to grant. If you think about that in relation to the Second Amendment, you will understand what he is saying.

Governmental regulations and laws should not supersede the Constitution. It seems only a few people are offended by this unconstitutional practice for items concerning safety and the environment. Still as long as the Constitution stands the citizens have the power to make these official abide by our standard of freedom. Why don't we do that?

The adversarial trial procedure bothers me, but not as bad a criminal justice system that does not treat everyone equally. I think Juvenal Court is wrong. Why is this age discrimination by our courts permitted? Seems to be a violation of the 14 Amendment to the Constitution where it states in Section 1:

"...nor shall any State deprive any person of life, liberty, or property, without due process of law; nor deny to any person within its jurisdiction the equal protection of the law."

Granting special treatment to Juvenal offenders is not equal protection. But our nation has a fondness for children, even when they commit the evil act of murder. Please do not misunderstand, we need Criminal Procedures, without them there would be no rule of law or professional ethics. I was very impressed with manner in which the three trials were held for Alfred Vaughan in 1894-95-96. It was not at all like a Hollywood movie about the old west. But it was very different from a trial today. It was speedy and there was no ridiculous penalty phase for these trials. Certainly, it was better then than today's tactics of stalling and then stalling some more. A man recently confessed to murdering seven persons, but the Public Defender said he is not guilty and his civil rights were violated. The local District Attorney says it will be three years before this person comes to trial. This is totally absurd.

What about Alfred's plea of Not Guilty being based on Self-Defense? Alfred knew that he would be asked, "Did you do it?" He couldn't say "No." He would have to say. "Yes, BUT!" I've heard the test for a plea of self-defense is only justified when the defendant believes the use of deadly force was necessary as a result of an attack upon the defendant and to save themselves they used deadly force. Also, this belief must be reasonable for the common person. We all know that it is not good to kill a person, but it is better than letting someone kill you. If it were true that Johnny pulled a pistol and fired four shots at point blank range at Alfred and Willie charged him with an axe, we would all agree that Alfred acted in self-defense.

Alfred's attorney certainly could not have used the insanity defense. Most of us would agree those committing criminal acts have some degree of diminished mental capacity, but not to the point where they cannot determine right from wrong. Recall, Alfred said he was going to town to tell the Sheriff. Yes, he knew right from wrong.

What happens when a person commits homicide? In Alfred's day it was simple if murder were done in the first degree, the sentence was hanging. Could the jury have found Alfred guilty but in the second degree or for manslaughter? The degrees of homicide have evolved: Manslaughter has been distinguished from murder. Murder generally is understood to be a cold-blooded killing of a human. The law adds the condition of malice aforethought to murder. And from the criminal justice system we will learn that malice aforethought doesn't mean would you might assume. It has nothing to do with malice or forethought. In law it means or stands for the state of mind, which must meet the legal definition required to convict a person on a charge of murder. Murder has been separated into first and second degrees Basically, first degree murder involves willful killing while second degree murder would not. Manslaughter has evolved and is said to be voluntary when it linked to an act of provocation and while the act may be involuntary when a homicide occurs as a result of negligence...

Recalling Judge Mack's instruction from the second trial regarding malice aforethought. There does not have to be a time delay to consider the murder before the act is committed. But the Jury must agree about the defendant's state of mind when the murder took place. Assuming that you did not believe Alfred's testimony about defending himself, then you really are left with only murder in the first-degree. It is impossible to call his act of homicide second-degree or manslaughter.

Also, I would like to comment about our society and the mass media. The media seems so concerned that someone will be offended by what others say. So the government has created a new code of conduct for us. Everyone must be "politically correct" when we speak or suffer the consequences of the government's political wrath. You can be shunned, ostracized, fired from your job and confronted with a legal action. Heaven help us if we accidentally slip and say something they consider wrong. Few have the courage today to speak or should I say tell a stranger what they really believe. Those that say, "I'm offended" are really saying you don't have the right to speak because you do not think properly. This started when the news media and a political party realized they could manipulate segments of people in their effort to win an election. The basic gimmicks are the race card, cultural diversity, poverty, schools (that have never gotten better) and the environment. Issues like these have made it possible for them to collectively control voting blocks and create single issue voters. We are not a "United We Stand" nation on any issue, although these words sound so nice.

Many living in this country today are not even Americans first because of the loyalty they have to their native homeland and the foreign culture, which they refuse to give up. Perhaps their children will learn about an American Culture, but not if the "Globalist-Diversity People" can help it. Can America continue with this type of fragmentation? What are we, just a collection of the World's emigrants? Am I wrong by thinking many of these new emigrants are totally unlike those that came prior to the last century? Now, it seems they are only coming to take advantage of the economic opportunities found here in the United States. Perhaps you too are a little frustrated by the lack of common sense from our elected officials regarding immigration. Have you noticed many of these same official are the ones working to re-define our nation's history?

Being less serious, I wonder how Hollywood would recreate this western crime story? The problem of scripting for most historical events comes from the fact that too many people are involved. While I think W. D. Jones should be the leading character of the story, I must admit it would difficult to make him the center of focus as required for movie audiences. Also, the total story here would certainly take longer than the typical two hour movie. Perhaps the adaptation by a screenwriter would only use a few elements of the story. These could be the events prior to Alfred's three trials or maybe the focus would fixed on just the three trials and let the details of the murder come as the witnesses are called to testify.

Surely, you can think of actors to play the characters of this story. We all know that it is seldom to see a celebrity hero in real world. Most of the time we see people in the Criminal Justice System doing their jobs like those people from Lander County, following Alfred's murder of Johnny and Willie.

Suppose a story like this could reach a large audience and the focus was on the impact to the many lives hurt by the act of murder. Would we benefit? I do not think so because the criminal mind is self-centered and blind to the consequences as they continue to reflect of Cain's hatred.

I would like to thank you for reading my personal thoughts

in this epilogue. You may only agree with parts of my observations and comments. However, I hope we could agree and recognize that the American Culture has been under heavy attack during these last fifty years. What can we do to save our history? It appears only a remnant of the American Culture from the 1800s and early 1900s will be correctly remembered. This survival is important and it is a responsibility.

America like most nations is limited. Our nation is restrained by the way the citizen collectively think about the American History. Especially, the history of those that fought to procure or defend the freedoms we enjoy. In spite of what a modern history revisionist might say, we are indebted to those that settled and civilized this Great Country.

Appendix:

Bibliography

Biography

Photos

Johnny's Letter

Census

Election Results

Nevada Central Railroad

The GAP at Water Canyon

Austin Courtroom

Old Lister Ranch

Vicinity Map

BIBLIOGRAPHY

BOOKS:

Browne, J. Ross. *Mining Adventures California & Nevada, Paisano Press, 1961*

Carlson, Helen S. *Nevada Place Names.* University of Nevada Press, 1974.

Curriden, Mark and Phillips Jr. Leroy. *Contempt of Court,* First Anchor Book Edition, February 2001

Davis, Sam P. *History of Nevada, Vol. I and Vol. II,* (1913?)

Douglas, William and Nylen, Robert A. *Letters from the Nevada Frontier,* University of Oklahoma Press, 1992

Fradkin, Philip L. *Stagecoach,* Simon & Schuster, 2002

Myrick, David. *Railroads of Nevada and Eastern California,* University of Nevada Press

O'Brien, J. P. *History of the Bench And Bar of Nevada, 1913,* Bench and Bar Publishing Company

Paher, Stanley W. *Nevada Ghost Towns & Mining Camps,* Howell-North Books, 1980

Scrugham, James, History of Nevada, The American Historical Society, Inc. 1984

Thompson & West, *History of Nevada, 1958 Edition, Introduction by David F. Myrick,* Howell-North Publisher

Wren, Thomas. *A History of The State of Nevada Its Resources and People,* The Lewis Publishing Company, 1904

Yenne, Bill. *The Opening of the American West,* Chartwell Books, Inc.1993

REPORTS:

Annual Labor Review: *W. D. Jones,* Nevada Labor Temple Review 1914-15

Report of Cases: *The Supreme Court of the State of Nevada,* January Term 1896

Report of Cases: *The Supreme Court of the State of Nevada,* January Term 1895

NEWSPAPERS:

Reese River Reveille (Austin)

Reno Gazette-Journal

TRANSCRIPTS:

In the District Court of the Third Judicial District of the State of Nevada, Lander County

State of Nevada, Plaintiff vs. Alfred Vaughan, Defendant Filed August 10, 1894.

Vol. I Examination of Jurors

Vol. II Witness Testimony (This volume has been lost)

Vol III Witness Testimony

State of Nevada, Plaintiff vs. Alfred Vaughan, Defendant Filed July 26, 1895.

Vol. I Examination of Jurors

Vol. II Witness Testimony

Vol. III Witness Testimony

NOTES:

William W. Christian, Lander County Clerk, Notes for 1895 Trial, State of Nevada, Plaintiff vs. Alfred Vaughan, Defendant

ARTICLES & PAMPHLETS:

Anderson, Jim. *Lost in Austin,* article from the Nevada Magazine

Austin Chamber of Commerce. *Welcome To Austin*

Austin Chamber of Commerce. *Austin's Central Nevada Discovery Driving Tours*

Nevada's Silver Triangle. *Journey to the Middle of Nowhere by David W. Toll*

Tri-County Development Authority. *Lander County Nevada*

Nevada State Historic Preservation Office. *A Guidebook to Nevada's Historical Markers*

WEB SITES:

www.americanwest.com/trails/pages/ponyexp1.html

www.ghosttowns.com/states/nv/austin.html

www.the-onramp.net/battlemountain/

BIOGRAPHY

WILLIAM DUDLEY JONES

Copied from: A History of The State of Nevada, Its Resources and People; Lewis Publishing Company, 1904:

HON. W. D. JONES, of Austin, is one of the leading citizens of Nevada. He was born December 24, 1850, in Jackson county, Tennessee where his father was an overseer of Negroes on a plantation. In 1858 his father left Tennessee intending to go to Texas and build a cabin on the prairie in which he might have a home for his wife and five children. At Natchez on the Mississippi, while crazed with drink he leaped from the steamboat and found a grave in the great Mississippi. W. D. Jones who was the oldest of the children and at that time eight years old, took the place of the father of the family, and struggled with all his boyhood strength to maintain his mother and brothers and sister. He was afterward taken into the family of Major Joseph Harlan, who lived six miles from Gallatin the Hartsville turnpike, in Sumner County, Tennessee. Miss Sue B. Harlan became his adopted mother, and a strong affection existed between the boy and the head of the Harlan family in the person of Miss Harlan. Miss Harlan died in 1877, and her remains are resting in the garden of the Harlan homestead.

Leaving Tennessee in 1866, young Jones came to Austin, Nevada on January 26, 1868, and has made his home here ever since. For a year or so he was a clerk and was then a cowboy and rancher. In 1871 he was committee clerk, and in 1881, assistant chief clerk of the Assembly of Nevada. He was elected district attorney of Lander County in 1886. He was then thirty-six years old, and without any school education, having lived the rough uncultured life of a cowboy for many years. He had begun the reading of law at such intervals as he could find, and then began the practice of law at Austin without any equipment or books. By his great industry and keen judgment he at once attracted public notice, and was immediately recognized as a formidable opponent at the bar. He filled the office of district attorney for ten years with marked ability until he was elected attorney general of Nevada in 1898. In December of that year he moved his family to Carson City, and was installed in the office on the first Monday in January of the following year. He continued in that position for two years, and his success is indicated by the large number of state and other cases, which were tried by him, and which are given in the Nevada reports. In 1901 Governor Sadler recognizing Judge Jones ability, tendered him the office of judge of the third judicial district of Nevada composed o Lander Nye and Eureka counties. Judge Jones resigned his other position during the term, refusing to be a candidate for election 1902. He then resumed his successful practice, and since his retirement from the bench has enjoyed a splendid private clientage and is one of the leading lawyers of Nevada bar. While he was attorney for the state he won the celebrated cases against the C. P. Company; the boundary line case between Eureka and Lander counties; convicted A. Vaughan of the murder of the two Litster boys three times in succession- after two years of almost constant labor was senior counsel for Senator Ernst in the tax case in the district and supreme courts, which was finally decided in favor of Ernst on the very point first raised by his senior counsel.

January 3, 1876, Judge Jones, married Miss Laforga F. Birchim, the adopted daughter of John G. and Adaline C. Birchim, who were pioneers to Nevada from California, living on Reese River near Austin from 1864 till their death. Mrs. Jones was but twelve years old when her foster parents made the trip from California, and she helped drive the cattle from Sacramento County, oftentimes on foot. Mrs. Jones, who is a native of Ohio and but two months younger than her husband, was two years of age when her parents, whose name was Allison, died of the cholera. They were on the plains on the way to the west, and her uncle cared for her until she arrived in Placerville, California, when he gave her to the Birchims. Mr. and Mrs. Jones have a son and two daughters, all horn in Lander County and all grown. The son is Dr. J. B. Jones, a graduate from the University of Nevada and from the dental department of the University of California; he is a model young man, and is now located in a successful dental practice Reno, Nevada. The two daughters, Addle J. and Edna T., are bright, some young women, and are popular with all who know- them. There is a grave in the Austin cemetery that marks the spot of a lovely daughter's resting place, and if living she would now he twenty years of age.

Mr. and Mrs. Jones are both pioneers of Nevada. And each possesses in a marked degree the strongest attributes of good citizenship, being leaders every charitable, social and public movement. Mrs. Jones is a lady of great force of character and ability to do things and is one of the pillars of strength in the Methodist church, of which she has long been a devoted member, and she is a noble wife and mother.

Judge Jones is a thirty-second degree Mason and a member of the Eastern Star, is past grand chancellor of the order of Knights of Pythias of Nevada, and is the supreme representative of the Grand Domain of Nevada to Knights of Pythias supreme lodge of the world, and is a member of Ancient Order of United Workmen, of the Elks, and the Rathbone Sisters. He has as wide and favorable acquaintance in Nevada as any man the State, and his neighbors say that he is one of the best politicians, in the State. As a life-long Democrat he has done all in his power to promote interests of the party; he has frequently stumped the state during the campaigns, and was with Hon. George W. Cassidy in the latter's last campaign for Congress. He is a supporter of the Silver cause, and has done effective work in the organization of party lines. For nine years he was editor of the People's. Advocate and of the Reveille.

Mr. and Mrs. Jones are the highest type of the kind of material used to make the high standard of citizenship found throughout the Nevada. Judge Jones has had a remarkable career. Only wonderful will power and tenacity of purpose combined with a strong mentality grained character could effect a rise from a poor, hard-working orphan at the age of eight, through subsequent years when he had no opportunity for gaining education and the equipment with which most boys start their careers, carry him through the hard struggles for a living at the rough work of rancher and cowboy, then give him courage for the unaccustomed digging necessary for the mastery of the jealous mistress of the law, and thence to the courts, to higher offices and one of the most important judicial positions in the commonwealth, from which he has retired with wealth of honor and the esteem of all his fellow citizens.

Another Biography was copied from: The Nevada Labor Temple Review published in 1914-15 Annual Labor Review has the following biography:

W. D. Jones, one of the oldest members of the Nevada Bar and a resident of Reno for the past ten years, left Tennessee at the close of the Civil War and located at Austin, Nev., in 1868, and has been a resident of this state ever since, his law offices being in the Clay Peters building, and his home at 137 Nest Liberty street.

Judge Jones, during his residence at Austin, Nev. was a clerk and miner, and then went upon the ranges of Reese River and Smith Creek and worked as a cowboy and rancher until 1886, when he was elected district attorney of Lander County, to which office he resigned in 1901 to accept the judgeship of the Third Judicial District comprising Lander, Nye and Eureka Counties.

With the exception of the time Judge Jones was on the district bench, he has been an active practitioner at the bar of this state, from 1886 until the present time, and has been engaged in some of the most important cases in -Nevada. He was a member of the Assembly, from Washoe County, at the session of 1911 and general and special session of 1912, and for the past six years has been a member of the Board of School Trustees.

In 1893, Alfred Vaughan shot and instantly killed John and William Litster in Boone Canyon, Lander County, Nevada. Judge Jones being District Attorney of Lander County at the time took up the prosecution of the case, which lasted for nearly three years, and convicted Vaughan of murder in the first degree three times. The judgment of conviction in the first case wasreversed on the definition of “malice aforethought," and the second, judgment conviction was reversed by the disqualification of a juror. The case was then transferred from Lander to Washoe County and Vaughan was tried before Judge Cheney in Reno, where he was again convicted of murder in the first degree, and an hour or so after the return of the verdict, Vaughan took poison in his cell in the Court House and died that afternoon. During the several trials of Vaughan, his brothers and mother frequently threatened to take. Judge Jones' life (W. D. was the District Attorney at that time)..

Since locating in Reno. Judge Junes has successfully defended several important murder cases, among them being the case of Kucks for killing "Slim" in the Palace saloon; Stanley Peak for killing an Italian: Dr. Wichmann in his first trial for murder by means of abortion; Joe Palazaro for killing a countryman, and several other noted cases. He has also successfully settled some of the largest and many smaller estates of deceased persons in this and other counties in this state. Judge Jones' only son, Dr. J. B. Jones, is a dentist in high standing in Sacramento, Cal. and his only daughter is married and resides in Reno. Judge Jones has always been a strong Democrat, and is declared by those who know him best, as being loyal and true friend.

The third biography was copied from: “History of the Bench and Bar of Nevada”, Edited by J. P. O'Brien, published in 1913. Most of the biographies' are accompanied with a photo, however this was not the case for W. D. Jones. This is the only place where I seen his full name in print. Throughout the story of the Vaughan Trial he is always referred to as W. D. Jones.

William Dudley Jones: Residences, 137 West Liberty Street; office 200-1 Clay Peters Building, Reno. Born in Tennessee, December 24, 1850. son of Alfred M. and Mary R. Jones. Moved to Austin 1868. Married January 3, 1876, to La Forga F. Birchim. Educated in public schools for a short period before the Civil War. Admitted to the bar to Nevada 1892. Engaged in the general practice of law alone to the present time, except two years co-partnership with W. H. A. Pike. District Attorney of Lander County, Nevada, ten years, from 1886. District Judge of Lander, Nye and Eureka Counties. Attorney General of Nevada elected 1897. Member of Assembly 1911-12. Member of Masonic Order; B.P.O.E.; Knights of Pythias; F.O. E. and Moose Fraternities. Member of the State Bar Association. Served in the Confederate Army during the Civil War. Democrat.

WILLIAM EASTON, 1854-1921

The following edited biography for Willaim Easton was partially copied from: "A HISTORY OF NEVADA" found at the Nevada State Library.

He is a native of Canada, where he was born on the 1st of January 1854. His grandfather, William Easton, Sr. a native of Scotland, immigrated to Canada in 1800, where his family had their residences about thirty miles south of the city of Montreal. His son, Neal Easton, was born on the family homestead there, and married Bliss Ann Jamieson, also a native of Scotland, and they became the parents of seven children. The mother passed away in death in 1866. Neal moved to London, Ontario where died at the age of seventy-seven years.

William Easton, the only member of his father's family in Nevada, received his early education in Canada, and when fourteen years of age went to London, Ontario, to learn the blacksmith's trade. From there he went to Bismarck, on the Canada Southern Railroad, and thence came to Austin, Nevada in 1875, where he was employed as mining engineer by the Manhattan Company, also doing their blacksmithing.

In 1890 he was elected Sheriff and Assessor and held that office for four terms of two years each. He was the Sheriff that arrested Alfred Vaughan for killing John and William, Jr. Litster on December 28, 1893. Mr. Easton in 1899 purchased the International Hotel, a building one hundred by one hundred feet in dimensions, with twenty-three sleeping apartments, a large hall for theatres and parties, a large dining room and all modern conveniences to be found in a first-class hotel. He also owns a half interest in a livery stable in Austin, and was one of the town's successful businessmen.

Mr. Easton was formerly identified with the Republicans, but when his party abandoned its bimetallic principles he became an active organizer of the Silver Party. He later decided that he would be an Independent in his political affiliations. In 1899 he was Sergeant-At-Arms in the State Legislature. In 1902 he was again elected Assessor of Lander County, making ten years that he held that office. This last term did not combine the office of Sheriff.

In January 1888, Mr. Easton married Miss Lucy Anna Stow a dative daughter of California. She was born in San Francisco. They have three children: Neil Stow Easton; Della Louise Easton; and Melville H. Easton. The family attended the Methodist Church. Fraternally, Mr. Easton was a Free Mason and held the office of senior warden in the blue lodge and was the treasurer of the chapter. He has also filled all the offices in the lodges of the Independent Order of Odd Fellows and the Knights of Pythias.

William Easton's daughter Della married George Watt Litster in 1910. William is Marilou Colson's great grandfather. After William severed two terms in the Nevada State Senate, he and his wife moved to San Francisco. It was his wish to be buried in the cemetery at Austin. Here the inscription reads: "Native of Canada, Died in San Francisco, 1921, Aged 67, Rest in Peace".

William Easton was the Sheriff at Austin in 1893, 94,95, and 96. He married Lucy Stow in San Francisco and for time he was the owner of the International Hotel. His daughter had one child, William Glenn Litster. William Easton was buried at Austin near the Litster Family Plot.

WATT, GEORGE, 1831-1899 by Donald Colson

George Watt: There are five persons listed with the named George Watt in the California 1860 Census. Only one fits the George Watt of Silver Creek Nevada. Four were from Scotland. Three were listed as laborers and one was a Stock Dealer in Yolo County. The stock dealer is Lander County's George Watt.

His gravestone states that he died Jan. 5, 1899, Aged 67 years, 11 mo. 23 days. Therefore his born date was Jan. 12, 1831. He would have been 29 yr. old Jan. 12, 1860. There is a problem because 1860 census lists George at age 37. Often as in the cases I reviewed the handwriting was extremely poor, perhaps the 37 was really meant to be 29. Or could this have just been George's heavy Scottish accent. Perhaps, he was misunderstood when he said his age.

The book "Letters from the Nevada Frontier" has notes on page 346 that copy's the following from the Reese River Reveille: *George Watt was born in Dunfermline, Fife, Scotland. He came to California in the late 1850's. In 1863 he drove a herd of cattle into Central Nevada from California, settled in Austin and raised livestock to supply meat for Austin. He later acquired the Silver Creek Ranch. Watt served in the Nevada Assembly in 1875, and again in 1879.*

Tasker Oddie's letter dated November 20, 1898, mentions going to the Watt Ranch. He left Austin at about 11 o'clock and got there at 2 o'clock that afternoon. This was a 3 hour 16 mile ride. He said the Watt's were very nice people and they are Scotch people. The letter can be found in the book by *William Douglas, and Robert A. Nylen: Letters from the Nevada Frontier, University of Oklahoma Press, 1992.*

The letter states that Mr. Watt came to Lander County many years ago and that he owns several ranches. Mrs. Isabella (Litster) Watt was said to be a bright and entertaining lady. The family includes five sons and four daughters and the children were all musical. They had a piano and a violin and the children either played an instrument or sang. He said: *Almost all the girls in this country can play the piano.* The boys were said to be a fine lot and they were all good horseman. Especially Jim, *he delights in getting on the hardest bucking horse he can find and scarcely ever gets spilled off.* He sounds like a Willie Litster the type of buckaroo Oddie mentioned how hard it is to stay on one of these wild bucking horses. *The best riders get bucked off, but they seldom get hurt* He said: *all the men swear like troopers all the time.*

Oddie said the Watt's had a pleasant little house. It is noted that Tasker came from a wealth eastern family and not doubt he was raised in a large house. He said it should be understood that people living here don't have the advantages found in a city. They had a country dance that lasted till six in the morning the night he was at the Watt's. I've noted most all the dances back at that time were all night affairs. One rancher family that came had traveled 30 miles all day just to be there.

George Watt is listed as a member: The Society of Reese River Pioneers was organized on the 11th of June 1873. It was comprised of males who were residents of the Reese River Mining District prior to the 31st of Dec. 1864 and also the male descendants of persons eligible for membership. Reference: *Thompson & West, History of Nevada.*

I've found George Watt did own several ranch properties by 1893. He was rich man by the standards of that time. This biographical summary does not consider any genealogical research. However, he might possibly be related to the famous Scottish inventor, James Watt, 1736-1819, who invented an improved steam engine. James gave us the term "horsepower" and the British Association named the unit of electrical power to honor him, thus we have stamped on our light bulbs the word "watt". James might have left a large family an inheritance and he could have been George's grandfather? I really should not speculate. George did seem to have a lot more money then the typical settler. He even traveled back to Scotland in the late 1860's where he married Isabella Litster. The Watt's are listed in the 1870 census for Lander County, NV. Their first of nine children was born in 1871.

George was also elected to the State Assembly in 1875 and 1879. Robert Eason was George's half brother.

Marilou (Litster) Colson

Photo, 1953, the great granddaughter
of William and Elizabeth (Glenn) Litster
and William and Lucy (Stow) Easton

Litster Family

From left to right: Louis 10, James 20, Elizabeth 52, Lizzie 16, William 53, and George 13. The photo here may have been taken in 1898, about four years after the death of Johnny and Willie. One of the books on the table appears to be the family Bible.

Elizabeth (Glenn) Litster

Date of photo is unknown, perhaps 1903

William Easton

State Senator William Easton and daughter Della at Reno, NV, January 16, 1907. Photo was taken during the 23rd Session of the State Senate. William also served in the 24th Session. William Easton was the Sheriff at Austin in 1893, 94,95, and 96. He married Lucy Stow of San Francisco. And for time he was the owner of the International Hotel. His daughter married George Watt Litster. William Easton was buried at Austin near the Litster Family Plot.

Della (Easton) Litster

Date of photo is unknown.
Della married George Watt Litster, August 5, 1910; she died in 1915 at the age of 24. Della and George had one child, William Glenn Litster.

George and Louis Litster

Photo date unknown, appears to be about 1903.
Louis at the left would have been 15 and George
would have been 18 years old.

Austin Methodist Church

Photo taken in September 1996.
This is the church where the service was held
December 30, 1893 for Willie and Johnny Litster.

Austin Courthouse

The Austin Courthouse was completed in 1869. This is where the first and second trials of Alfred Vaughan were held. The cornice covering the front entrance can be seen. Richard Jennings was lynched from this cornice in 1881 for killing John A. Barrett. The details of the Jennings lynching can be found in Chapter 4. Six other lynching were recorded in Nevada during 1882 to 1944, while 4708 lynching were recorded in the U.S. and 2733 of these lynching took place during the years prior to 1900.

Johnny & Willie's Gravestone

Johnny and Willie Litster's Gravestone Reads:
Come Ye Blessed
John G. Litster
Aged 19 yrs
William Litster
Aged 16 yrs
Died Dec. 28, 1893

Johnny's Letter

Date: December 26, 1893, See Chapter 1, page 25

First Page:

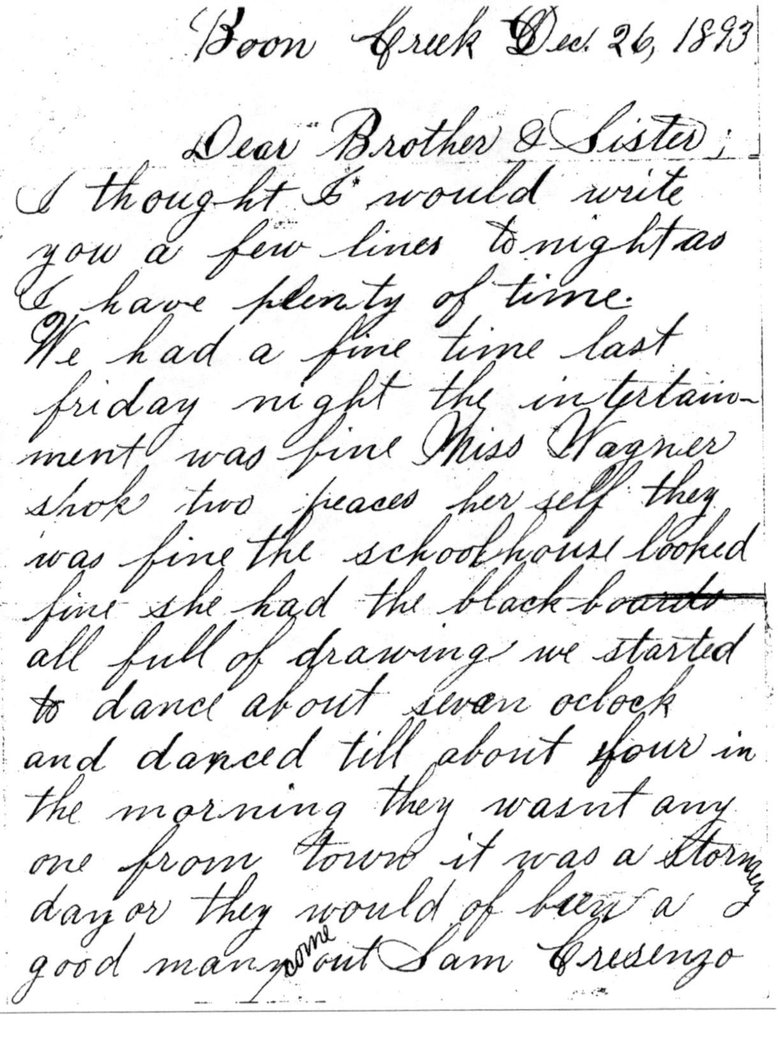

Boon Creek Dec. 26, 1893

Dear Brother & Sister;

I thought I would write you a few lines tonight as I have plenty of time. We had a fine time last friday night the intertainment was fine Miss Wagner shok two peaces her self they was fine the school house looked fine she had the black boards all full of drawings we started to dance about sevan oclock and danced till about four in the morning they wasnt any one from town it was a stormy day or they would of been a good many come out Sam Cresenzo

Page Two

said he was goeing to bring
out a buss load. We plained
the floar and cut six wax
candles and I tell you it was fine
wish you only was here Miss
Wagners Sister and Husband and
his Brother and Cousin was their
we will send you a programe
when we get an envalope all the
neighbors was their but Aunt
Isa Uncle George went home
with the girls after the intertain
ment was over. We received your
letter Friday but you forgot to
~~put in the samples of Walts shirts~~
it must be pretty good cloth for
10¢ a yard Mama says she hopes
you will have good luck with them.
The Steers are doeing fine they are
fat as hogs now the stock Cattle
are loking fine to we feed them
one lode a day that is when it is

Page Three

starming when it is good weather
we dont feed them. Will Wills
have got two colts up breaking
they are daisies to buck they are pretty
gentle now
Is Will Sholtes got back to
Cortez yet he said he was going
to try to be back for Xmas.
Lizzie is writing to Reto to
night and sending her a new years
card. Jane Eason got home
yesterday she is going to stay
till the fifteenth. Mama got
the cover for your bowl when
she was in town from Mr.
Dalton I guess I will close as
I havnt any more news wishing
you both a happy new year and
many of them. Your Loving
Brother

John G. Litster

CENSUS

This census summary checked the following years for various character found in the book: 1870, 1880, 1900, 1910 and 1920.

1870, Watt: George, age 38, wife Isabella, age 21.

1870, Eason: Robert, age 24; wife Ellen age 25; J. Eason, age 20; E. Eason, age 23. (J. Eason and probably his wife E. Eason are only seen in this Lander County census.) It is logical that this young Scotsman worked for George Watt and he probably came to Lander County when George drove a herd of cattle here in 1864.

1880, Litster: William, age 34; wife Elizabeth, age 30; Mary, daughter age 10; John, son age 5; William, son age 3, (James was not listed, however his was born in March of that year.)

1880, Watt: George, age 49, wife Ima (Isabella), age 29; Cressa, daughter age 9; George Jr. son age 7; James, son age 5; Robert, son age 3; James Litster, age 76 and Christina Litster, age 71 were listed as boarders. (Litster was misspelled Loelster. They were Isabella's father and mother.)

1880, Dunsdon: Thomas, age 38; wife Emily, age 35; Emily, daughter age 18; Annie, daughter age 13; John, son age 11; Nathan, son age 8.

1880, Eason: Alex, age 36; wife Mary, age 32; Jane, age daughter 4; Ellen, daughter age 1. (Her son, Joseph was not born until July 1881.)

1880, Eason: Joseph, age, 25; wife Isabella, age 25; Jeanette, son age 9; Joseph Jr., son age 7; Andrew, son age 5; Alexander, son age 3; Ellen, daughter age 1/12. (Eason name was spilled Esson in census.)

1880, Eason: Robert, age 34; wife Elleen, age 35; Joseph son age 9; James, son age 8; Robert Jr. son age 6; Cressa, daughter age 4; Ellen, daughter age 3.

1880, Vaughan: Lee, age 56; wife Isabella, age 45; Frank, son age 14; Charles, son age 9; Alfred, age 7; Harry, son age 5.

1890, The records for the 1890 Census were destroy in a fire in Washington D.C.

1900, Litster: William, born June 1844, age 55; wife Elizabeth, born June 46, age 53; James, born Mar. 1880, age 20; Elizabeth, born Sept. 1883, wife age 16; George, born July 1885, son age 14; Louis, born May 1888, son age 12.

1900, Watt: (George died Jan. 5, 1898) Isabella, age 48; living with their mother were four sons and three daughters, they were: James, age 22, Robert, age 21; William, age 19; Helen, age 16; Isabella, age 13; Jessie, age 10; Oliver age 6. Margaret White, servant, age 19; Cara Rutherford, guest, age 23; Joseph Eason, boarder, age 26.

1900, Dunsdon: Thomas, born Oct. 1844, age 55; wife Emily, born Feb. 1842, age 58; John, born Nov. 1870, age 29; Nathan, born Jan. 1873, age 27 (Nathan's occupation is listed as a Civil Engineer.); Daisy, born Apr. 1881, age 19. (Note: John and Nathan rode to Austin from Silver Creek to get the doctor for Willie Litster, Dec. 28, 1893.)

1900, Watt, Jr.: George, age 27; wife Estella, age 18.

1900, Easton: William, age 46; wife Lucy (Stow), age 36; Neil, son age 10; Della, daughter age 7.

1900, Eason: Mary, age 53; (her husband Alexander died in 1891) Jane, daughter age 25, Nellie (Eason) Oates, daughter age 21; Joseph (Joe), son age 18; John, son age 11; Mary Oates, granddaughter, age 18 mo.

1900, Eason: Joseph, age 48; wife Isabel, age 49; Alex, age 21; Isabel, age 16. (Joseph appears to be Mary Eason's brother in-law.)

1900, Eason: Andrew, age 25; wife, Winnie, age 23; Chester son, age 18mo.

1900, Rast: John, age 49; wife Elizabeth, age 47; Herbert, son age 25; Lizzie, daughter age 23; Nicholas, age 48

(Nicholas was the State's key witness during the three trials. Nick was living with his brother's family. Nick name was not found in the 1910 or 1920 census, but death records for State lists Nick's death 6/7/1922 at age 70.)

1910, Litster: Elizabeth, age 63; (William died Apr. 3, 1903) Louis, son age 21; James, son age 30; Rose, wife age 30, (Rose is James wife.)

1910, Watt: Isabella, age 59; Isabella, daughter age 23; Jessie, daughter age 19; Oliver, son age 16.

1910, Watt: Robert, age 32; wife Cora, age 33; Kenneth, son age 7; George, son 4.

1910, Watt, Jr.: George, age 36; wife Estella, age 27; Genie, daughter age 7; Rolland, son 5; Thomas, son age 2

1910, Christian: William, age 46; wife Mary, 40; George Litster, brother-in-law, age 24

1910, Dunsdon: John, age 39; Warren, brother age 34.

1910, Easton: William, age 56; wife Lucy, age 47: Neil, son age 20; Della, daughter age 17; Melville, son age 12

1910, Eason: Joseph, age 37; wife Maud, age 33; David, son age 5; Clarence, son age 3.

1920, Litster: Elizabeth age 72; Louis, son age 31; Ida, daughter-in-law age 20; Louis Jack, grandson, age 5mo.

1920, Litster: James, age 39; wife Rosalia, age 40; Caroline, daughter age 3; Ethel, daughter age 12.

1920, Watt: Oliver, age 25; wife May, age 19; Dorothy, daughter age 9 mos.

1920, Watt: James age 44; wife Irene, age 25; Jack Oliver, son age 18 mo. (James and Oliver's mother was Isabella Litster Watt. Hear Death Certificate lists her date of death as 10/14/1922, at age 75.)

Election Results

Results of the November 1894 Election in Lander County was interesting. This election definitely influenced Alfred Vaughan's second and third trial. There were fewer votes than you might expect. Consider the fact that women did not vote, nor did the Chinese or Indians living in Lander County. The combined total vote for District Attorney was 485 and this can be compared to 479 votes that were cast for the office of County Clerk. The number of those that could have voted, but did not is unknown. The history of this story could have changed had more men exercised their right to vote.

You may recall W. D. Jones was not happy about James Egan agreeing to assist James Dennis, Alfred's attorney, during the second trial. Also, you can see that Jones nearly lost the election to Egan. He had only nine more votes than this runner up. Egan had worked in the District Attorney's office prior to the election and during Vaughan's first trial. Egan changed his mind about assisting Dennis after Judge Mack told him that he could be disbarred due to a conflict of interest resulting from his participation in the first trial.

Mr. Truman also ran for District Attorney Jones and he garnered nearly a third of the votes too. He was twenty-five shy of Jones. Nevertheless these two gentlemen obviously had a good professional relationship. Truman assisted Jones during all three trials. It appears that had either Truman or Egan decided not to run against Jones that he might not have been the D.A. during the second and third Vaughan trials. This reasoning is based on the logic that Jones, the incumbent had 173 of the 485 votes that were cast. The following is a summary of the vote tally for District Attorney:

Jones, W. D.	173	Votes Silver Party
Egan, James B.	164	Votes Silver Party
Truman, D. S.	148	Votes Silver Party

The office for County Clerk was wide open as the

incumbent retired. William Christian won this position with only 30 percent of the vote total. His wife was the sister of the two brothers that Alfred Vaughan murdered. Recall, Dennis was very suspicious of Christian's work while he assisted the County Commissioners summons people for jury duty. William was the County Clerk during the second and third Vaughan trials. The following is a the summary of the voting:

Robinson, F. H.	86	Votes
Grasser, L.C.	128	Votes
Malloy, John J.	118	Votes
Christian, W. W.	147	Votes

The combined office for Sheriff and Assessor had 511 votes cast. This race had 26 more votes cast than that or District Attorney and William Easton won his race by 15 votes. His daughter, Della Easton, married George Watt Litster in 1910. George is 8 years old little boy that rode for help on the day his two brothers was killed. Della is Marilou (Litster) Colson, Grandmother.

McCourt, Thomas	248	Votes
Easton, Wm.	263	Votes

The State of Nevada also elected a Regent to the University. H. S. Starratt won this position by a landside. Recall, Starratt was the man Alfred Vaughan drew and pointed his pistol at while visiting the Litster Ranch three years before this election in 1890-91. The discovery of this event revealed the beginning of the feud between the Litster and Vaughan brothers. The reason for Starratt visit was never said. The following is a summary of the voting:

Patterson, W. H.	45	Votes	Rep.
Starratt, H. S.	374	Votes	Silver
Wiseman, A. H.	23	Votes	Dem.

The Honorable C. E. Mack, District Judge of the First Judicial District of Nevada presided at the second Vaughan trial. Judge Mack is a very able man and that he bears the distinction of being one of the best jurists in the State. He defeated Judge Rising, who had been in office for 30 years at the November 1894 election. The Judge has succeeded in making himself very popular with the citizens during the short time that he lived in Austin according to the May 22, 1895 Reese River Reveille.

Nevada had four District Judges running for office in Silver Party, 1894: They were all elected.

First District: C. E. Mack, Storey. Presided over second Vaughan trial 1895.

Second District: A. F. Cheney, Washoe. Presided over trial Vaughan trial 1896,

Third District: A. L. Fitzgerald, Eureka. Presided over first Vaughan trial 1894.

Fourth District: G. T. Talbot, Elko

The performance of the three judges: Fitzgerald, Mack and Cheney were distinctly different. Judge Fitzgerald made a mistake with his instructions to the jury as well as refusing to answer the foreman of jury when he asked for a clarification regarding the degrees of murder.

Judge Mack was sent to Austin to preside over the second trial following the Supreme Courts ruling for a new trial. His instructions to the jury for homicide could be used for a legal textbook. He knew what the Supreme Court said about the first trial. However, the judge allowed Dennis to make a mockery of the court's decision to replace the perjured juror, A. A. Flint. Why didn't the Judge Mack hold Dennis in contempt of court? Dennis knew exactly what he was doing by not participating in the selection of the replacement juror.

Judge Cheney appears to have been a very efficient judge. He was able to give the case to the jury on the fourth day of the trial. No transcript was made for this trial so it is impossible to appreciate his work or the way he handling these attorneys. It would have been interesting to read the closing statements. These were not recorded at any of the three trials. Judge Cheney did not ask these attorneys for any input regarding his instructions to the jury as did the other two judges.

Nevada Central Railroad

The Nevada State Railroad Museum located in Carson City has several old restored locomotive engines including those used for narrow gauge tracks like those for the Nevada Central Railroad. This short line ran from Battle Mountain to Austin. Service officially began on March 1, 1880 to Austin's extended city limits at Ledlie or as it was then called the Austin Junction which is actually about seven miles west of Austin. This junction is about one mile northeast of the old abandoned sites of Jacobsville and the Pony Express Station that was adjacent to the Reese River. The railroad was abandoned in 1938.

You can still see evidence of the old railroad grade from Highway 305 as it traverses the Reese River Valley. This short line used narrow 36-inch gauge for the tracks instead of the standard gauge tracks that have 4 feet 8½ inch spacing between the rails. The short line was approximately 93 miles in length after extension was added to Clifton at the base of Pony Canyon below Austin in 1888.

The construction for the railroad was behind schedule and it was apparent the rail line would not to reach Clifton within the allotted time for construction. Therefore, Austin's town fathers move the city limits to Ledlie, thus allowing NCR to fulfill the terms of the contract. The story about financing and construction for this short line railroad between Battle Mountain and Austin is long and complicated. Ledlie (Austin Junction) continued to be used as station for freight teams destine to Ione, Grantsville, Silver Peak and Jefferson. I've read that there were times when as many as 250 mules were used for sixty wagons hauling freight to be transferred at this station.

The initial travel time from Battle Mountain to Austin was nearly nine hours and this included a one-hour meal stop for the travelers. The outgoing passengers had a meal at Hallsville and the passengers coming had the meal at Bridges. There were several stops and a five-mile per hour speed limit was used as the train passed each of the 13 sidings. This slowed the average speed between the two terminuses to 11 miles per hour. The one-way passenger fare was $9.00 or 10 cents a mile. Freight was shipped at one cent per hundred pounds for each mile traveled. Service was improved by the fall of 1880. Travel time was cut to five and one-half hours and the meal stops were eliminated. A daily train leaving Austin at 8:00 a.m. and would arrive in Battle Mountain 1:30 p.m. While a train from the oppose direction would departing from Battle Mountain at 7:30 a.m. and arrive 1:10 p.m. at Austin (Clifton).

The 1880 census lists Austin's population at 1679 and Battle Mountain's 522. Austin's silver boom had passed by this time. Rail service certainly improved the quality of life in Austin. Recall, Johnny Litster sent a letter dated December 26, 1893, from Boone Canyon to his sister living at Cortez. The letter was post marker in Battle Mountain that very same day.

Alfred Vaughan's attorney, James F. Dennis had his home in Battle Mountain. He must have logged many hours traveling between these two towns. His train fare plus hotel accommodates was a considerable cost to the Vaughan's. Nothing was found about the Litster's using the NRC for their travel to and from Austin. They most likely traveled the 22 miles by wagon. Wagon travel would allow them to visit with their relatives at the Watt Ranch.

The following sketch shows the places where the Nevada Central Railroad sidings and the distance in miles from Austin. The terminus station at Clifton would have been better location for the town by today's standards instead of the hillside canyon development in Austin. Originally, these two locations were competing town sites. Austin won by offering free lots to merchants and miners provided that they would help build the road up the grade for the main street into Austin. This road is still the US Highway 50 alignment. The people controlling the Clifton property really lost for a couple of reasons. Though the high price they were asking for building lots was not the main reason. Basically, the miners did not want to live that far from where they worked and if you have ever been to Austin, then you know those miners didn't want a long morning uphill walk going to work. They wanted to live near the mines and the stores. Clifton did provide a good location for the terminus of the NRC. Austin became the County seat in fall of 1863 and that ended the competition.

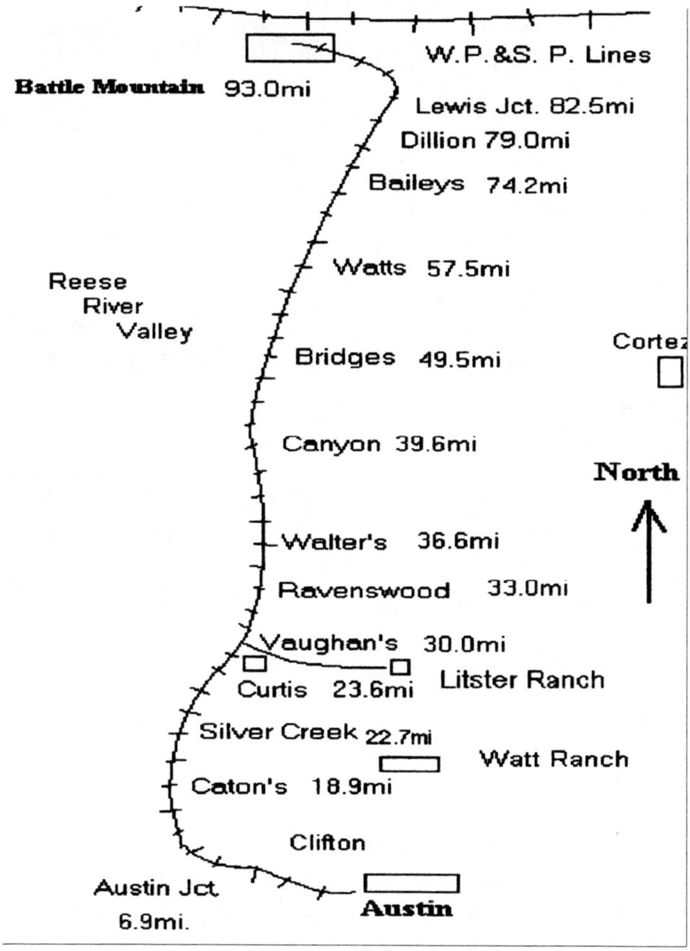

The GAP at Water Canyon

The open area is the only location that fits the testimony describing the former fence line with the GAP. You can visualize a wagon road crossing the flat heading toward the Water Canyon road by the trees. The truck in the foreground is parked on the main road in Boone Canyon. The old Litster Ranch house is about one mile down the Canyon which is to the right in the above picture. Boone Creek is barely noticeable along the base of the convex sloping hillside from where I am standing for this picture.

Austin Courtroom

I am sitting in the chair where witnesses testified during Alfred Vaughan's two trials in Austin. Look how close the jury box is to

the witness stand. You can see two rails at the floor in the jury box. They are brass boot rails for the juror's foot rest. There is one large table in the foreground and I assume this would have been shared by the both prosecution and the defense attorney's. The old courtroom is on the second floor of this historic 1869 Courthouse. The old Sheriff's Office and jail cells were located downstairs on the first floor during the time when Alfred was in jail.

Old Litster Ranch Map

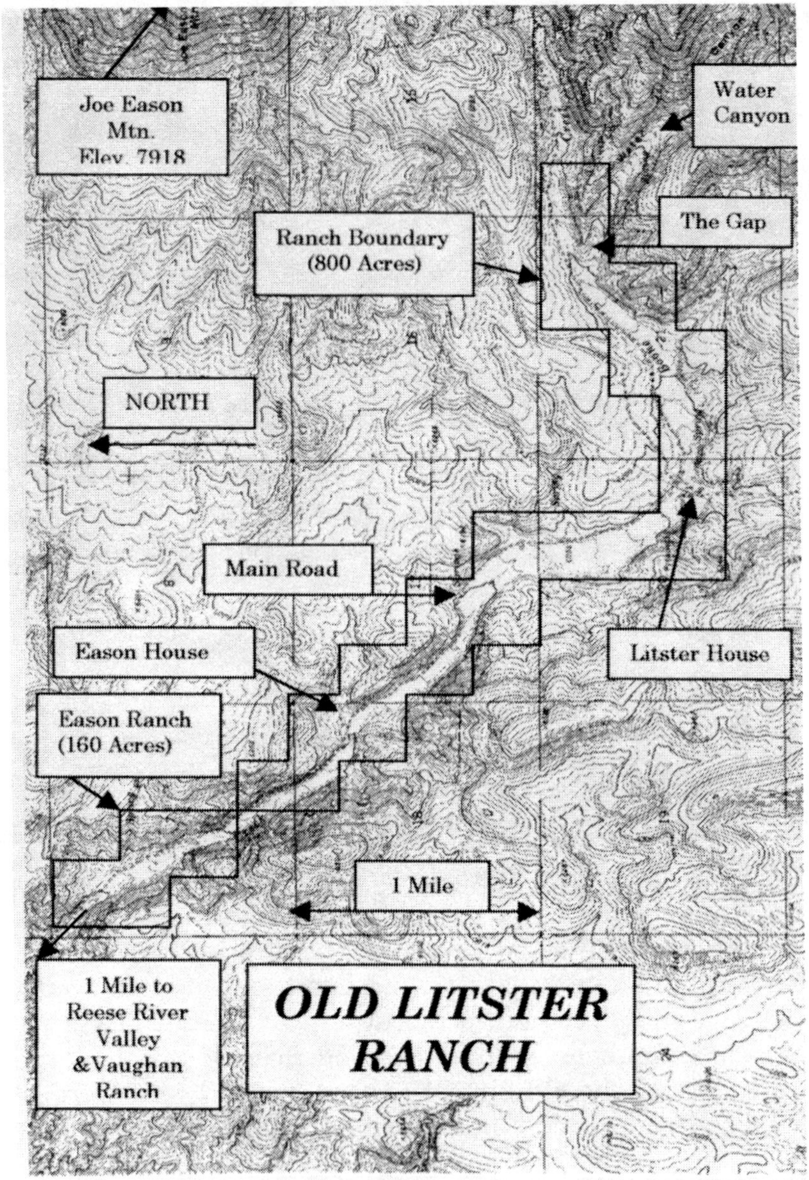

The main road in Boone Canyon from Hwy 305 passes the Vaughan Ranch and continues through the old Litster Ranch.

Vicinity Map

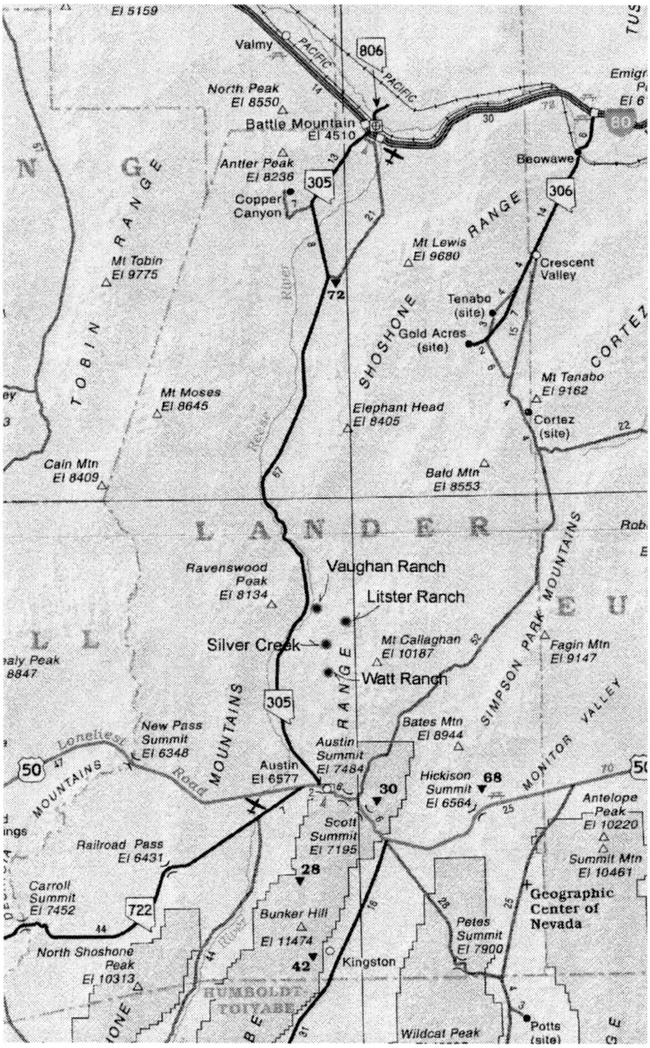

Traveling State Highway 305: Austin is 89 miles south of Battle Mountain. The old Litster Ranch was about 22 miles north of Austin and 4 miles east of the highway. The sign for the old Vaughan Ranch can be seen next to the highway at the mouth of 'Boone Canyon. The old Watt Ranch is now the Silver Creek Ranch and it is about 16 miles north of Austin. The ghost town site of Silver Creek is between the Litster and Watt ranches.